"This Series May Soon do For Travel Guides What Hitchcock did for Film." —Chicago Tribune

"An Insider With Attitude." —Newsday

"A New Series From Genius Dan Levine." —Elle Magazine

"Ultra Hip Travel Tomes." —Atlanta Journal-Constitution

"This Book Understands All That." —Chicago Tribune

"At Once Witty and Irreverent." —Toronto Sun

"Sharp Writing and a Thrilling Layout." —San Francisco Examiner

"If it's Cutting Edge You Want in a City That Teeters Between Conservative and Revolutionary, This is the Book to Buy." —Toronto Sun

"It's Hip to be There." —Chicago Sun-Times

"Slangy and Wired, Yet so Explicit and Well-Written." —Prague Post

"No Other Guide Captures so Completely and Viscerally What it Feels Like to be Inside the City." —San Francisco Bay Guardian

"Brutally Honest Insiders Give You the Straight Scoop on Where to be Seen so You Don't Feel or Look Like a Tourist." —Fitness Magazine

"Biting." —Library Journal

"Refreshingly Frank." —MSNBC

"Razzle-Dazzle Design." —USA Today

"Refreshingly Sharp." —Consumer Reports

"One Guide That Doesn't Shrink From Expressing Opinions." —Boston Globe

"Opinionated, Mildly Caustic and Very Stylish." —Baltimore Sun

Time Warner Center and Trump International Hotel

## About Series Director Daniel Levine

Daniel Levine is a leading international trend hunter with a sharp eye for discovering pioneers in the world's ever-changing cultural landscape. He has written 10 best-selling guidebooks, produced travel television for HBO and NBC, and appeared as a travel trend expert on every major TV network in the US. Described as a "genius" by Elle magazine, Daniel has also been called the 21st-century Arthur Frommer for his stylish writing and contemporary approach to the world of travel. Daniel began his career researching and writing significant portions of the legendary guidebook *Europe on $50-a-Day*. During eight years with publishing giant Simon & Schuster he also wrote nine other best-selling travel books, from California and Florida to London and Italy. Daniel splits his time between Avant-Guide offices in the US and Europe.

## Avant-Guide Online

avantguide.com is the place to discover all the latest developments on all that's new, unique and fashionable via Daniel Levine's Travel Trends Blog. And when you sign up for the free Avant-Guide Communiqué, you'll receive twice-monthly updates on the world's newest hotels, restaurants, shops and sights. You can also test your knowledge and skill with the weekly Avant-Guide Travel Challenge, as well as make real-time reservations for almost every hip hotel in the world. As a service to the Avant-Guide community, we negotiate low rates directly with many hotels and have tapped directly into the reservations systems of many more. Our goal is to offer preferred rates and service for every hotel recommended by Avant-Guide.

## Avant-Guide Lifestyle Network—A Private Members Club

The Avant-Guide Lifestyle Network (AGLN) offers members exclusive benefits including international concierge services that provide access to the inaccessible. AGLN members also benefit from hotel upgrades, preferred restaurant reservations, priority line passes and invites to special Avant-Guide events, showroom sales and more. See avantguide.com for details.

## Our Select Network Of Destinations And Venues

Avant-Guide is a global-lifestyle media company offering a robust range of stylish, information-based products and services related to travel and entertainment. By identifying and creating new, unique and fashionable experiences in the world's most exciting places, Avant-Guide is focused on being the foremost authority on progressive destinations, goods, services and experiences worldwide. In the process we are assembling an influential community of contemporary travelers and a select network of destinations, merchants and service providers who cater to them. Members of the Avant-Guide community are welcome to nominate avant destinations, but should be aware that being recommended by Avant-Guide is at our sole discretion and we never accept discounts or payment in return for positive coverage.

## Write To Us

Keeping our ears close to the ground includes listening to what our readers have to say. People often send us great stories about their avant experiences and we love to hear your comments. See what others have to say on our website and write to us at VIP@avantguide.com. Our hard-working interns respond personally to every email!

## Our Future

Avant-Guide is growing rapidly, covering an increasing number of locations worldwide. Our goal is to be the world's leading source of stylish destination information across all media, including printed guidebooks, digitally and on the Web. Let us know what you think.

# THE AVANT-GUIDE MANIFESTO

**Life is a Sensory Pilgrimage to be Enjoyed & Savored**
Avant-Guide continuously wanders the contemporary cultural landscape in search of hip hotels, extraordinary restaurants, unique shops and the best nightlife. We are particularly attracted to unique places and one-of-a-kind experiences that we haven't encountered before, especially when they are innovative and have distinctive personalities. We work hard to make each Avant-Guide culturally courageous in exactly the same way, with informed listings, stylish prose and a sexy package that doesn't make you stick out like a tourist.

**You Are Free to Choose What You Want**
Life is too short to wade through exhaustive lists. We go to great lengths to accurately research and edit the information you need. And we deliver it in a way that's both easy and pleasurable to use. Each listing is heavily cross-referenced, painstakingly mapped and intensively indexed. And Avant-Guide understands the importance of drawing a bright line between what you have to experience and what is not worth getting out of bed for.

**Stay Independent & Trustworthy**
Avant-Guide never accepts discounts or payments in exchange for positive coverage. Our worldwide network of informational omnivores are passionate about spotting emerging experiences long before they devolve into popular trends. But our visits to restaurants, clubs and other establishments are anonymous and expenses are paid by Avant-Guide. Few other guides can make this claim.

# LISTINGS KEY

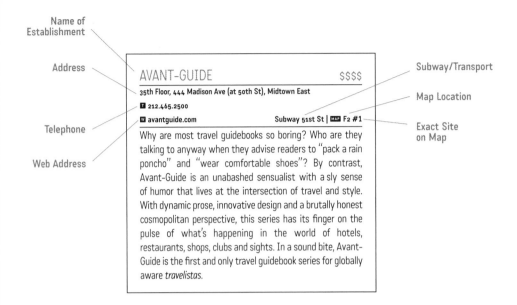

Name of Establishment

Address

Telephone

Web Address

## AVANT-GUIDE $$$$
35th Floor, 444 Madison Ave (at 50th St), Midtown East
☎ 212.465.2500
🌐 avantguide.com    Subway 51st St | **MAP** F2 #1

Why are most travel guidebooks so boring? Who are they talking to anyway when they advise readers to "pack a rain poncho" and "wear comfortable shoes"? By contrast, Avant-Guide is an unabashed sensualist with a sly sense of humor that lives at the intersection of travel and style. With dynamic prose, innovative design and a brutally honest cosmopolitan perspective, this series has its finger on the pulse of what's happening in the world of hotels, restaurants, shops, clubs and sights. In a sound bite, Avant-Guide is the first and only travel guidebook series for globally aware *travelistas*.

Subway/Transport

Map Location

Exact Site on Map

## WHAT THE $$$$ MEAN

### RESTAURANTS
Our $ estimates are based on the average price of one meal.

$ . . . . . . . . under $20
$$. . . . . . . . $20–$40
$$$ . . . . . . . .$41–$60
$$$$ . . . . . . . .over $60

### HOTELS
Our $ estimates are based on a twin room. These can swing dramatically, depending on season, so use this as a guide.

$ . . . . . . . . under $200
$$. . . . . . . $200–$350
$$$ . . . . . . $351–$500
$$$$ . . . . . . . over $500

**Empire Press Media, Inc.,** New York www.avantguide.com | vip@avantguide.com **Series Director** Daniel Levine **Photo Editor** Peter N. Jones **Design** >o< Mowshe Studio | ka+li6+mig+push+ya5 | www.mowshe.cz **Writers** Andre Stenson, Cloe Anderson, Patricia Stewart, JP Lewis, Michael Gross, H. Victor Thomas, Tanisha Bell, Marilyn Wood **Associate Editor** Andy Markowitz **Chief Copy Editor** Peter Metzenbaum **Fact Checking** Prescott Mills, Amy Thompson **Back Cover Photography** Cornelis van Voorthuizen **Additional Photography** Terje Sørgjerd **Digital Cartography Copyright** © Empire Press Media, Inc. **Strategy & Partnerships** Gabor George Burt **Communications Director** Westley Overcash **Website Coding** motiongang. com **Interns** Kurt Heidemann, Kendall Beaudry, Ryan Rosen **Font** KATARINE by Tomáš Brousil **Very Special Thanks** Fran & Alan Levine, Jonathan Pontell, Marilyn Wood, Simon Doonan, Daniel Libeskind, Charlie Palmer, Kevin Roberts, Michael Stipe, Da Jamb, Declan King, Pinky, James Kinsella, PB8, Lisa-Kim Ling Kuan, Jim Kwiatkowski

# Contents

# SLEEP

# 1

It's been twenty years since Ian Schrager opened the world's first hip hotel, Morgan's on Madison Avenue. Today, this New York City landmark is joined by some 50 other style-driven hotels, a trend that is only growing stronger as major players from the worlds of fashion, food and nightlife transform themselves into chic hoteliers. The hotels in this book represent the very best in each price category that New York City has to offer. All offer something new, unique or fashionable, and are special in the way of local color and character. And we have gone to great lengths to uncover the very best of the city's budget hotels. Every establishment listed here meets our strict criteria for service, facilities and value. Hotels get extra points for shower power, room service reaction time, a sound system when you want it, and silence when you don't.

**Getting the best hotel deal is definitely avant. for the best rates and exclusive extras reserve on avantguide.com**

## RESERVATIONS

Getting the best deal is definitely avant. Before booking a hotel, check out avantguide.com where you can make real-time reservations for many of the establishments we recommend. As a service to the Avant-Guide community, we negotiate low rates directly with a large number of hotels and have tapped directly into the reservations systems of many more. Our goal is to offer preferred service for as many of the hotels listed in every Avant-Guide book as we can. However, our reviewers are fiercely independent and have no relationship whatsoever with any of the establishments we recommend. Members of the Avant-Guide Lifestyle Network (AGLN) can also score many extras, including preferred rooms, automatic late checkouts, and special services and amenities appropriate to making our members feel like the VIPs they are. See our website for details.

## BEST HOTELS TO...

### SPOT CELEBRITIES
Chambers, The
Gansevoort, Hotel
Mandarin Oriental
Mercer, The
Tribeca Grand Hotel
W Union Square

### KICK BACK WITH KIDS
Alex Hotel, The
Arlington Hotel
Beacon Hotel
Hard Rock Hotel
Radio City Apartments

### PRETEND YOU'RE ROCK ROYALTY
Bryant Park, The
Kitano New York
Morgans
Royalton, The
W New York

### PARTY HARDY
60 Thompson
Hudson
Maritime Hotel, The
Soho Grand
Soho House New York

### BE AN ARTSY BOHEMIAN
Carlton Arms
Chelsea Hotel
East Village Bed and Coffee
Gershwin, The
Hotel 17

### HAVE A SECRET ROMANCE
Benjamin, The
Blakely, The
Casablanca Hotel
Dream Hotel
Franklin, The
Muse, The

### GET DOWN TO BUSINESS
70 Park Avenue
Four Seasons, The
New York Palace
RIHGA Royal
Trump International Hotel

### LIVE STYLISHLY ON THE CHEAP
Cosmopolitan, The
Larchmont Hotel
Park South Hotel
Roger Smith, The
Thirty-Thirty, Hotel
Time, The

## WHAT THE $$$$$ MEAN

Our $ estimates are based on a twin room. These can swing dramatically, depending on season, so use this as a guide.

| | |
|---|---|
| $ | = under $200 |
| $$ | = $200–$350 |
| $$$ | = $351–$500 |
| $$$$ | = over $500 |

Alex

## 60 THOMPSON $$$

60 Thompson St (at Broome), Soho

☎ 212.431.0400 or 877.431.0400

🖥 60thompson.com  MAP K1 #1

Style lovers flock to this self-consciously cool Soho style spot owned by the same trio of Pomeranc brothers who run the stylish Sagamore Hotel in South Beach, Miami. Eclectic design by Thomas O'Brien of Aero Studios includes high-end flea-market finds in the lobby, and guest rooms featuring sleek dark wood headboards set against a wall of paneled leather. And while prices are uniformly large, some standard guest rooms can be small. The best and most spacious room is the Loft, a spectacular duplex penthouse with double-height ceilings, a stone fireplace, private deck and roof garden. Details are attended to in all rooms, including Philosophy bath products, linens by Frette, minibars stocked by Dean & DeLuca and staff uniforms by Nino Cerruti. There's an excellent restaurant (Kittichai), and lobby and rooftop bars that are chic enough to lure trendy locals.

**100 Rooms:** a/c | tv | tel | web | minibar | stereo | rm svc

## 70 PARK AVENUE $$$

70 Park Ave (at 38th), Midtown

☎ 212.973.2400 or 877.707.2752

🖥 70thparkave.com  MAP I1 #2

San Francisco-based Kimpton Group comes to Manhattan with this stylish new hotel designed by Jeffrey Bilhuber, who's clients include David Bowie, Anna Wintour and Hubert de Givenchy. It's a suitably good looking place, built with the group's trademark stone fireplace in the lobby, comfortable rooms fitted with good linens and oversized plasma TVs and touch-screen telephones that let you order room service electronically. Standard rooms are tiny, as are the bathrooms. But they are well stocked with luxuries that include coffeemakers and free WiFi. Upgrade to a King Premier room if you're planning to do anything here other than sleep, though even here walls could be thicker. The best suite, on the 17th floor, comes with a wrap-around terrace. Silverleaf Tavern is a very good lobby-level restaurant. Pets are welcome and dog walkers are on staff. And yogis are catered to with a 24-hour in-house yoga channel. There's no gym, but guests have access to a nearby health club.

**205 Rooms:** a/c | tv | tel | web | minibar | stereo | rm svc

## ABINGDON GUEST HOUSE                    $

**13 Eighth Ave (at 12th), Greenwich Village**

☎ 212.243.5384

🌐 abingdonguesthouse.com                    MAP H2 #3

Precisely because it is one, Abingdon feels just like a high-quality home. Situated in twin townhouses, all nine smoke-free units are crisply decorated, have firm beds (some four-posters), good lighting and TVs with VCRs. Many have wood floors, exposed brick walls and tin ceilings. All rooms have a private bath, though a few are situated off the hall. There are four floors and no elevator. Located above a coffeehouse directly on Eighth Avenue, this is not the quietest place in the city, but the absence of street-level signage, your own key to the front door and complimentary breakfast downstairs will make you feel like a native.

**9 Rooms:** a/c | tv | tel | web

## ALEX HOTEL, THE                    $$$

**205 East 45th St (at Third), Midtown**

☎ 212.867.5100

🌐 thealexhotel.com                    MAP E2 #4

Designer David Rockwell created this small and stylish place with all the amenities that comfort-addicted guests expect from a fashionably contemporary hotel. Crafted with stainless steel and leather, rooms are quiet and cozy. The best have good views of the Chrysler Building. Bathrooms are limestone and can be small, but they are packed with amenities that include flat-panel TVs, rain showers, Frédéric Fekkai toiletries and Frette robes. Suites come with fully equipped Poggen Pohl Kitchens, complete with Sub-Zero refrigerators and Miele dishwashers. We found members of the black-clad staff, who wear Secret Service-type ear plugs, to be unusually attentive. But because they use the same small elevators as the guests, waits can be long. The lobby is home to a small DJ bar and the terrific Riingo restaurant.

**203 Rooms:** a/c | tv | tel | web | minibar | stereo | rm svc | gym

## ARLINGTON HOTEL                    $

**18 West 25th St (at Broadway), Flatiron District**

☎ 212.645.3990

🌐 hotelarlington.com                    MAP H1 #5

A good-value hotel (read: very basic and without a lot of perks), the Arlington is a solid choice for traveling cheapskates who don't need a lot of extras. Wear is evident throughout, but the location is great, rooms are clean and the beds and baths are fine. Features include a mini-fridge, safe and digital alarm clock. It's the kind of place in which a small deposit is required to make external telephone calls.

**85 Rooms:** a/c | tv | tel

## BEACON HOTEL                    $$

**2130 Broadway (at 75th), Upper West Side**

☎ 212.787.1100 or 800.572.4969

🌐 beaconhotel.com                    MAP C1 #6

The Beacon is a value-packed standby offering decent-sized, renovated rooms with good beds, standard furnishings and great views for those lucky enough to be on the upper stories. It's also got a great Upper West Side location that's close to Lincoln Center, good shopping and Central Park. Most accommodations include hair dryers, coffeemakers and fully-stocked kitchenettes. And there's a nonstop coffee shop on the ground floor.

**230 Rooms:** a/c | tv | tel

## BELVEDERE, THE                    $$

**319 West 48th St (at Eighth), Midtown**

☎ 212.245.7000 or 888.468.3558

🌐 belvederehotelnyc.com                    MAP D2 #7

Clean, friendly and well-located, The Belvedere is a thoroughly pleasant inexpensive hotel. Rooms are decent sized, competently furnished and include a fridge, microwave, hair dryer and iron. In all, a very recommendable place to stay for not too much money.

**400 Rooms:** a/c | tv | tel | web | gym

## BENJAMIN, THE                    $$

**125 East 50th St (at Lexington), Midtown**

☎ 212.715.2500 or 888.423.6526

🌐 thebenjamin.com                    MAP E2 #8

Built in 1927 by architect Emery Roth (and featured in a painting by Georgia O'Keeffe, who had an apartment across the street), The Benjamin is a mid-priced Midtowner that was transformed into a hotel in 1999 by the interior design firm Di Leonardo International. There's nothing flashy about the modern rooms, but all feature large, comfortable beds topped with Frette linens, and guests can choose from a menu of ten different pillows. Most, but not all, rooms are well-sized. The best are stocked with microwaves, coffeemakers, a large fridge and Aveda bath products. The worst, in the "06" line, have miniscule bathrooms and TVs hung from the ceiling, hospital-like. The quietest rooms are on higher floors facing 50th Street.

*The Chambers*

Service is uniformly excellent. The hotel is also home to the highly-regarded Affinia Wellness Spa.

**209 Rooms:** a/c | tv | tel | web | fax | minibar | rm svc | gym

## BLAKELY, THE $$

**136 West 55th St (at Sixth), Midtown**

☎ 212.245.1800 or 800.735.0710

🖥 blakelynewyork.com  |  **MAP D2 #9**

While not as hip or designy as many others in its class, this excellent Midtowner offers unusually spacious rooms filled with all the requisite amenities, like free WiFi, flat-panel TVs, marble Jacuzzi baths, Frette robes and complimentary coffee and tea. And all rooms have full kitchenettes. Beds are über-comfortable, dressed with feather mattress toppers, down pillows and duvets. Rooms on low floors can be dark and noisy, the staff could be better and the elevators are slow as molasses. But The Blakely is an excellent mid-priced island in an otherwise pricey sea.

**119 Rooms:** a/c | tv | tel | web | stereo | rm svc | gym

## BRYANT PARK, THE $$

**40 West 40th St (at Sixth), Midtown**

☎ 212.869.0100 or 877.640.9300

🖥 bryantparkhotel.com  |  **MAP H1 #10**

Fashionistas, primarily, flock to this avant hotel with a nightclub vibe and a stellar location across from its namesake park. Set in the American Radiator building, a landmark black-and-gold tower, the hotel features loft-like rooms that are designy and minimalist, set with comfortable, modern furnishings on hardwood floors. Sizes vary, but each has flat-panel TVs and great marble bathrooms with tubs large enough for two. And the attitude-free service is tops. Suites are extremely spacious and the best overlook the park. A few even have balconies. Avoid rooms on lower floors, where muffled noise from the hotel's hyped-up Koi sushi restaurant and trendy Cellar Bar can sometimes be heard into the wee hours. And forget about getting a room here during Fashion Week, when puffy-lipped models take over the hallways.

**127 Rooms:** a/c | tv | tel | web | fax | minibar | stereo | rm svc | gym

## CARLTON ARMS $

**160 East 25th St (at Third), Midtown**

☎ 212.679.0680

🖥 carltonarms.com  |  **MAP I1 #11**

The Carlton Arms is probably the wackiest place to stay in Manhattan. Every room, every corridor and seemingly every surface in this elevator-less five-story bohemian dive is covered with lively murals by local artists, many of whom have worked on the hotel's staff. Some of the art has even developed into major installations, resulting in an over-the-top hodgepodge that is anything but cookie-cutter. It's a fun place that lives down to all expectations, playing to young student/artist types who don't need TVs and don't plan to spend much time indoors. Rooms can be small, they are not the cleanest around and the shared showers are less than inviting. But the location is good and the vibe is truly, well, unique.

**54 Rooms:** a/c

## Casablanca Hotel $$

**147 West 43rd St (at Sixth), Midtown**

**T 212.869.1212 or 888.922.7225**

**W casablancahotel.com** MAP D2 #12

An intimate boutique hotel hard by Times Square in the heart of the Theater District, the Casablanca pleases us with a luxurious Moroccan style that truly indulges each guest like a pasha, with beautifully appointed rooms, and a plethora of amenities including VCRs, terry bathrobes, complimentary soft drinks and fresh flowers in every room. An excellent continental breakfast is served, along with all-day cookies and coffee, and evening wine and cheese. Light sleepers should ask for a room facing the interior courtyard.

**48 Rooms:** a/c | tv | tel | web | minibar | stereo | rm svc

## Chambers, The $$$

**15 West 56th St (at Fifth), Midtown**

**T 212.974.5656 or 866.204.5656**

**W chambershotel.com** MAP E2 #13

The Chambers is a white-hot hotel packed with sophistication and sleek touches. All the hallmarks of hip hoteling are in place at this exceptional place, including killer public areas that double as party venues and small, minimalist David Rockwell-designed rooms swanked out with MTV touches that include power showers, etched-glass bathroom doors and a roll of butcher paper you can pull over the glass writing desk for notes or cleanliness. The excellent Town restaurant is downstairs.

**77 Rooms:** a/c | tv | tel | web | minibar | stereo | rm svc

## Chelsea Hotel $$

**222 West 23rd St (at Seventh), Chelsea**

**T 212.243.3700**

**W chelseahotel.com** MAP H1#14

The historical Chelsea is one part hotel, two parts mysterious phenomenon. Throughout the 20th century, the building has been a shabby chic flophouse for a roster of bohemian transients, from Mark Twain to the members of Jefferson Airplane. *Titanic* survivors with second-class tickets were lodged here for a few days, and in 1953, at age 39, the hard-drinking poet Dylan Thomas collapsed in his room here, later dying in nearby St. Vincent's Hospital. Andy Warhol made a film here and Sid killed Nancy in room 100. Guestrooms run the gamut from decent to horrible. Like a proverbial box of chocolates, you never know what you're going to get. Some are tiny, some are huge. Some are renovated and some are not. Some are fitted with huge, carved 19th-century furnishings, and some contain 1950s-era tubular steel dinettes. Suites are the best bets, as many retain their Victorian layouts and have spectacular carved-marble fireplaces that still work.

*The Benjamin*

**400 Rooms:** tv

## City Club Hotel $$$

**55 West 44th St (at Sixth), Midtown**

**T 212.921.5500**

**W cityclubhotel.com** MAP E2 #15

Wonderful interiors by Jeffrey Bilhuber and room service from chef Daniel Boulud's DB Bistro Moderne conspire to make this a good, if pricy, choice in Midtown. City Club is an intimate place for moneyed guests who shy away from staying in hotels in which the lobby doubles as a nightclub. Indeed there is hardly a lobby here at all. Standard rooms can be small for the price. Some are very small, have no dressers and tiny closets. But all are beautifully lit and well decorated with original art and furniture, feather beds and TVs cleverly hidden behind mirrors. Book a Deluxe King room if you want room enough to swing your pearls.

**65 Rooms:** a/c | tv | tel | web | stereo | rm svc

Hudson Guestroom

its large circular aquarium, mimics equally fanciful blue-illuminated rooms featuring giant plasma TVs and Molton Brown toiletries. Guestrooms are helpfully labeled Small, Medium, Large and Extra Large, but even these appellations are misleading, as the small ones are positively tiny and some don't even have windows. iPods programmed with 2,000 songs are theoretically available for guests' use, but there are too few of them to guarantee you'll get one. The hotel is also a base for a trio of drinkeries that include the cavernous subterranean Subconscious Bar, a whimsically striped lobby lounge, and Ava, a dreamy rooftop lounge that, unfortunately, is often closed to guests in favor of private events.

**228 Rooms:** a/c | tv | tel | web | minibar | stereo | rm svc | gym

## EAST VILLAGE BED AND COFFEE      $

110 Ave C (at 7th), East Village

☎ 917.816.0071

🖥 bedandcoffee.com      **MAP** J2 #18

Staying at this budget-priced alternative accommodation truly gives you the experience of being a New York native. You can live well, in spacious and nicely decorated rooms, or you can live cheaply in the Chalet, which is accessible by ladder. Either way, you will be in a unique neighborhood that is both amazingly lively and surprisingly quiet. Bathrooms, which are spotless, are shared, as is a living room, library and fully equipped kitchen. Most guests seem to enjoy meeting other travelers, many of whom seem to be from Europe, despite the fact that smoking is prohibited.

**7 Rooms:** a/c | stereo

## FOUR SEASONS, THE      $$$$

57 East 57th St (at Madison), Midtown

☎ 212.758.5700 or 800.819.5053

🖥 fourseasons.com      **MAP** E2 #19

A flashy IM Pei-designed showstopper built for visiting celebs and globo-bosses, the Four Seasons 53-story limestone tower is nothing if not dramatic. It's a huge hotel that happily flaunts its wealth of space, which, of course, is Manhattan's most precious commodity. Guestrooms are some of the largest in the city. They are also super luxurious, designed with contemporary prints, top-quality custom furnishings and unusual extras that include power-operated silk drapes opened via bedside switch, and turbo bathtubs that fill in just 60 seconds. Suites include walk-in closets with tie racks large enough to accommodate 50 ties, and private balconies on higher floors open onto unobstructed

## COSMOPOLITAN, THE      $

95 West Broadway (at Chambers), Tribeca

☎ 212.566.1900 or 888.895.9400

🖥 cosmohotel.com      **MAP** K1 #16

Situated in the heart of Tribeca, just five blocks north of the World Trade Center site, The Cosmopolitan is a clean, well-lighted place with simple furnishings and muted colors. It's a relatively inexpensive hotel with an atmosphere to match: welcoming and modern, relatively quiet and laid-back. Service is lacking and it is somewhat noisy. But the price is light in a happening neighborhood that has few hotels.

**105 Rooms:** tv | tel

## DREAM HOTEL      $$

210 West 55th St (at Broadway), Midtown

☎ 212.247.2000 or 866.437.3266

🖥 dreamny.com      **MAP** D2 #17

Actor/model/hotelier Vikram Chatwal (**Time**) and surrealist fashion photographer David LaChapelle teamed up to create this mid-priced hotel with supercool design that sometimes favors form over function. The stylish lobby lounge, with

*The Gershwin*

city views. Superb service catering to any type of neurotic need, plus a famously well-connected concierge keep this hotel at the top of our list.

**370 Rooms:** a/c | tv | tel | web | fax | minibar | stereo | rm svc | gym

## FRANKLIN, THE $$

**164 East 87th St (at Lexington), Upper East Side**

☎ 212.369.1000 or 800.607.4009

**W** franklinhotel.com     **MAP** B2 #20

If you're young and avant and want to stay on the Upper East Side, then The Franklin is your hotel. "Affordable, chic, boutique" should be the motto of this slightly eccentric fashion-industry charmer that was transformed from a former crack house into a proverbial house of style. Minimalist design emphasizes a few important pieces in otherwise clutter-free rooms. Look for brushed steel furnishings, canopy beds, cedar closets, fresh flowers and VCRs. A sleek place at plain prices, The Franklin represents good value in one of the city's toniest neighborhoods. Rates include breakfast, in-room movies, parking and tea each afternoon in the lobby.

**51 Rooms:** a/c | tv | tel | web | stereo

## GANSEVOORT, HOTEL $$$

**18 Ninth Ave (at 13th), Meatpacking District**

☎ 212.206.6700 or 877.426.7386

**W** hotelgansevoort.com     **MAP** G2 #21

Designed by architect Stephen B. Jacobs and interior designer Andi Pepper, the zinc-colored metal-clad Gansevoort is a colorful beacon in one of Manhattan's hottest neighborhoods. Just past the tall illuminated glass entrance columns you'll find modern and minimalist rooms with cream and gray fabrics, dark wood furnishings and leather headboards. And plasma TVs are everywhere, even in the elevators. The best rooms overlook the action on Ninth Avenue and from high floors you can see the river from the comfort of your feather-topped bed. Deluxe Rooms are substantially larger than Standard Rooms and many have step-out balconies. Topped by retractable glass, the rooftop lounge is the hotel's showpiece, featuring twin seating areas, a heated swimming pool and wonderful views that include the **Soho House** pool across the street. Of course, chic boutiques, cool bars and a bit too much noise is just outside the front door too. And, for the moment at least, you can still get a side of beef on the next corner.

**187 Rooms:** a/c | tv | tel | web | minibar | stereo | rm svc | gym

*Mandarin Oriental*

## GERSHWIN, THE $

**7 East 27th St (at Fifth), Flatiron District**

☎ 212.545.8000

🌐 gershwinhotel.com          MAP H1 #22

The rest stop of choice for traveling alternateens and boho Europeans, The Gershwin offers inexpensive funky lodgings and interestingly "decorated" rooms. A fun, pop-art lobby gives way to guest quarters so spartan that ceiling cracks become decoration. Very clean but exceedingly bohemian, the hotel has the atmosphere of an upscale youth hostel that was opened in a week. Inexpensive doubles are augmented by super-cheap, eight-bed multi-shares—each a global village in microcosm. Closet space is non-existent. Messages? Fugetaboutit. The Red Room, a dark and cheap bar, is the hotel's piece de resistance, reeling in guests and locals with live music seven nights a week.

**147 Rooms:** a/c | tv | tel | web

## HARD ROCK HOTEL $$

**235 West 46th St (at Broadway), Midtown**

☎ 212.764.5500 or 800.225.7474

🌐 hardrock.com          MAP D2 #23

This former Ian Schrager hotel is rebranding as the Hard Rock, the third American venture (Chicago was the first) for the Spanish-based Sol Meliá hotel group, the largest resort hotel company in the world. This hotel features contemporary design in modern surroundings right in the heart of Times Square. Whether it will attract Jenny Craig rejects from the Midwest, or waify AMWs (actress/model/whatever's) from the city is to be seen.

**610 Rooms:** a/c | tv | tel | web | minibar | rm svc | gym

## HOTEL 17 $

**225 East 17th St (at Second), Gramercy**

☎ 212.475.2845

🌐 hotel17ny.com          MAP I2 #24

Hotel 17 is the ultimate budget-priced downtown dive with shared baths, packed with impoverished young trendies who read about it in Details magazine. A former welfare hotel, 17 has a heroin-chic allure that has landed almost as many fashion shoots as guests. Close to the East Village without actually being in it, the hotel thrives on its edgy image to the extent that carpet stains remain unchallenged by the house cleaners. That said, Hotel 17 is not life threatening, it's great for late-nighters and it has a unique atmosphere that is authentically hip.

**120 Rooms:** tv

Morgans

## HOTEL 31 $

120 East 31st St (at Park), Midtown

☎ 212.685.3060

🖳 hotel31.com      MAP I1 #25

Europeans, especially, seem to gravitate to this budget savior because it's cheap, clean, safe and has good beds and showers. On the harsher side, the design is awful and old-fashioned, there are no views, and it can be a little noisy. You'll pay a bit more for a private bathroom, and it's well worth it. All in all, this is one of the best budget finds in Manhattan.

**60 Rooms:** a/c | tv | tel

## HOTEL ON RIVINGTON, THE $$

107 Rivington St (at Ludlow), Lower East Side

☎ 212.475.2600 or 800.915.1537

🖳 hotelonrivington.com      MAP L1 #26

Originally begun in conjunction with designy Surface magazine, a partnership that soon fizzled, this hip hotel amid the tenements of the Lower East Side plays to German camera crews, visiting designers and style sensitive others looking for a hip place to stay that won't break the bank. The LES location is at once high-energy and sketchy, which, of course, is a big part of the charm. Accommodations at THOR are thoughtfully laid out and incredibly comfortable, though the quality of the workmanship is questionable and showing wear. There are slate tubs and heated floors in the bath, plasma TVs and minibars stocked with healthful items from Teany, Moby's vegan restaurant down the street. Guestrooms are thrillingly bright and those on higher floors enjoy striking views of Manhattan—even from some bathrooms. Corners facing southeast take in the Financial District and all three downtown bridges. And blackout drapes sweep around the room at the touch of a button. The lovely bar, designed by Piero Lissoni, is a sexy place for a drink.

**109 Rooms:** a/c | tv | tel | web | minibar | stereo | rm svc

## HUDSON $$

356 West 58th St (at Eighth), Midtown

☎ 212.554.6000 or 800.444.4786

🖳 hudsonhotel.com      MAP D2 #27

Designer Philippe Starck was enlisted to create Ian Schrager's (Gramercy Park Hotel, **Morgans, Royalton**) biggest hotel yet: a stunning party-in-a-box designed with whimsical gathering places, bars and eateries. Even the fitness facilities are imbued with stylish fun, encompassing a David Barton gym (with an

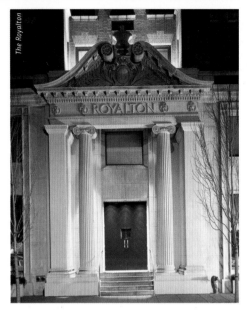

*The Royalton*

natural wood floors, shoji paper screens, a deep-bathing tub and futons on tatami mats. There is no gym, but guests have free access to New York Sports Club.

**149 Rooms:** a/c | tv | tel | web | minibar | rm svc

## LARCHMONT HOTEL  $

**27 West 11th St (at Fifth), Greenwich Village**

☎ 212.989.9333

🌐 larchmonthotel.com  **MAP** H2 #29

A haven for debt-ridden aristocrats, young couples and students on a tight budget, the Larchmont is an alluring little inn on a perfect Greenwich Village street. The antithesis of a corporate hotel, this place is homey and unique. Rooms are small, and none comes with private bath. But each is well decorated in muted earth tones, very clean and equipped with good lighting, a writing desk, ceiling fan, bathrobe and slippers.

**58 Rooms:** a/c | tv | tel

## MANDARIN ORIENTAL  $$$$

**Time Warner Center, 80 Columbus Circle (at 60th), Upper West Side**

☎ 212.805.8800 or 866.801.8880

🌐 mandarinoriental.com  **MAP** D2 #30

Easily one of the most striking and sophisticated hotels in Manhattan, the Mandarin Oriental occupies floors 35 to 54 of the Time Warner Center, offering amazing views, top-of-the-line service and spectacularly sleek high-tech rooms. Every guest room has large marble baths and separate showers with amenities by Aromatherapy Associates, flat-panel HD TVs with surround sound, laptop chargers in the safe and floor-to-ceiling windows. The best face Central Park. Of course, prices are also in the stratosphere, but that's no impediment for the celebrities and C-level power professionals (CEO, CFO and the like) who can often be spotted swanning through Asiate restaurant and the swanky **Lobby Lounge**.

**250 Rooms:** a/c | tv | tel | web | fax | minibar | stereo | rm svc | gym

Olympic-sized pool), a bowling alley, and basketball, volleyball and archery courts. "Dorm Chic" guest rooms are small, but still manage to contain a suite of visually rich objects, including stainless steel tables, gold-leaf stools, upholstered headboards and dramatic bedside light boxes designed by Francesco Clemente. The Columbus Circle location is great and the space-age Hudson Bar remains a swoony place for a drink.

**1000 Rooms:** a/c | tv | tel | web | fax | minibar | stereo | rm svc | gym

## KITANO NEW YORK  $$

**66 Park Ave (at 38th), Midtown**

☎ 212.885.7000 or 800.548.2666

🌐 kitano.com  **MAP** I1 #28

In an ever-increasing sea of sameness, the Kitano offers luxurious service, simple elegance and distinctive Japanese calm. The hotel is something of a poor man's Mandarin Oriental. But not too poor. Along with Japanese green tea making facilities, standard rooms come with good beds, marble baths, high-speed Internet, plasma TVs, bathrobes, soundproofed windows that open and Shiseido bath products. Premier rooms, located in the building's corners, are larger and include a separate sitting area. As is usual, the best rooms are on high floors. Samurais with deep pockets will want to splash out for the top floor Tatami Suite, a stylish playpen furnished with

## MARITIME HOTEL, THE  $$

**363 West 16th St (at Ninth), Chelsea**

☎ 212.242.4300

🌐 themaritimehotel.com  **MAP** G2 #31

Built in 1966 as a training center for the National Maritime Union, this unique 12-story building with porthole windows was transformed by Sean MacPherson and Eric Goode, America's premiere restaurant and nightlife impresarios, into a highly styled boutique hotel. Standard guest rooms are snug and very

Trump International Hotel

"The Life Aquatic." Resembling a cabin on a cruise liner, they're decked out with ocean-themed fabric, teak furnishings, great bathrooms, plasma TVs and, of course, a round window that can open and close. Most importantly to most guests, The Maritime blurs the boundary between hostelry and entertainment venue, offering a spacious outdoor lounge, a couple of excellent bars (**The Cabanas**, **Hiro**)and the terrific **Matsuri** restaurant, all of which are thick with scenesters.

**125 Rooms:** a/c | tv | tel | web | minibar | stereo | rm svc

## MERCER, THE                                    $$$

**147 Mercer St (at Prince), Soho**

☎ 212.966.6060 or 888.918.6060

🌐 mercerhotel.com                        MAP K1 #32

The Mercer is an ultra-trendy hot spot with a tranquil atmosphere and understated design that's meant to contrast with Ian Schrager's dazzling party palaces. Run by André Balazs (**QT**), the hotel offers spacious, loft-like studios that are expensive, roomy, minimalist and just oh so Soho. Conceived by designer Christian Liaigre, Zen-like serenity is achieved with luxurious woods, custom made furnishings and extra-large marble bathrooms, many of which have two-person tubs. Room features include a table large enough for dining or working, a suite of chairs and minibar stocked

by Dean & DeLuca. Unusually for such stylish places, the staff here is as capable as it is good-looking. The bamboo-and-brick Mercer Kitchen, downstairs, is under the control of Manhattan mega-chef Jean-Georges Vongerichten (Jean Georges, JoJo, Vong).

**75 Rooms:** a/c | tv | tel | web | fax | minibar | stereo | rm svc

## MORGANS                                    $$$

**237 Madison Ave (at 37th), Midtown**

☎ 212.686.0300 or 800.444.4786

🌐 morganshotel.com                        MAP H1 #33

Despite an unstylish Murray Hill location and Armani-clad staff (yawn), Morgans remains one of the best hip hotels in Manhattan. A vanguard of cool when it was opened two decades ago by former Studio 54 partners Steve Rubell and Ian Schrager (Gramercy Park Hotel, **Hudson**, **Royalton**), the hotel has retained its image as a sophisticated address for high-level creatives and B-list celebrities who aren't in desperate need of an audience. With just a small brass nameplate by the door, the hotel features minimalist guest rooms with suede headboards, corduroy ottomans, bronze floor lamps and built-in maple cabinets and window seats. Baths are particularly striking, designed with black-and-white tiles and granite floors, along with stainless steel

fixtures and Jacuzzi baths. The penthouse, one of the premiere places to stay in New York, sprawls out with two terraces, a multimedia room and a private greenhouse. The hotel is also home to Asia de Cuba restaurant.

**154 Rooms:** a/c | tv | tel | web | fax | minibar | stereo | rm svc

## MUSE, THE                                     $$$

130 West 46th St (at Sixth), Midtown

☎ 212.485.2400 or 877.692.6873

ⓦ themusehotel.com                         **MAP** D2 #34

Fashionable surroundings and a terrific location in the heart of the Theater District are the best attributes of this hotel. Rooms are small, but attractively furnished with contemporary light cherry furnishings and very comfortable beds. Some even have balconies. There's also a full raft of luxuries, including in-room coffeemakers. The staff can be harried, and the interior could use some updating. Choose a high floor to minimize street noise.

**200 Rooms:** a/c | tv | tel | web | minibar | stereo | rm svc | gym

## NEW YORK PALACE                               $$$

455 Madison Ave (at 50th), Midtown

☎ 212.888.7000 or 800.697.2522

ⓦ newyorkpalace.com                         **MAP** E2 #35

This landmark hotel unites a contemporary 55-story tower with the 1882 Villard Houses, a group of six historical brownstone mansions designed by McKim Mead and White, Auguste Saint-

Gaudens and Louis Comfort Tiffany. The result is a beautiful and well run old-world hotel that is geared for serious business but allows for plenty of pleasures. The courtyard entrance and lavish public areas exude a unique elegance. And guest rooms are as luxe as the lobby is plush. Each has a large, firm bed, executive-size desk and good lighting. Fine views over St. Patrick's Cathedral make west-facing rooms on higher floors more expensive than those below. Rooms on executive floors include access to a private lounge with complimentary continental breakfast, and hors d'oeuvres and beverages each evening. A terrific, full service gym includes a rollerblade training machine.

**963 Rooms:** a/c | tv | tel | web | fax | minibar | stereo | rm svc | gym

## PARK SOUTH HOTEL                              $$

122 East 28th St (at Lexington), Midtown

☎ 212.448.0888 or 800.315.4642

ⓦ parksouthhotel.com                        **MAP** I1 #36

Chic surroundings, friendly professional service, sophisticated small rooms and well-within-this-stratosphere pricing conspire to make this one of the best-value finds in Manhattan. It's a great little hotel with Sealy Posturpedic beds, bathrobes, free large continental breakfast and Internet. The best face the street and have no views to speak of, but are quieter than those facing the interior of the building and are closer to the air conditioning system.

**41 Rooms:** a/c | tv | tel | web | fax | stereo | gym

## QT HOTEL                                                 $$

**125 West 45th St (at Sixth), Midtown**

☎ 212.354.2323

🌐 hotelqt.com                                    **MAP** D2 #37

This stylish no-frills offering by hotelier André Balazs (**Mercer**) is such a decidedly mixed bag that even the owner jokingly refers to it as "the sub-Standard." Enthusiasts love the Times Square location, the very cool design by New York architect Lindy Roy and the playful little ground floor swimming pool that's just big enough to make a splash. And there's a little cedar paneled DJ bar with cork stools and pink leather banquettes. Otherwise, check-in is at a simple counter just inside the front door, there is no lobby to speak of and guestrooms are incredibly compressed, so much so that many contain platform beds and/or bunk beds, and not much else. The quietest (note we did not say "quiet") rooms are on the top floors. Extras include flat-panel TVs, small refrigerators, safes and free WiFi, as well as a miniature gym, sauna and steam room. This one's for youthful adventurers.

**140 Rooms:** a/c | tv | tel | web | gym

## RADIO CITY APARTMENTS                                    $

**142 West 49th St (at Sixth), Midtown**

☎ 212.730.0728 or 877.921.9321

🌐 radiocityapartments.com                        **MAP** D2 #38

RCA gets the Avant-Guide nod of approval because it represents one of the best space-to-price ratios in Manhattan. For not too much money you get your own little apartment with one, two or three rooms, in addition to a well-equipped kitchenette. Furnishings are not designy, or even especially comfortable. Bathrooms can be cramped, showers are weak and some wear is evident. But the beds are fine, it's relatively quiet and the Rockefeller Center location is great.

**85 Rooms:** tv | tel | web

## RIHGA ROYAL                                              $$$

**151 West 54th St (at Sixth), Midtown**

☎ 212.307.5000 or 877.746.6225

🌐 rihgaroyalny.com                               **MAP** D2 #39

This luxurious Midtowner is a flamboyant, all-suite hotel with huge rooms at medium prices. Its 54 stories cater to well-to-do mortals and a wide spectrum of rich and famous, from Emperor Akihito to the rock band Oasis. And it's particularly great for families. In addition to great Central Park views (from north-facing rooms on high floors), the hotel offers in-room ice-makers, free limos to Wall Street and 24-hour in-suite dining with china, crystal and silver. The top of the line Pinnacle suites have state-

of-the-art features that include videophones and the ultimate in Japanese technology: electronic bidet-toilets.

**500 Suites:** a/c | tv | tel | web | minibar | stereo | rm svc | gym

## ROGER SMITH, THE                                         $$

**501 Lexington Ave (at 47th), Midtown**

☎ 212.755.1400 or 800.445.0277

🌐 rogersmith.com                                 **MAP** E2 #40

James Knowles, the Roger Smith's owner and "Creative Strategist" likes to think of his hotel as a place for artists and art-lovers with a lobby that is something of a gallery for contemporary paintings and statues. Indeed, entry-level pop groups and other creatives seem to like this hotel's well-sized rooms, each of which is uniquely furnished with B&B foundlings and full of character. Service can be uneven, but there's a generosity of spirit in this cozy inn, nestled amongst the skyscrapers of Midtown. Rooms come with refrigerators and coffeemakers, there's a video lending library and a good breakfast, free to all guests.

**130 Rooms:** a/c | tv | tel | web

## ROYALTON, THE                                            $$$

**44 West 44th St (at Fifth), Midtown**

☎ 212.869.4400 or 800.635.9013

🌐 royaltonhotel.com                              **MAP** E2 #41

In 1988, when disco kings Steve Rubell and Ian Schrager (Gramercy Park Hotel, **Hudson**, **Morgans**) hired Philippe Starck to create this new hostelry, the idea was to design an entertaining and provocative frolic pad. Starck took a historic hotel and rendered it unrecognizable, with a playroom lobby full of oversized furniture, showplace guestrooms and a modelicious, black-clad staff. Today the sleek modish beds, serene neutral-tone furnishings and steel, slate-and-glass bathrooms with round tubs feel very 1990s. And low lighting and small desks are the epitome of form over function. But bathrooms are large and bedrooms are comfortable, equipped with VCRs and stereos. Some even have working fireplaces. The lobby-level **Round Bar**, almost literally a watering hole, is one of the coziest places in the city for a drink.

**168 Rooms:** a/c | tv | tel | web | minibar | stereo | rm svc | gym

## SOHO GRAND                                               $$$

**310 West Broadway (at Canal), Soho**

☎ 212.965.3000 or 800.965.3000

🌐 sohogrand.com                                  **MAP** K1 #42

The Soho Grand is an over-the-top, self-consciously stylish spot in a unique location, within walking distance to Soho's

*W Union Square*

shaped bathtubs big enough for two. The best are mini-suites, in which a thick curtain divides the bed and sitting areas. And guests have access to all the club's bars.

**24 Rooms:** a/c | tv | tel | web | stereo

## THIRTY-THIRTY, HOTEL $

**30 East 30th St (at Madison), Midtown**

☎ 212.689.1900 or 800.497.6028

🌐 thirtythirty-nyc.com     **MAP** H1 #44

A value-conscious hotel that is as no-nonsense as its name, 30-30 offers rooms that are clean, comfortable and have a modern, minimalist look. Beds have padded bedheads and black side tables. But space is limited so that TVs are suspended from the walls, and the single chair is likely tucked into a corner. The best rooms have twin queen beds and views of the Empire State Building, the worst rooms have bunk beds and views of nothing at all.

**240 Rooms:** a/c | tv | tel | web

## TIME, THE $$

**224 West 49th St (at Broadway), Midtown**

☎ 212.320.2900 or 877.846.3692

🌐 thetimeny.com     **MAP** D2 #45

If we didn't warn you to look out for it, you'd miss the tiny unprepossessing entrance to this midtown style spot by Vikram Chatwal (**Dream**). A large glass elevator lifts you to a candle-lit lounge/reception area with wall holograms and low-rider leather seating that is sometimes a gathering place for a theater/media crowd. Designed by Adam Tihany, the hotel's guestrooms are fun and colorful, but unanimously snug and lightly showing wear. The location is great, but there's no view. If you can score a great deal you should consider staying here. If not, keep shopping.

**200 Rooms:** a/c | tv | tel | web | fax | minibar | stereo | rm svc | gym

## TRIBECA GRAND HOTEL $$$

**2 Sixth Ave (at Church), Tribeca**

☎ 212.519.6600 or 877.519.6600

🌐 tribecagrand.com     **MAP** K1 #46

A hotspot for local film execs and capitalists working in the nearby Financial District, the Tribeca Grand has a striking interior that begins with a soaring eight-story atrium and vast lounge/restaurant featuring windows that stretch one whole block. The drama continues in the contemporary guestrooms equipped with wireless Internet keyboards, ergonomic chairs, and built-in bathroom TVs with water-proof remotes. Additional luxuries include Frette bathrobes and

art galleries and shops. The wonderful, post-modern interior is clearly influenced by the neighborhood's commercial roots. Guests enter past bouncer-like doormen into a dramatic dance-club interior that grooves with high-volume chill-out music. A glowing staircase of translucent coke bottle glass and cast iron suspended from the ceiling by tensile cables, leads to the main lobby-salon, a trendy showplace of colossal art where great-looking people dressed in black gather in front of enormous windows treated with muslin and velvet. Cool gray and beige guestrooms are small and minimalist, designed with overscale furniture, original photographs from a local gallery and heavy velvet drapes. Pampering comes in the form of Frette linens and velour bathrobes, fleece throws, Kiehl's toiletries, and non-fat-munchie-stocked minibars.

**369 Rooms:** a/c | tv | tel | web | fax | minibar | stereo | rm svc | gym

## SOHO HOUSE NEW YORK $$$

**29 Ninth Ave (at 13th), Meatpacking District**

☎ 212.627.9800

🌐 sohohouseny.com     **MAP** G2 #43

Most people who know Soho House only know it as a members-only restaurant and night club. But it's also a small luxury hotel that's open to non-members. And it's one of the coolest places to stay downtown. Rooms have an industrial loft feel, range in size from large to huge and feature exposed beams, brick walls and sumptuous furnishings that include crystal chandeliers, Asian rugs, giant plasma TVs and egg-

linens, toiletries from Kiehl's, and a luxurious, private 98-seat screening room. As you'd imagine celebrities are commonplace and the bar scene is stellar. But beware late night noise from all the revelry below. And do you really need to pay so much and still be kept behind the velvet rope?

**203 Rooms:** a/c | tv | tel | web | fax | minibar | stereo | rm svc | gym

## TRUMP INTERNATIONAL HOTEL $$$$

1 Central Park West (at Columbus Circle), Upper West Side
☎ 212.299.1000 or 888.448.7867
🌐 trumpintl.com                                    MAP D2 #47

Grudgingly we admit that The Donald gives great hotel. The Versace of real estate transformed one of the nation's ten worst buildings into a neighborhood beacon and helped restore an entire district in the process. The hotel's black and gold exterior attracts the kind of nouveau riche European that thinks the Trump trademark is one of sophistication. Yet the interior honestly is all class. Guestrooms are designed with rich textures and tasteful colors, and fitted with sensuously stained wood furnishings, enormous closets and elegant marble baths. Some even have kitchens. On the higher floors the hotel's floor-to-ceiling windows offer amazing, unobstructed views over Central Park. Suites include telescopes amongst the furnishings, as well as good-sized Jacuzzi tubs. And there's a terrific fitness center, complete with a lap pool and spa. Of course all this finery isn't cheap, but for those lucky enough to occupy a corner room facing northeast and holding dinner reservations at Jean-Georges downstairs, it's easy to identify with the owner and feel like you're far more than an apprentice.

**167 Rooms:** a/c | tv | tel | web | fax | minibar | stereo | rm svc | gym

## W NEW YORK $$$

541 Lexington Ave (at 49th), Midtown
☎ 212.755.1200 or 877.946.8357
🌐 whotels.com                                    MAP E2 #48

The very first link in the growing chain of Ws, this stylish hotel rides the fence between corporate and cool. Designed by David Rockwell, it's the perfect vibe for fashionable midtowners who love lounging in the lobby, drinking at Rande Gerber's Whiskey Blue, dining in Drew Nieporent's Heartbeat restaurant, and pampering at the large Bliss49 spa. And who doesn't? Fashionable interior design includes walls of running water in the dark lobby, organic cuisine in the restaurant, and even pots of wheatgrass in the small rooms. And there's always terrific music—that's the key to all the W hotels.

**722 Rooms:** a/c | tv | tel | web | fax | minibar | stereo | rm svc | gym

## W THE COURT $$$

130 East 39th St (at Lexington), Midtown
☎ 212.685.1100 or 877.946.8357
🌐 whotels.com                                    MAP I1 #49

The least expensive, and least exciting, of the quartet of Manhattan Ws, The Court has a very dark and sexy lobby and public areas that include Scott and Rande Gerber's stylish Wet Bar. Small guestrooms feature stylish furnishings and very good beds. And tiny bathrooms are stocked with thick robes and Bliss products. From check-in to the concierge, the black-clad staff can be hit or miss. Overall, this W feels like a good-value hip hotel.

**198 Rooms:** a/c | tv | tel | web | minibar | stereo | rm svc | gym

## W TIMES SQUARE $$$

1567 Broadway (at 47th), Midtown
☎ 212.930.7400 or 888.625.5144
🌐 whotels.com                                    MAP D2 #50

Stylish and busy, this swanky hotel is a good choice for urban adventurers looking for an energetic location, a throbbing bar scene and trendy minimalist surroundings. Small rooms with low lighting and tiny bathrooms with doorless showers are minuses. And the youthful clientele and thin walls keep noise levels relatively high. The best rooms have Times Square views, and all have great beds and good bath products.

**509 Rooms:** a/c | tv | tel | web | fax | minibar | stereo | rm svc | gym

## W UNION SQUARE $$$$

201 Park Ave South (at 17th), Union Square
☎ 212.253.9119 or 877.946.8357
🌐 whotels.com                                    MAP I2 #51

This relentlessly stylish hotspot is so right it feels like it was designed by a focus group. It's got an awesome location too, on the northeast corner of Union Square in the handsome Beaux-Arts Guardian Life building. Guests enter to a double story lobby lounge furnished with clusters of plush velvet sofas. Each W hotel has a signature object, and here it's board game tables that are dotted throughout. Rooms are luxe comfortable, furnished with down comforters, a chaise lounge and a decent sized desk. Todd English's terrific Olives restaurant is a good choice for dinner, and the hip Underbar is a sexy place for a drink. In all, the best of the NYC Ws.

**270 Rooms:** a/c | tv | tel | web | fax | minibar | stereo | rm svc | gym

## KEVIN ROBERTS

**Kevin Roberts is the New York-based Worldwide CEO of Saatchi & Saatchi, one of the world's leading creative organizations. Before joining the agency in 1997, Kevin held leadership positions with some of the world's great brands, among them Procter & Gamble, Pepsi and Gillette. Kevin's radical optimism, uncompromising style, visionary ideas and straight-talking manner have situated him at the leading edge of global commerce. He is also a prolific traveler and the author of two books, most recently *Lovemarks: the future beyond brands*.**

Avant-Guide: What five non-essential items do you never travel without?

Kevin Roberts: iPod and speakers, plus Bose headphones, to create my own world; A Philips micro dicta player, for those 3am world-changing ideas; My Adidas gym shoes, to keep the metabolism working; Imovane, a sleeping pill to get you over jetlag; and 5 spare Mont Blanc Rollerball refills (I write a lot).

=∧= Describe your perfect hotel room of the future. What kind of architecture, furniture, facilities and services would you like it to have?

KR: It would be just like the Zen Suite at Hotel Zazou in Dallas. Tranquil, flat surfaces; a 40GB iPod loaded with tracks by today's Texan country rocker, Robert Earl Keen; a barista with Brazilian coffee; a DVD playing *The Sopranos* **and** *Deadwood* (all episodes); and a big, long desk to work on.

=∧= What can you get in New York City that you can't get anywhere else?

KR: Original Pucci, Mary Quant and Paco Rabanne dresses from the '60s, in the vintage hideaways in Nolita.

=∧= Where do you take out-of-towners when you want to show them a one-of-a-kind New York City experience?

KR: Madison Square Garden: New York excess in all its glory!

=∧= What is it about New York City that you dream about when you're away?

KR: Breakfast at the Cub Room in Soho [131 Sullivan St, at Prince]. The turkey sausage is healthy hedonism.

=∧= Where are your favorite places in New York City to shop?

KR: Moss, the best design store in the world; and Dean & DeLuca, the working exec's kitchen.

=∧= What aspect of your profession do you most enjoy?

KR: Interacting with ideas people, because ideas are the currency of the future.

=∧= What is your fallback job?

KR: Restaurateur in Auckland or St. Tropez. I love food, wine and people, and I have homes in both places.

=∧= What is your favorite motto or catch phrase?

KR: Nothing is Impossible.

| Map | # | Area | Hotel | Address | Phone | Website | Style Driven | Theme Driven | Club/Bar Scene | Spa | Pool | Business Sense | Kid Friendly |
|---|---|---|---|---|---|---|---|---|---|---|---|---|---|
| | | | **Inexpensive $** | | | | | | | | | | |
| H2 | 3 | Greenwich Village | Abingdon Guest House | 13 Eighth Ave | 212.243.5384 | abingdonguesthouse.com | | | | | | | ★ |
| H1 | 5 | Flatiron District | Arlington Hotel | 18 West 25th St | 212.645.3990 | hotelarlington.com | | | | | | | |
| I1 | 11 | Midtown | Carlton Arms | 160 East 25th St | 212.679.0680 | carltonarms.com | | ★ | | | | | |
| K1 | 16 | Tribeca | Cosmopolitan, The | 95 West Broadway | 212.566.1900 | cosmohotel.com | | | | | | | |
| J2 | 18 | East Village | East Village Bed and Coffee | 110 Ave C | 917.816.0071 | bedandcoffee.com | | | | | | | |
| H1 | 22 | Flatiron District | Gershwin, The | 7 East 27th St | 212.545.8000 | gershwinhotel.com | ★ | ★ | | | | | |
| I2 | 24 | Gramercy | Hotel 17 | 225 East 17th St | 212.475.2845 | hotel17ny.com | ★ | | | | | | |
| I1 | 25 | Midtown | Hotel 31 | 120 East 31st St | 212.685.3060 | hotel31.com | | | | | | | |
| H2 | 29 | Greenwich Village | Larchmont Hotel | 27 West 11th St | 212.989.9333 | larchmonthotel.com | | | | | | | |
| D2 | 38 | Midtown | Radio City Apartments | 142 West 49th St | 212.730.0728 | radiocityapartments.com | | | | | | | ★ |
| H1 | 44 | Midtown | Thirty-Thirty, Hotel | 30 East 30th St | 212.689.1900 | thirtythirty-nyc.com | ★ | | | | | | |
| | | | **Moderate $$** | | | | | | | | | | |
| C1 | 6 | Upper West Side | Beacon Hotel | 2130 Broadway | 212.787.1100 | beaconhotel.com | | | | | | | ★ |
| D2 | 7 | Midtown | Belvedere, The | 319 West 48th St | 212.245.7000 | belvederehotelnyc.com | | | | | | | |
| E2 | 8 | Midtown | Benjamin, The | 125 East 50th St | 212.715.2500 | thebenjamin.com | ★ | | ★ | | | ★ | ★ |
| D2 | 9 | Midtown | Blakely, The | 136 West 55th St | 212.245.1800 | blakelynewyork.com | | | | | | ★ | |
| H2 | 10 | Midtown | Bryant Park, The | 40 West 40th St | 212.869.0100 | bryantparkhotel.com | ★ | ★ | | | | ★ | |
| D2 | 12 | Midtown | Casablanca Hotel | 147 West 43rd St | 212.869.1212 | casablancahotel.com | | ★ | | | | | |
| H1 | 14 | Chelsea | Chelsea Hotel | 222 West 23rd St | 212.243.3700 | chelseahotel.com | | | | | | | ★ |
| D2 | 17 | Midtown | Dream Hotel | 210 West 55th St | 212.247.2000 | dreamny.com | ★ | ★ | | | | | |
| B2 | 20 | Upper East Side | Franklin, The | 164 East 87th St | 212.369.1000 | franklinhotel.com | ★ | | | | | ★ | ★ |
| D2 | 23 | Midtown | Hard Rock Hotel | 235 West 46th St | 212.764.5500 | hardrock.com | | | ★ | ★ | | | ★ |
| L1 | 26 | Lower East Side | Hotel on Rivington, The | 107 Rivington St | 212.475.2600 | hotelonrivington.com | ★ | ★ | | | | | |
| D2 | 27 | Midtown | Hudson | 356 West 58th St | 212.554.6000 | hudsonhotel.com | ★ | ★ | | | | | |
| I1 | 28 | Midtown | Kitano New York | 66 Park Ave | 212.885.7000 | kitano.com | | | ★ | | | ★ | ★ |
| G2 | 31 | Chelsea | Maritime Hotel, The | 363 West 16th St | 212.242.4300 | themaritimehotel.com | ★ | ★ | | | | | |
| I2 | 36 | Midtown | Park South Hotel | 122 East 28th St | 212.448.0888 | parksouthhotel.com | ★ | | | | | | |
| D2 | 37 | Midtown | QT Hotel | 125 West 45th St | 212.354.2323 | hotelqt.com | ★ | ★ | | ★ | | | |
| E2 | 40 | Midtown | Roger Smith, The | 501 Lexington Ave | 212.755.1400 | rogersmith.com | | | | | | | ★ |
| D2 | 45 | Midtown | Time, The | 224 West 49th St | 212.320.2900 | thetimeny.com | ★ | ★ | | | | | |
| | | | **Expensive $$$** | | | | | | | | | | |
| K1 | 1 | Soho | 60 Thompson | 60 Thompson St | 212.431.0400 | 60thompson.com | ★ | ★ | | ★ | | | |

| Map | # | Area | Hotel | Address | Phone | Website | Style Driven | Theme Driven | Club/Bar Scene | Spa | Pool | Business Sense | Kid Friendly |
|---|---|---|---|---|---|---|---|---|---|---|---|---|---|
| **Expensive $$$** | | | | | | | | | | | | | |
| I1 | 2 | Midtown | 70 Park Avenue | 70 Park Ave | 212.973.2400 | 70thparkave.com | ★ | | | | | ★ | ★ |
| E2 | 4 | Midtown | Alex Hotel, The | 205 East 45th St | 212.867.5100 | thealexhotel.com | ★ | ★ | | | | ★ | ★ |
| E2 | 13 | Midtown | Chambers, The | 15 West 56th St | 212.974.5656 | chambershotel.com | ★ | ★ | | | | ★ | |
| E2 | 15 | Midtown | City Club Hotel | 55 West 44th St | 212.921.5500 | cityclubhotel.com | ★ | | | | | | |
| G2 | 21 | Meatpacking Dist. | Gansevoort, Hotel | 18 Ninth Ave | 212.206.6700 | hotelgansevoort.com | ★ | ★ | | | | ★ | ★ |
| K1 | 32 | Soho | Mercer, The | 147 Mercer St | 212.966.6060 | mercerhotel.com | ★ | ★ | | | | ★ | ★ |
| H1 | 33 | Midtown | Morgans | 237 Madison Ave | 212.686.0300 | morganshotel.com | ★ | ★ | | | | ★ | |
| D2 | 34 | Midtown | Muse, The | 130 West 46th St | 212.485.2400 | themusehotel.com | ★ | | | | | ★ | |
| E2 | 35 | Midtown | New York Palace | 455 Madison Ave | 212.888.7000 | newyorkpalace.com | | | | | | ★ | ★ |
| D2 | 39 | Midtown | RIHGA Royal | 151 West 54th St | 212.307.5000 | rihgaroyalny.com | | | | | | ★ | ★ |
| E2 | 41 | Midtown | Royalton, The | 44 West 44th St | 212.869.4400 | royaltonhotel.com | ★ | ★ | | | | ★ | |
| K1 | 42 | Soho | Soho Grand | 310 West Broadway | 212.965.3000 | sohogrand.com | ★ | ★ | | | | ★ | |
| G2 | 43 | Meatpacking Dist. | Soho House New York | 29 Ninth Ave | 212.627.9800 | sohouseny.com | ★ | ★ | | | | ★ | ★ |
| K1 | 46 | Tribeca | Tribeca Grand Hotel | 2 Sixth Ave | 212.519.6600 | tribecagrand.com | ★ | ★ | | | | ★ | |
| E2 | 48 | Midtown | W New York | 541 Lexington Ave | 212.755.1200 | whotels.com | ★ | ★ | ★ | | | ★ | ★ |
| I1 | 49 | Midtown | W The Court | 130 East 39th St | 212.685.1100 | whotels.com | ★ | ★ | | | | ★ | |
| D2 | 50 | Midtown | W Times Square | 1567 Broadway | 212.930.7400 | whotels.com | ★ | ★ | | | | ★ | ★ |
| **Very Expensive $$$$** | | | | | | | | | | | | | |
| E2 | 19 | Midtown | Four Seasons, The | 57 East 57th St | 212.758.5700 | fourseasons.com | ★ | ★ | ★ | | | ★ | ★ |
| D2 | 30 | Upper West Side | Mandarin Oriental | 80 Columbus Circle | 212.805.8800 | mandarinoriental.com | ★ | ★ | ★ | | | ★ | ★ |
| D2 | 47 | Upper West Side | Trump International Hotel | 1 Central Park West | 212.299.1000 | trumpintl.com | ★ | ★ | ★ | ★ | ★ | ★ | ★ |
| I2 | 51 | Union Square | W Union Square | 201 Park Ave South | 212.253.9119 | whotels.com | ★ | ★ | ★ | | | ★ | ★ |

| Pack it | | | | |
|---|---|---|---|---|
| aspirin | cd's | handcuffs | picnic blanket | sunglasses |
| backgammon set | clock | hat, scarf, gloves | playing cards | sunscreen |
| batteries | condoms | kite | power adapter | swim suit |
| beach towel | corkscrew | magazines | rolling paper | swiss army knife |
| binoculars | dvd's | massage oil | scented candles | umbrella |
| books | flip-flops | mp3 player | scrabble | video camera |
| camera | frisbee | phone charger | sexy underwear | warm sox |

W 118th St
W 117th St
W 116th St

*Morningside Park*

E 118th St
E 117th St
E 116th St
E 115th St

Frederick Douglass Blvd
Manhattan Ave

W 114th St
W 113th St
W 112th St
W 111th St
W 110th St

Seventh Ave
Lenox Ave
St Nicholas Ave

Fifth Ave
Madison Ave
Park Ave
Lexington Ave
Third Ave
Second Ave

E 113th St
E 112th St
E 111th St
E 110th St

Morningside Drive

**1**

W 109th St
W 108th St
W 107th St
W 106th St
W 105th St
W 104th St
W 103rd St
W 102nd St
W 101st St
W 100th St

E 109th St

**SPANISH HARLEM**

Harlem Meer

West Drive

*Conservatory Garden*

*Pool*

East Drive

E 108th St
E 107th St
E 106th St
E 105th St
E 104th St
E 103rd St
E 102nd St
E 101st St
E 100th St
E 99th St

**1**

W 97th St
W 96th St
W 95th St
W 94th St
W 93rd St
W 92nd St
W 91st St

97th St Transverse Rd

E 98th St

*Central Park*

Columbus Ave
Central Park West
West Drive

E 97th St
E 96th St
E 95th St
E 94th St
E 93rd St
E 92nd St
E 91st St

**2**

W 90th St
W 89th St
W 88th St
W 87th St
W 86th St
W 85th St
W 84th St
W 83rd St
W 82nd St
W 81st St

**UPPER WEST SIDE**

*The Reservoir*

East Drive

85th St Transverse Rd

*Great Lawn*

**UPPER EAST SIDE**

E 90th St
E 89th St

20

E 88th St
E 87th St
E 86th St
E 85th St
E 84th St
E 83rd St
E 82nd St
E 81st St
E 80th St

**2**

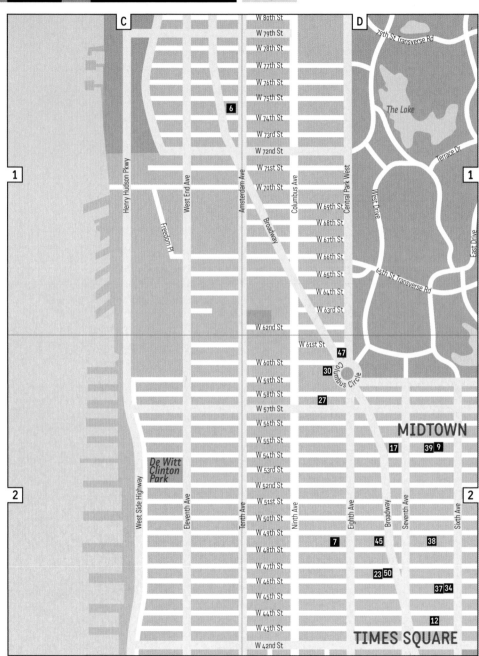

E

F

E 79th St
E 78th St
E 77th St
E 76th St
E 75th St
E 74th St
E 73rd St
E 72nd St
E 71st St
E 70th St
E 69th St
E 68th St
E 67th St
E 66th St
E 65th St
E 64th St
E 63rd St
E 62nd St
E 61st St
E 60th St
E 59th St
E 58th St
E 57th St
E 56th St
E 55th St
E 54th St
E 53rd St
E 52nd St
E 51st St
E 50th St
E 49th St
E 48th St
E 47th St
E 46th St
E 45th St
E 44th St
E 43rd St
E 42nd St

Cherokee Pl

John Jay Park

Conservatory Water

Roosevelt Island

1

1

Fifth Ave
Madison Ave
Park Ave
Lexington Ave
Third Ave
Second Ave
First Ave
York Ave
Franklin D Roosevelt Dr

Zoo

Queensboro Bridge

Sutton Pl

2

Beekman Pl

2

Park Ave S

Vanderbilt Ave

19

13

35

8

48

40

4

15

41

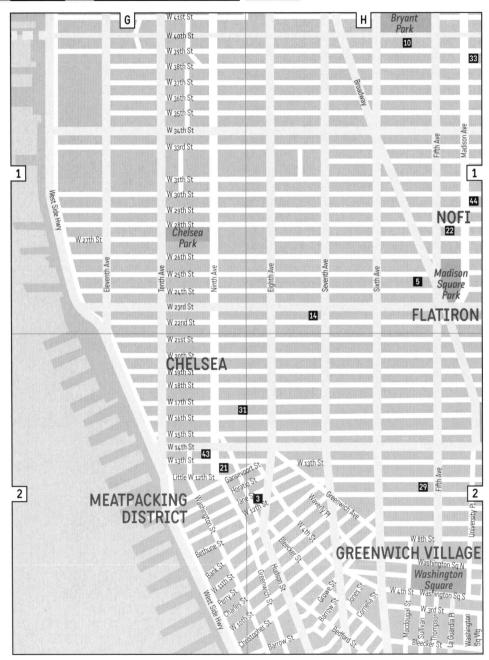

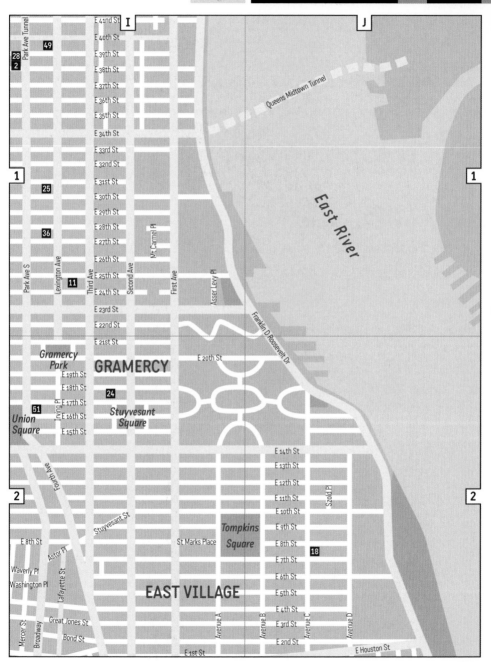

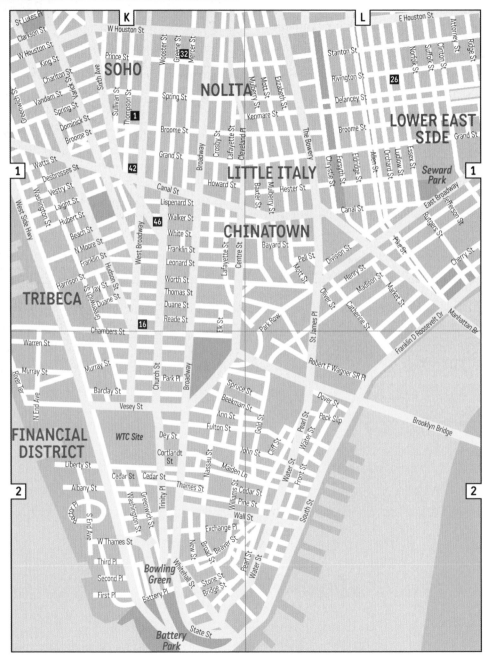

EAT

# 2

Contemporary New York dining has recently gone in directions that that few could have guessed, to embrace lots of tequila-drenched Mexican places, a slew of barbeque joints both down and haute, and a raft of super-high-end Japanese restaurants that go well beyond sushi and soba. And as globalization intensifies, its becoming increasingly more difficult to classify cuisines without the use of hyphens. Our recommendations take you all over the city, from the celebrity-studded showplaces of Soho and the Meatpacking District to the outer reaches of the city where knowing gastronauts hide out with the talented young chefs of tomorrow. Restaurants recommended by Avant-Guide represent the finest in each price category that the city has to offer. All present something new, unique or fashionable or are very special in the way of local flavor and character. And we have gone to great lengths to uncover the very best of the city's lesser-known places. Regardless of budget—from hot dogs to time-consuming stock reductions—with Avant-Guide in tow there's no excuse for a bad meal.

**Our reviewers have no relationship to any restaurant listed in this guidebook. All visits are anonymous, and expenses are paid by Avant-Guide.**

## THE RESERVATIONS GAME

As sure as death and taxes, there's always a restaurant of the moment; one in which every night is like a movie premiere filled with film stars, models, musicians, the media elite, athletes, restaurateurs, garmentos and generic rich people. Within the first two weeks of opening everyone will trample through, before quickly heading off to the Next New Thing. If you want to be there too, it's time to use some muscle, work the phones and call-in favors. When white-hot slows to simmering, street-wise mortals can get reservations about a week in advance. Unless you have connections, or don't mind being seated at 6pm or 11pm, we advise you to reserve a table as far in advance as possible. Call now.

## WHO'S WHO: NY'S AVANT MULTI-RESTAURATEURS

| | |
|---|---|
| Mario Batali | Babbo, Bar Jamón, Casa Mono, Lupa |
| Jimmy Bradley | The Harrison, Red Cat |
| Bobby Flay | Bar Americain, Mesa Grill |
| Eric Goode & Sean MacPherson | La Bottega, Matsuri |
| Steve Hanson | Atlantic Grill, Blue Fin, Vento |
| Nobu Matsuhisa | Nobu, Nobu 57 |
| Keith McNally | Balthazar, Lucky Strike, Pastis, Schiller's Liquor Bar |
| Danny Meyer | Blue Smoke, Tabla |
| Jean-Georges Vongerichten | 66, Mercer Kitchen, Perry Street, Spice Market, Vong |

## WHAT THE $ MEAN

Our $ estimates are based on the average price of one meal.

| | |
|---|---|
| $ | = under $20 |
| $$ | = $20-$40 |
| $$$ | = $41-$60 |
| $$$$ | = over $60 |

## BEST RESTAURANTS TO...

**SPOT CELEBRITIES**
66
Matsuri
Mercer Kitchen
Mr. Chow
Nobu
Spice Market

**HAVE A ROMANTIC TRYST**
Boat House
Dylan Prime
Holy Basil
Megu

**KICK BACK WITH KIDS**
Blue Smoke
Golden Unicorn
Markt
Public

**FOR POWER LUNCHMANSHIP**
Bar Americain
Brasserie
Keens Steakhouse

**HAVE A FOODGASM**
Babbo
Tabla
Vong
WD-50

**GO FOR BRUNCH**
Ideya
Mesa Grill
Public
Schiller's Liquor Bar
Spotted Pig, The
Vento

**EAT DESSERT FIRST**
ChikaLicious
Ferrara
Il Laboratorio Del Gelato

**HAVE A MIDNIGHT SNACK**
Bao
Blue Ribbon
Coffee Shop
Florent
LoSide Diner
Veselka

**HAVE A TRUE NEW YORK EXPERIENCE**
John's Pizzeria
Oyster Bar, The
Sammy's Roumanian
Second Avenue Deli
Tal Bagels
Tavern on the Green

**WISH YOU LIVE IN THE NEIGHBORHOOD**
Atlantic Grill
Aquagrill
Bottino
Chow Bar
Harrison, The
Red Cat

**EAT, DRINK AND BE VERY**
Balthazar
BED New York
Freemans
La Bottega
Pastis
Tao

**HAVE A QUICK BITE**
Caracas Arepa Bar
Daisy May's BBQ USA
Gray's Papaya
La Casa De Los Tacos
Little Italy Pizza
SobaKoh

66

## 66 $$$

241 Church St (at Leonard), Tribeca

☎ 212.925.0202 ☑ jean-georges.com

CHINESE                                     MAP K1 #1

Specializing in freestyle Shanghai cuisine created by Jean-Georges Vongerichten (**Mercer Kitchen**, **Perry Street**, **Spice Market**, **Vong**), 66 is a sleek and pricey scene spot with good sightlines and a very stylish crowd that usually includes a handful of celebrities. It's a great looking, Zen-like space designed by Richard Meier with Eames chairs and Saarinen tables set with lazy susans. Dressed in uniforms by Vivienne Tam, even the staff looks great. There's a long communal table up front, which is often available for walk-ins, and a more secluded dining area in back, for which reservations are required, often far in advance. Recommended dishes include chilled honeydew melon soup with peekytoe crab, lobster noodles with green chili, and shrimp and foie gras

dumplings. However, few diners would argue that the food alone warrants such high prices.

## AQUAGRILL $$$

210 Spring St (at Sixth), Soho

☎ 212.274.0505 ☑ No Website

SEAFOOD                                     MAP K1 #2

Aquagrill is all about the sea and being seen. A great Soho location and an amazingly extensive oyster bar (24 varieties at last count) play to all manner of downtown fish-lovers and shellfish-ionados. Good chefs and top ingredients converge daily in Aquagrill's hard-working kitchen where a fresh ocean catch like halibut, cod, monkfish, and tuna are brought in each morning and handled with utmost care. Choose your *poisson* and have it cooked to your specifications: roasted, poached or grilled. Side dishes are as good as the main courses, and we usually order several. Good lighting, comfortable seating and

fair prices help make Aquagrill a king of all things fishy. It's especially great in summer, when tables spill onto a sidewalk terrace.

## ATLANTIC GRILL $$$

1341 Third Ave (at 77th), Upper East Side

☎ 212.988.9200 ◫ brguestrestaurants.com

SEAFOOD      **MAP** E1 #3

A smart-casual jewel in the crown of Steve Hanson's food empire (**Blue Fin**, **Vento**), Atlantic Grill plays to rich, young Upper Eastsiders with very good seafood and a happening fishbowl dining room. Squeeze past the smartly dressed folks at the polished wood bar and settle into a booth for a meal that might include freshly shucked oysters and plump crab cakes to excellent maki rolls and wood-grilled halibut with light caper vinaigrette. Make reservations and you still may be asked to wait.

## BABBO $$$$

110 Waverly Pl (at MacDougal), Greenwich Village

☎ 212.777.0303 ◫ babbonyc.com

ITALIAN      **MAP** H2 #4

The Italian restaurant to best all Italian restaurants, Babbo is chef Mario Batali's (**Casa Mono**, **Lupa**) much-praised gourmet paradise: the perfect union of food, service, wine and atmosphere. Both high energy and homey, the enchanting bi-level townhouse dining room is perfect for truly inventive yet unpretentious meals that don't shy away from salt, fat and offal. Think ravioli stuffed with crushed squab liver and beef cheeks. It's explosive cooking that's not for the faint of heart, or wallet. There are a few tables by the bar for walk-ins, but even Jesus would have a tough time getting a reservation on a Saturday night. Cross your fingers and call.

## BALTHAZAR $$$

80 Spring St (at Crosby), Soho

☎ 212.965.1414 ◫ balthazarny.com

FRENCH BRASSERIE | OPEN LATE      **MAP** K1 #5

Keith McNally (**Lucky Strike**, **Pastis**, **Schiller's Liquor Bar**) created this sophisticated, brilliantly faux brasserie, in which golden light bounces off huge ormolu mirrors illuminating red leather banquettes, distressed tile flooring and handsome, white-aproned waiters. Ultimately, good food is what keeps regulars regular, and Balthazar delivers with flavorful and creative renditions of French classics that include the house's specialty shellfish platter, a decadent two-tier *plateau de fruits de mer* brimming with oysters, clams, sweet jumbo shrimp, scallop ceviche, sea snails and more. Other excellent entrees include sautéed skate with capers, steak au poivre, and roasted bacon-wrapped monkfish. Desserts are tops,

BED New York

and while the all-French wine list offers no bargains, several drinkable whites are priced under $30.

## BAO 111 $$$

111 Ave C (at 7th), East Village

☎ 212.254.7773 ⓦ bao111.com

**VIETNAMESE NEW | OPEN LATE** 🗺 J2 #6

Vietnamese goes hip at this energetically youthful restaurant that pairs an inventive kitchen with a trendy dining room. Hidden deep in Alphabet City, this intimate, amber-lit restaurant with embroidered pillows on wooden banquettes plays to both dates and groups with excellent noodle soups swimming with crab and shrimp, tender short ribs infused with lemongrass, scallops with bacon, and spring rolls served with crisp lettuce and mint leaf wrappers. Wash it down with house-infused sakes in flavors like lemongrass and pomegranate. Plus, they serve most nights until 2am. Truly a hidden treasure.

## BAR AMERICAIN $$$

152 West 52nd St (at Sixth), Midtown

☎ 212.265.9700 ⓦ baramericain.com

**AMERICAN NEW** 🗺 D2 #7

Food Network star chef Bobby Flay (**Mesa Grill**) created a loud American expense-account brasserie in a soaring bi-level space designed by David Rockwell with a zinc bar, massive mirrors and a caring, black-aproned waitstaff. The Iron Chef puts American twists on French favorites that include Vidalia onion soup, skate with caper sauce, grilled steaks, and triple-tiered shellfish platters. And, unlike most places in Paris, portions are large and there's a full bar mixing creative cocktails for post-work suits. Choose a seat facing the open kitchen if you want to see the chefs in action.

## BED NEW YORK $$$

530 West 27th St (at Tenth), Chelsea

☎ 212.594.4109 ⓦ bedny.com

**AMERICAN NEW** 🗺 G1 #8

You can lean like it's Passover every night at this beautifully lit, mattress padded restaurant in which patrons are encouraged to dine while reclining. Yes, it's yet another bed restaurant, like Supper Club in Amsterdam, but without the artistic dinner-as-theater angle. Sprawling across a seductive sixth floor dining room and equally enticing rooftop garden (with glass-enclosed gazebo for year-round use), the restaurant mimics the swoony and pulsating atmosphere of its sister, BED Miami, a mecca of eater-tainment in which DJs spin, scene and style is paramount and guests are asked to slip off their Manolos and into slippers. Meals are offered both à la carte and *prix fixe*, and might start with rice paper wrapped crab cakes, duck leg

*Blue Fin*

## BLT FISH $$$

21 West 17th St (at Fifth), Union Square

☎ 212.691.8888 🌐 bltfish.com

**SEAFOOD** ‖ MAP H2 #10

A bistro that's named not for a lowbrow sandwich, but for high-minded chef/owner, Laurent Tourondel, BLT Fish is a good restaurant with a dual personality. On the ground floor it's clam shack casual, reservations are not accepted, and blackboard specials include steamed clams, meaty lobster rolls and apple pie. Upstairs is far more formal, a place in which corporate card carriers dine beneath a fantastic retractable skylight roof and chow on wonderful dishes like grilled octopus salad and whole citrus-infused sea bass that's filleted tableside.

## BLUE FIN $$$

W Times Square, 1567 Broadway (at 47th), Midtown

☎ 212.918.1400 🌐 brguestrestaurants.com

**SEAFOOD** ‖ MAP D2 #11

There's not a lot of competition and it's certainly not cheap, but Blue Fin is probably the hippest restaurant on the Great White Way. Part of the Steve Hanson empire (**Atlantic Grill**, **Vento**), this bi-level style spot is large, loud, lively and architecturally dazzling. The food plays to fish eaters with an enormous raw bar, very good sushi and straightforward chowders, crab cakes and grilled fish. There's a good bar too with a fun, fishbowl view of Times Square. In short, it's an excellent choice for fin-icky eaters in what is otherwise a culinarily-challenged neighborhood.

## BLUE RIBBON $$$

97 Sullivan St (at Spring), Soho

☎ 212.274.0404 🌐 blueribbonrestaurants.com

**AMERICAN NEW | OPEN LATE** ‖ MAP K1 #12

Fashionable, fun and jammed at all hours, it's hard to imagine a more successful scene spot than this polished Soho dining room. It's just an unpretentious rectangle storefront with tightly spaced tables, a tiny oyster bar by the window and a no-reservations policy that often translates into waits. But, the wonderful, eclectic menu and bustling atmosphere are like magnets for upscale downtowners. Blue Ribbon is known as the place where chefs from other restaurants go after their own kitchens close. The menu caters to both grazers and gorgers with everything from tofu ravioli and sesame-glazed catfish, to fried chicken and sweetbreads. The wonderfully rich and meaty paella is chunked out with lots of shellfish and savory sausage. It's a huge dish that you won't want to share.

confit spring rolls or seared foie gras with caramelized mango, then move to salmon and scallop "osso buco," sesame charred tuna steak, or free-range beef tenderloin.

## BILTMORE ROOM $$$$

290 Eighth Ave (at 25th), Chelsea

☎ 212.807.0111 🌐 thebiltmoreroom.com

**ASIAN NEW** ‖ MAP H1 #9

A turn-of-the-century marble interior salvaged from the old Biltmore Hotel and completely up-to-date New Asian cooking devised by consulting chef Gary Robins are the one-two punch of this extraordinary (and extraordinarily popular) restaurant. Recommended dishes include crunchy crab-stuffed squash blossoms, giant prawns wrapped in crispy noodles, cod in miso sauce, and fork-tender rack of lamb with Algerian spices. Even desserts are great. Of course, you can always just have some drinks and appetizers at the bar. Service can be attitudinal, but the supper club ambience is sexy and youthful, complete with retro chandeliers and a plush phone booth that has been whimsically repurposed for cellular chatterati.

## Blue Smoke $$

116 East 27th St (at Park), Midtown

☎ 212.447.7733 ✆ bluesmoke.com

AMERICAN REGIONAL     MAP I1 #13

After a rocky start, Danny Meyer (**Tabla**) is now turning out quality barbeque and stunning side dishes that are worthy of a great Missouri smokehouse. Traditionalists scoff at pit-smoked salmon and foie gras, as well as the inauthentically buzzy scene. But the tender baby back ribs, the chunky pulled pork sandwiches and the sublime baked beans with chopped burnt ends (crunchy barbequed pork) are state of the art. The sprawling dining room is casual and woody, with a skylight over large red-vinyl booths, the best of which are on the mezzanine. The full menu is also available in the Jazz Standard live music club, downstairs.

## Boat House $$$

in Central Park, East 72nd St (at Park Drive North), Upper East Side

☎ 212.517.2233 ✆ thecentralparkboathouse.com

AMERICAN NEW     MAP D1 #14

One of New York's most bucolic locations has a great restaurant to match. The Boathouse is a small, wood-framed building on the shore of The Lake in the middle of Central Park. The view from the outdoor dining deck is unparalleled, and lunchtime tables get mighty scarce when the weather turns nice. The kitchen turns out delicious and creative contemporary-American dishes that might include rich chestnut soup flavored with smoked duck and chives, tender short ribs braised in cabernet, and seared striped bass with sherry-vinegar sauce. Leave **Tavern on the Green** to the tourists and don't forget to bring a date.

## Bottino $$$

246 Tenth Ave (at 24th), Chelsea

☎ 212.206.6766 ✆ bottinonyc.com

ITALIAN NORTHERN     MAP G1 #15

Situated way over on the West Side, Bottino is a solid neighborhood restaurant in one of the city's most creative neighborhoods. Full with artists and dealers from local galleries, this light and chic-simple spot has the atmosphere of an oasis, one that's amplified by a bucolic back garden (make reservations). Food here is rustic, changes with the seasons and never fussy. Think tomato and arugula salad with shaved pecorino, spaghettini with clams, and roast chicken with mashed potatoes. Lunches are particularly special here and there's often a good happy hour crowd.

## Brasserie $$$

100 East 53rd St (at Park), Midtown

☎ 212.751.4840 ✆ restaurantassociates.com

FRENCH BRASSERIE | OPEN LATE     MAP E2 #16

Traditional brasserie and ultra-mod styling by the design firm Diller + Scofidio collide at this highly recommended Midtowner. Playing to local office workers as well as design types who are enchanted enough with this place to make the trip from downtown, the futuristic design includes closed-circuit TVs over the bar in which you can watch new arrivals prancing through the door. The Alsatian food is far more classic: onion soup, bistro burgers, cassoulet, coq au vin, steak frites, bouillabaisse... there's nothing you haven't seen before, but quality is tops and prices are right. And generous hours guarantee you can get a great meal long after most neighbors have called it quits.

## Calle Ocho $$$

446 Columbus Ave (at 81st), Upper West Side

☎ 212.873.5025 ✆ calleochonyc.com

LATIN NUEVO     MAP A2 #17

This colorful Miami-style restaurant has almost single-handedly heated up the Upper West Side scene, serving great food and cocktails to the neighborhood's best looking crowd. It's a large place with a dedicated lounge, high ceilings and a suitably energetic atmosphere that's mimicked by inventive Latin flavors that meringue around your mouth. Wonderful meals, beautifully plated, might include citrusy shrimp ceviche, goat cheese tamales, lobster empanadas, plantain-encrusted halibut, and steak with tomato escabeche. And the fabulousness continues all the way to dessert. A raft of fruity mojitos and other tropical drinks keep the bar hopping late into the night.

## Caracas Arepa Bar $

91 East 7th St (at First), East Village

☎ 212.228.5062 ✆ caracasarepabar.com

VENEZUELAN     MAP I2 #18

It's all in the name at this tiny, fast-casual Venezuelan food shop specializing in arepa: round, crispy corn muffins stuffed with seventeen varieties of fillings, from tofu and portobello mushrooms, to chicken and avocado, stewed meat and plantains, and shredded beef and cheddar cheese. Made to order, served in plastic baskets and sided with sour cream and fried plantains, it's the perfect antidote to pizza for a unique, succulent snack.

## Casa Mono $$$

**52 Irving Pl (at 17th), Gramercy**
☎ 212.253.2773 🌐 No Website
SPANISH NUEVO     🗺 I2 #19

## Bar Jamón $$

**125 East 17th St (at Irving), Gramercy**
☎ 212.253.2773     🗺 I2 #20

Superchef Mario Batali (**Babbo**, **Lupa**) is the toque behind these happening Spanish-ish twins serving amazing food in very tight and trendy surroundings. In theory, Bar Jamón, whose entrance is just around the corner, is something of a waiting room for the Casa Mono restaurant. In practice, however, 14-stool Jamón stands on its own as a fabulous place for a full-flavored Rioja along with delicious hams and cheeses. At bustling Casa Mono, the menu expands to include a huge range of inventive tapas, along with a short menu of grilled meats, creative pastas and pizzas. For gastronomical theater, the best seats are at the bar, facing the open kitchen.

## ChikaLicious $$

**203 East 10th St (at Second), East Village**
☎ 212.995.9511 🌐 chikalicious.com
DESSERT     🗺 I2 #21

You know those fancy restaurant *prix fixe* dinners that end with a parade of desserts? Now imagine the same thing, but without the dinner part. And, without the fancy restaurant part either, because this novel dessert bar specializes in super-high-end multi-course sweets, without any of the ancillary frou-frou. It's a tiny place—with portions to match—in which fabulously constructed three-course menus (including an *amuse bouche* and *petits fours*) will set you back about $15, without wine.

## Chow Bar $$

**230 West 4th St (at 10th), Greenwich Village**
☎ 212.633.2212 🌐 No Website
ASIAN     🗺 H2 #22

Chef Peter Klein was a pioneer of Chino-Latino cooking when he manned the stoves at China Grill in the 80's. Now this sexy and energetic dining room in the Village is the setting for an alluring menu of small plates like honey plum-glazed barbequed spareribs, steamed shrimp dumplings with red pepper miso sauce, and crispy crab spring rolls with red-chili cucumber sauce. And you've never tasted anything like the steak frites served here, bursting with the flavors of cilantro, shallots, garlic, ginger, soy and chili peppers. The room has zip too, thanks to the intense lime-green and orange color scheme, the buzzy scene and powerful cocktails that will keep you glowing.

## Coffee Shop $$

**29 Union Square West (at 16th), Gramercy**
☎ 212.243.7969 🌐 No Website
AMERICAN | OPEN EARLY & LATE     🗺 H2 #23

The 1980's hotspot that trendies love to hate is actually a great place for dining in those last hours before sunrise. Unlike real coffee shops, this one can always be counted on for decent Brazilian-style food, good music, flattering lighting and a great looking staff. Add a wonderful Formica counter seating from the restaurant's original incarnation and you have a top late-night standby. Nobody really needs a meaty Rio de Janeiro stew at four in the morning, but it's here if you want it, along with sandwiches and breakfast foods.

## Daisy May's BBQ USA $

**623 Eleventh Ave (at 46th), Midtown**
☎ 212.977.1500 🌐 daisymaysbbq.com
AMERICAN REGIONAL     🗺 C2 #24

In the burgeoning New York barbeque wars, pit master (and CIA graduate) Adam Perry Lang's remote smokery regularly comes out on top. Physically this place is a dive, which is one of the things it has going for it. Meats are slathered with thick spice pastes and complex sauces to create something exceptional that's tart, sweet, spicy and salty. Unfortunately, except for a narrow counter, there's no place to eat: It's takeout (and free citywide delivery) only. But the fact that so many are willing to find a nearby bench, or sit by the river, or eat God-knows-where, is testament to how far we will go for the holy grail of 'que.

## Diablo Royale $$

**189 West 10th St (at 4th), Greenwich Village**
☎ 212.620.0223 🌐 diabloroyale.com
MEXICAN     🗺 H2 #25

When you're in the West Village with a taste for some devilish Mexican, Diablo Royale has your 666. Sporting a playful red and black inferno-esque theme, the restaurant features a handsome little "t'kill ya" bar and a serious kitchen that turns out very good chicken in pumpkin seed-tomatillo sauce, seared tuna and avocado tacos, grilled whole shrimp with dried chilies and garlic, and braised spare ribs with adobo chilies and honey.

English Is Italian

## Dok Suni's $$

119 First Ave (at 7th), East Village

☎ 212.477.9506 ☒ No Website

**KOREAN** `MAP` I2 #26

We're not sure if Korean food will ever be hip, but this dark East Villager is as avant as Seoul food gets. Dok Suni's cuisine is not very authentic, but it is really flavorful and interesting: Vegetarian bi-bimbop—a stone pot of rice, vegetables and sauces with an egg on top—is a healthful take on the original and every bit as savory as the traditional versions served on 32nd Street. Braised short ribs smothered in a cloyingly tangy barbeque sauce is another winner. Appetizers and desserts are far less successful and should probably be avoided entirely. Wonderful, smoky aromas permeate the small dining room (and your clothes), which is papered with pages from old books and lighted with lanterns that are so ineffective you'll be tempted to whip out a flashlight. Good prices, fun food and something of a scene keep the hipsters coming. Arrive early or late to avoid a long wait.

## Dylan Prime $$$

62 Laight St (at Greenwich), Tribeca

☎ 212.334.4783 ☒ dylanprime.com

**STEAKHOUSE** `MAP` K1 #27

It's hard to imagine a hipper steakery than this sexy spot set with mood lighting, candlelit leather booths, a chillout soundtrack and a drink menu that extends into bellini territory. Ultimately, however, it's the food you've come for and Dylan doesn't disappoint. From rib-eyes to porterhouses, cuts are prime indeed, topped with the gently crusted "chapeaux" of your choice and paired with an "accessory" like bitter greens or wilted tomatoes with blue cheese.

## English Is Italian $$$

622 Third Ave (at 40th), Midtown

☎ 212.404.1700 ☒ chinagrillmanagement.com

**ITALIAN** `MAP` I1 #28

Boston-based chef Todd English (Olives) teamed up with the New York restaurant group China Grill Management (Asia de

Chikalicious

Cuba, China Grill, Ono) to create this set-price (about $40), all-you-can-eat Tuscan feeding frenzy in an underserved corner of Manhattan. The cavernous dining room is group- and family-friendly; a nice environment in which to gorge on a parade of mid-quality antipasti, pasta, meat and fish. Think about splurging on the buffalo mozzarella appetizer, in which the cheese is made fresh tableside. And, happily, the good wine list includes several bottles under $30.

## FERRARA $

195 Grand St (at Mulberry), Little Italy

☎ 212.226.6150 ☒ ferraracafe.com

**DESSERT ITALIAN**                         MAP L1 #29

Yes it's touristy. And no, it's not the best dessert you've ever eaten, but Ferrara is an over-the-top New York experience offering the kitschiest cannoli and cookies anywhere. Opened in 1892, it's the real deal; Little Italy like it used to be, with brightly lit cases groaning under colorful Italian desserts and more mirrors than Versailles.

## FLORENT $$

69 Gansevoort St (at Washington), Meatpacking District

☎ 212.989.5779 ☒ restaurantflorent.com

**FRENCH BISTRO | OPEN LATE**                MAP G2 #30

An early pioneer opened long before the Meatpacking District became fashionable, Florent Morellet's eponymous restaurant

has matured into one of New York's quintessential late-night landmarks. There are fewer strange-looking party monsters than there used to be, but one still goes to this colorful all-night diner for the scene as much as for the food (and the cute waiters). Sturdy bistro meals include onion soup, boudin noir, and steak frites, along with fantastic bread, budget wines and breakfast served all night.

## FREEMANS $$

Freeman Alley (at Rivington), Lower East Side

☎ 212.420.0012 ☒ freemansrestaurant.com

**AMERICAN NEW**                             MAP L1 #31

Hidden at the dead end of a tiny alley between Bowery and Chrystie streets that doesn't even appear on most maps, Freemans is the grunge-glam restaurant and bar of your dreams. Owner Taavo Somer, an architect who used to throw parties at the Pussycat Lounge and still designs a line of fake vintage T-shirts that sell at **Barneys**, has created a funky, laid back and very friendly place to drink and dine. Inside, old looking wooden tables are set on distressed plank floors and various taxidermied animal heads are pinned to painted cement walls like an urban hunting lodge. Correspondingly, gussied-up fish and game are the foods of choice, appearing in starters like wild boar pâté with raspberries, and mains like thyme-infused whole roast trout. Order a side of macaroni and cheese with everything. There's a well-priced wine list and great cocktails too. Reservations are accepted only for parties of six or more.

## Golden Unicorn $$

18 East Broadway (at Catherine), Chinatown
☎ 212.941.0911 🌐 No Website
DIM SUM                     MAP L1 #32

People come here for the great selection of dim sum, served daily from 9am to 3.30pm. Hidden on the second and third floors of a small building in the corner of Chinatown, Golden Unicorn is one of those exotic and wonderful Hong Kong-style hideaways that you would never find on your own (read: crowded, noisy, bullet service and lazy susans in the middle of big round tables). Piled high on carts, a huge variety of dim sum is piloted around the dining room by no-nonsense middle-aged waitresses. Hail one and start pointing to the little treats you want: steamed meat-filled dumplings, shrimp turnovers, rice-noodle rolls, savory pork triangles and much more. Other items are available from a vast Cantonese menu, but they somehow seem superfluous.

## Gray's Papaya $

402 Sixth Ave (at 8th), Greenwich Village
☎ 212.260.3532 🌐 No Website
AMERICAN | Open NONSTOP          MAP H2 #33
2090 Broadway (at 71st), Upper West Side
☎ 212.799.0243                   MAP D1 #34
539 Eighth Ave (at 37th), Midtown
☎ 212.904.1588                   MAP H1 #35

When your wallet is crying "uncle" and your stomach is not far behind, Gray's Papaya comes to the rescue 24/seven with perfectly grilled hot dogs at prices that can't be beat. These terrific, skinny pimp steaks are served on warm buns and topped with sauerkraut or onions and quality, spicy mustard. Their trademark Recession Special includes two dogs and a mysterious synthetic drink like coconut champagne. It's a true New York experience.

## Harrison, The $$$

355 Greenwich St (at Harrison), Tribeca
☎ 212.274.9310 🌐 theharrison.com
MEDITERRANEAN AMERICAN           MAP K1 #36

Stylish, understated and deliberately worn around the edges, The Harrison is Tribeca in microcosm. With realistic prices, very good food, and service to match, this corner restaurant exudes an old school atmosphere that does double duty as both

a simple neighborhood kitchen and a destination place, one in which moneyed locals rub well-clad shoulders with corporate geldings from Citigroup, visiting celebrities and others in-the-know. Co-owned by chef Jimmy Bradley (Red Cat), the emphasis here is on stylized, rich comfort foods like wood-smoked pork chops, endive-and-pear salad with walnuts and blue cheese, prosciutto-wrapped sweetbreads, and crispy fried clams with coriander-flavored aïoli for dipping.

## Hell's Kitchen $$$

679 Ninth Ave (at 47th), Midtown
☎ 212.977.1588 🌐 hellskitchen-nyc.com
LATIN NEW                        MAP D2 #37

Mexico meets modishness at this energetic taqueria with a nonconformist kitchen. Small as a bowling alley, and almost as loud, the beautifully lit dining room is a festive and theatrical setting for a zingy menu that includes excellent tuna tostadas, duck breast in mole sauce, salmon with spicy wilted greens, and huitlacoche fungus tamales. Chips and black bean sauce are served gratis to go down with any number of specialty margaritas. Unless you are arriving before 7pm, or are with a large group, reservations are not accepted.

## Holy Basil $$

2nd Fl, 149 Second Ave (at 9th), East Village
☎ 212.460.5557 🌐 holybasilrestaurant.com
THAI                             MAP I2 #38

Great food, good service, fair prices and a slightly sultry atmosphere conspire to make this our top pick for Thai in Manhattan. The second floor dining room is so dark you can't really see what you're eating, but that's a plus for PODs (people on dates), and it's just the right atmosphere to start your meal with an exotic-fruit cocktail. When it's time to order, feel free to be adventurous, as the kitchen is just as comfortable turning out traditional red curries and pad Thai, as it is with steak salad, pork with green beans, crispy duck in coconut sauce, and chicken massaman curry. And there's plenty for vegetarians to like too.

## Ideya $$

349 West Broadway (at Grand), Soho
☎ 212.625.1441 🌐 ideya.net
CARIBBEAN                        MAP K1 #39

Growing up eating dried out Jamaican Patties off hot dog carts didn't prepare us for the fabulous Caribbean food that's served at this casual and spirited windward-theme restaurant.

*Keens Steakhouse*

Playing to an oh so Soho crowd with a cool interior design, Ideya creates a transporting atmosphere that's no doubt made more effective by terrific mojitos served by the pitcher. The menu hopscotches around the islands to offer very good pressed Cuban sandwiches (ham, pork, cheese, pickle) and skirt steak with chimichurri sauce. And weekends bring one of the neighborhood's best brunches.

## IL LABORATORIO DEL GELATO $

95 Orchard St (at Broome), Lower East Side
☎ 212.343.9922 🖰 laboratoriodelgelato.com
**DESSERT**                                      🗺 L1 #40

It's worth the trek to the Lower East Side to get a mouthful of the city's best Italian-style ice cream. A dozen flavors are offered daily, all of which are made here in their exhibition kitchen from seasonal ingredients. We've had their explosive black sesame, lavender and ginger flavors, but the super-intense dark chocolate is the one that we dream about when we're away.

## INDOCHINE $$$

430 Lafayette St (at Astor), East Village
☎ 212.505.5111 🖰 No Website
**VIETNAMESE**                                   🗺 I2 #41

A hotspot for satay and celebs since 1984, Indochine proves that being trendy doesn't mean you have to be a flash in the pan. This place practically invented the French-Colonial dining scene and still draws black-clad, table-hopping loyalists with good food, clubby booths and beautiful servers. Models are still ordering nothing but can be seen everywhere. And over a decade later the delicate Franco-Vietnamese food still feels inventive, if not exotic. There is an interesting variety of crunchy hand rolls, paired with piquant dipping sauces, good filet of sole steamed in a banana leaf and bathed in coconut milk, and a sturdy sweet-and-sour soup is loaded with shrimp, pineapple, tamarind and tomatoes.

## INOTECA $$

98 Rivington St (at Ludlow), Lower East Side
☎ 212.614.0473 🖰 inotecanyc.com
**ITALIAN**                                      🗺 L1 #42

A good stylish vibe, with low prices to match, are the one-two punch of this solid corner Italian restaurant. Playing to twenty- and thirty-somethings, most of whom are probably crawling around the neighborhood's plethora of bars afterwards, the dining room is as sceney and urbane as you'd expect it to be. And when the weather heats up the entire glass front folds open for a semi-alfresco experience. Fueled by a vast wine list, the menu trends towards generously portioned "small" plates that run from prosciutto and cheese and spicy chicken sandwiches to meatballs in tomato-citrus sauce.

## John's Pizzeria $

278 Bleecker St (at Seventh), Greenwich Village

☎ 212.243.1680 🖥 No Website

PIZZA      🗺 H2 #43

408 East 64th St (at First), Upper East Side

☎ 212.935.2895      🗺 F1 #44

260 West 44th St (at Broadway), Midtown

☎ 212.391.7560      🗺 D2 #45

Whether John's is the best pizza in New York is debatable, but it's certainly one of the most popular. Some would argue that John's is not "real" New York pizza. Their perfectly charred, super thin crust pies are far closer to the coal-fired pizzas served in Naples than they are to the doughy slices this city made famous. John's doesn't even sell slices. It's a rustic, sit-down restaurant with bullet service and high turnover. Over fifty toppings are available, but tomato-and-cheese is the pie of choice, topped with fresh garlic—if you're not on a first date.

## Keens Steakhouse $$$

72 West 36th St (at Sixth), Midtown

☎ 212.947.3636 🖥 keens.com

STEAKHOUSE      🗺 H1 #46

Keens is the best steakhouse in Manhattan. There, we've said it. It's a manly man's meatery that looks so much like a steakhouse is supposed to look that it would burgeon on kitsch if it weren't the real McCoy. Opened in 1885, and designed with hundreds, if not thousands of clay pipes hanging from the ceiling, a meal here is like traveling to a time predating cardiologists, or Atkins for that matter (order a baked potato). Yet, somehow, this place is perfect for business, groups, dates, whatever. Upon seating, tables are topped with fresh warm bread and a plate of crudités and olives. Flintstone-sized mutton chops are the thing to order here, cut thick and perfectly cooked, charred on the outside and tender within. Of course other steaks are available too, along with terrific short ribs stewed with root vegetables. About 200 strong, Keens also has the city's best scotch selection.

## Kum Gang San $$

49 West 32nd St (at Broadway), Midtown

☎ 212.967.0909 🖥 No Website

KOREAN | Open NONSTOP      🗺 H1 #47

For an authentic Korean experience that approximates something you'd experience in Seoul (read: great food, rude waiters), you don't have to look further than 32nd Street, where some dozen Korean restaurants serve day and night. Kum Gang San is the best of the bunch, offering a huge, nicely decorated dining room (those waterfalls!) and great food served with lots of fiery "banchan" side dishes. All the hits are here, including bulgoki (grilled marinated beef, which you spread with bean paste and roll into lettuce leaves), and bibimbap (an everything-but-the-kitchen-sink bowl of fried beef and vegetables tossed with rice). The barbequed beef is terrific and lunch specials are offered daily.

## La Bottega $$$

Maritime Hotel, 88 Ninth Ave (at 16th), Chelsea

☎ 212.243.8400 🖥 themaritimehotel.com

ITALIAN      🗺 G2 #48

Eric Goode and Sean MacPherson's party palace is the place to choose when culinary theater is at the top of your agenda. Yeah, they serve good grilled sardines, truffle-scented tuna with white beans, a sturdy pappardelle with rabbit ragù, and some decent wood-oven pizzas, but it's the atmosphere you've come for and this trendy trattoria doesn't disappoint. Great looking servers, wonderful lychee martinis and an amazing outdoor balcony that overflows with beautiful scenesters all summer long make this one of the finest places to dine near the Meatpacking District. For truly top-notch cooking, look elsewhere. For great looking people on the make, your appetite will be satisfied.

## La Casa De Los Tacos $

2277 First Ave (at 117th), Spanish Harlem

☎ 212.860.6858 🖥 No Website

MEXICAN      🗺 B1 #49

In Southern California there are thousands of great divvy taquerias like this. In New York you have to trek to East Harlem for sweet-smelling corn tortillas chunked up with chicken, beef tongue, braised pork or chorizo. The tacos are cheap, the dining room is reassuringly ugly and, as a destination place, it's a great excuse to see the neighborhood.

## La Esquina $$

106 Kenmare St (at Cleveland), Little Italy

☎ 646.613.7100 🖥 No Website

MEXICAN      🗺 L1 #50

Just like a good burrito, this hot-as-a-tamale Mexican corner is really three places rolled into one: a hole-in-the-wall Formica-topped taco stand, a decent cafe with a short Mexican menu,

and a clandestine subterranean restaurant and bar that's accessed through the door marked "Employees Only." It's a cavernous, dark and sexy space with candlelit tables hidden in alcoves, and a small bar serving exceptional tequilas along with small plates of delicacies like crab tostadas, charred chorizo quesadillas, and rotisserie chicken taquitos. Grilled whole snapper, chipotle shrimp, and steaks with chimichurri sauce also make appearances. Don't forget to bring a date.

## LITTLE ITALY PIZZA $

| | |
|---|---|
| 55 West 45th St (at Sixth), Midtown | |
| ☎ 212.730.7575 🌐 No Website | |
| PIZZA | 🗺 D2 #51 |
| 1 East 43rd St (at Fifth), Midtown | |
| ☎ 212.687.3660 | 🗺 E2 #52 |
| 180 Varick St (at Charlton), Soho | |
| ☎ 212.366.5566 | 🗺 K1 #53 |
| 11 Park Pl (at Broadway), Financial District | |
| ☎ 212.227.7077 | 🗺 K2 #54 |

What makes a great slice of New York pizza? It's the holy trinity: crispy crust, well-spiced sauce and mounds of real mozzarella cheese. That's why we pray at the Formica altars of LIP, a quartet

of downscale dives in which slices are consumed standing at counters. Regulars swear by the thick Sicilian style slices too.

## LOSIDE DINER $

157 East Houston St (at Eldridge), Lower East Side
☎ 212.254.2080 🌐 losidediner.com
AMERICAN | OPEN LATE　　　　　　　　🗺 L1 #55

LoSide is just a diner, but one that takes the festive sensibility of the neighborhood to heart, with good music, dodgy service and lots of late-night choices that appeal to alcohol-soaked revelers. Built with exposed brick and black booths, it's a sceney and easy-on-the-pocket place to scarf down everything from breakfast and burgers to classic American comfort foods like meatloaf and turkey pot pie.

## LUCKY STRIKE $$

59 Grand St (at West Broadway), Soho
☎ 212.941.0479 🌐 luckystrikeny.com
FRENCH BISTRO | OPEN LATE　　　　　　🗺 K1 #56

Keith McNally (**Balthazar**, **Pastis**, **Schiller's Liquor Bar**) is the master of creating stylish restaurants that never die. His secret? Doing things right, and not just *right now*. Once the boîte du jour, this aging hipster heaven has matured into a classic standby and a cherished Soho institution with a weathered charm that can always be counted on for decent food and a happy, bustling atmosphere. The casual, copper-topped brasserie decor is made lively with excellent music and an active multi-culti bar scene that hits its stride between midnight and 2am. Spaghetti with oil and garlic, steak frites, and turkey burgers are sure-fire hits from a menu of continental pub grub reliables that always includes choices of fish, fowl and farm.

## LUPA $$$

170 Thompson St (at Houston), Greenwich Village

☎ 212.982.5089 🌐 luparestaurant.com

ITALIAN                                    MAP K1 #57

Mario Batali (**Babbo**, **Casa Mono**) conceived Lupa as a casual, tighter, noisier and lower-priced alternative to his other Manhattan restaurants. But there is nothing cut-rate about the food. From pastas and sausages to oils and wines, almost everything here is custom-made for this kitchen. Once you've tasted the bucatini alla amatriciana loaded with the flavors of bacon, onions and cilantro, or the orecchiette and spicy broccoli rabe with sweet sausage, you'll never feel as good about plopping down $20 for an ordinary bowl of pasta again. Ditto for main courses like the classic saltimbocca or the pollo alla diavola, which has a kick worthy of its name. Needless to say, this place buzzes and it's tough to get in. Arrive early or expect to wait.

## MARKT $$$

401 West 14th St (at Ninth), Meatpacking District

☎ 212.727.3314 🌐 marktrestaurant.com

BELGIAN                                    MAP G2 #58

Markt was a pioneer in the Meatpacking District and it remains wildly popular in summer, when their outdoor tables are some of the most coveted real estate in the neighborhood. It's a Belgian-style bar and brasserie, which means there are numerous Belgian brews (along with a fine selection of other liquors) served in a good looking wood-and-brass interior. And of course, where there's Belgian beer, there's mussels, steamed in garlic and wine, along with very good steaks, fries and other traditionals.

## MATSURI $$$

Maritime Hotel, 369 West 16th St (at Ninth), Chelsea

☎ 212.243.6400 🌐 themaritimehotel.com

JAPANESE                                   MAP G2 #59

This swanky restaurant in the Maritime Hotel has a diminutive entrance, through an unassuming little door that can hardly

prepare you for the enormous, wooden barrel vaulted dining room inside; a spectacular subterranean space that's so fabulous it verges on the majestic. And the modelicious crowd isn't far behind. Matsuri's meals are designed by chef de cuisine Tadashi Ono, a Tokyo native who mastered French technique at some of New York's top restaurants. His specialty is *izakaya*, Japanese small plates that include fluke sashimi brushed with ponzu, boiled spinach in dashi, raw Kobe-style beef with a dash of mustard sauce, seared and sauced sushi, and various yakitori. Not surprisingly, sake cocktails are the drinks of choice, and plenty of penny-pinching lookie-loos just go straight to the mezzanine bar.

## MEGU $$$$

62 Thomas St (at Church), Tribeca

☎ 212.964.7777 🌐 megunyc.com

JAPANESE                                   MAP K1 #60

Japanese cooking reaches its zenith in this dramatically contemporary restaurant by Koji Imai, one of Japan's most successful high-end restaurateurs. Set with round booths around a large Buddha ice sculpture that's carved nightly, the dining room is nothing if not spectacular. Happily, so is the food. The complicated 12-page small plates menu encompasses literally dozens of other Nipponese treats that you never know existed. And it's all ridiculously high end. Yakitori are made from the most expensive Japanese chickens, scallops are perfectly cooked in eel-sly broth with truffles and foie gras, and raw Kobe beef strips are served with a fiery stone for tabletop grilling. Amish farmers in Ohio grow edamame to their exact specifications—no joke. Meals (and great sake drinks) are also served in the swanky upstairs lounge. An extravagantly memorable meal will set you back about $200. Don't forget the platinum.

## MERCER KITCHEN $$$

Mercer Hotel, 99 Prince St (at Mercer), Soho

☎ 212.966.5454 🌐 jean-georges.com

FRENCH, AMERICAN NEW                       MAP K1 #61

A dozen years on, Jean-Georges Vongerichten's (66, Perry Street, Spice Market, Vong) celebrity-studded Soho outpost is still one of the finest restaurants around. That's a testament to the superchef's trademark meals; exquisite dishes such as mint-scented tuna carpaccio, pumpkin ravioli with sage and brown butter, crab salad with mango mustard, or lemon risotto with bay scallops. And the forgiving brick-walled dining room plays to both fun (at one of the long communal tables) and romance (secreted in a subdued corner booth). Even desserts are outstanding.

*Perry Street*

## MESA GRILL $$$

102 Fifth Ave (at 15th), Union Square

☎ 212.807.7400 🌐 mesagrill.com

AMERICAN REGIONAL      MAP H2 #62

Other restaurants may come and go, but chef Bobby Flay's (**Bar Americain**) Southwestern standby soldiers on. We love the palate piquing combinations like the spice-rubbed pork tenderloin with bourbon ancho-chili sauce, and blue-corn crusted red snapper with buttermilk chipotle and roasted red pepper relish. Weekend brunches offer similarly spicy specialties (tequila-smoked salmon quesadilla, chicken-and-sweet potato hash served with a green chili hollandaise). In addition to a great selection of predominantly American wines, the bar boasts top-shelf tequilas and an extensive list of margaritas. The quietest seats are on the balcony of this soaring Flatiron district space that's decked out in southwestern colors, ranging from clay reds to avocado greens. We prefer to be in the middle of the rodeo on banquettes decorated with cowboys on bucking broncos.

## MR. CHOW $$$$

324 East 57th St (at Second), Midtown

☎ 212.751.9030 🌐 mrchow.com

CHINESE      MAP E2 #63

Of the two glamorous gourmet Chinese restaurants in Manhattan (the other is Shun Lee) this swanky place gets our nod for amazing food that's a world away from the greased-out noodle shops of Chinatown. Regulars here include lots of stars and generic rich people who let the waiters order for them. The waiters will press you, but don't you do the same. Ask for squab lettuce wraps, chicken satay, crispy orange beef, spicy green shrimp or gambler's duck. And be prepared to pay big time for the experience.

## NOBU $$$$

105 Hudson St (at Franklin), Tribeca

☎ 212.219.0500 🌐 myriadrestaurantgroup.com

JAPANESE PERUVIAN      MAP K1 #64

## NOBU, NEXT DOOR

105 Hudson St (at Franklin), Tribeca

☎ 212.334.4445      MAP K1 #65

## NOBU 57

40 West 57th St (at Fifth), Midtown

☎ 212.757.3000      MAP E2 #66

Ever since chef Nobu Matsuhisa, a Japanese-Peruvian-Los Angeleno, introduced a new kind of fusion to the world, there has been no looking back. Today the Nobu empire extends to some dozen restaurants across three continents, and in some ways has the whiff of a high-end chain—portion control and all. Still, if it's perfect yin-yang combinations like raw yellowtail with jalapeño peppers, barely cooked sashimi drizzled with garlic- and ginger-flavored olive oil, and monkfish-liver pâté with soy dressing and a gleaming dollop of caviar, then Nobu is your place. Regulars begin with shots of Masu sake, served tequila-style in small cedar cups with salted rims. If you can't get reservations, you can try your luck at Next Door Nobu, where only walk-ins are accommodated with a menu that rivals its neighbor at slightly lower prices. Nobu 57, the chef's more recent Carnegie Hall-area spin-off, is in a mammoth, two level David Rockwell-designed space.

## NOOCH $

**143 Eighth Ave (at 17th), Chelsea**
☎ 212.691.8600 ☷ No Website
**PAN ASIAN**                              `MAP` H2 #67

A fabulously trendy noodle shop chain from Singapore, Nooch is the kind of place in which lowly ramen is elevated to designer status with rich broths and served in Karim Rashid-designed bowls. There's even a full bar and a DJ booth. Udon and soba meals are meaty and slurping is smiled upon. And they close when they run out of their key ingredient: Soup. It's **Republic** for the Chelsea set.

## ODEON $$$

**145 West Broadway (at Thomas), Tribeca**
☎ 212.233.0507 ☷ theodeonrestaurant.com
**FRENCH BISTRO | OPEN LATE**            `MAP` K1 #68

Famous since Warhol's day, and immortalized in Jay McInerney's novel *Bright Lights, Big City*, Odeon was arguably the first hip New York bistro. Today it's a downtown fixture known to everyone from local families to curious visitors who come here day and night for great steak frites and monster martinis. Success persists because Odeon refuses to rest on its laurels: The retro-bistro dining room is well maintained, service is snappy and Grey Goose has replaced Absolut. The tried-and-true brasserie menu features perfect steak au poivre, a wonderful seared tuna sandwich enriched with arugula and wasabi mayonnaise, fine country salads and big juicy burgers. Not incidentally, there's a great bar, which still sees plenty of star power. People watching improves by the hour, culminating with a late-night party of club kids and fashionistas.

## OYSTER BAR, THE $$$

**Grand Central Terminal, Lower Level, 89 East 42nd St (at Vanderbilt), Midtown**
☎ 212.490.6650 ☷ oysterbarny.com
**SEAFOOD**                                `MAP` E2 #69

Opened in 1913, The Oyster Bar is old skool New York—a haven from the highfalutin dining that's now happening everywhere

else. The best seats are for walk-in singles or duos, to the right of the entrance at a long Formica counter where you can watch the famously gruff chefs in action. Others take tables in the tiled main dining room, a comfortable enough space with vaulted ceilings that can get aggressively noisy if a large party is in the house. The emphasis of course is on seafood, and oysters are the specialty. About two dozen varieties are in stock at all times. The pan roast is a forté. It's basically an instant stew made by combining clam juice, cream, Worcestershire sauce, spices and a handful of fleshy oysters. The rest of the arm's length menu reads like a survey of mid-Atlantic regional cooking and includes good clam chowders, coquille St. Jacques, crab cakes, Maryland she-crab soup, fried clams and an extensive fish selection. An equally long wine list attracts plenty of grape nuts. On weekdays, just after offices close, this place can get as crowded as, uh, Grand Central Station. The Oyster Bar is closed Saturdays.

## PASTIS $$$

**9 Ninth Ave (at Little West 12th), Greenwich Village**
☎ 212.929.4844 ☷ pastisny.com
**FRENCH BISTRO**                          `MAP` G2 #70

Keith McNally's (**Balthazar, Lucky Strike, Schiller's Liquor Bar**) Pastis is a cacophonous restaurant with a theatrical appeal that takes a page out of Parisian life and inserts it into New York. Although the restaurant's mirrors, marble-topped credenzas, zinc bar, signs and other accouterments may have been sourced locally, it looks like they're straight out of old Les Halles. And celebrities still arrive to this buzzing Meatpacking District bistro by the limo load. Culinarily, it's *vrai* Français—onion soup with a thick crust of cheese, croque monsieur served on a wooden board, skate with capers in black butter, roast leg of lamb with flageolets, and steak frites served with béarnaise sauce. House wines are served by the carafe, accompanied by sturdy tumblers. Show up at an off hour or expect to wait.

## PEARL OYSTER BAR $$

**18 Cornelia St (at 4th), Greenwich Village**
☎ 212.691.8211 ☷ pearloysterbar.com
**SEAFOOD**                                `MAP` H2 #71

Lots of knowledgeable locals claim that Pearl is their favorite place to nosh. It's quick and easy to drop into this upscale New England-style seafood shack, grab a stool at the marble bar, or one of the elevated tables, and enjoy up to-the-minute fresh shell and fin fish. The PEI mussels with wine are out of this world, and so too is the bouillabaisse. You'll find us at the bar, slurping down one of their wonderful bowls of clam chowder, which is made with just a hint of bacon.

## PERRY STREET                                                    $$$

176 Perry St (at Washington), Greenwich Village

☎ 212.352.1900 ☒ jean-georges.com

**FRENCH NEW**                                          MAP G2 #72

Superchef Jean-Georges Vongerichten (**66**, **Mercer Kitchen**, **Spice Market**, **Vong**) gets back to basics with this small, minimalist and less formal eatery in a glass-wrapped, Richard Meier–designed residential tower hard by the Hudson River. Both the L-shaped dining room and the menu here are far less flamboyant then his other splashy restaurants, but that hardly means they are tame. Meals on the frequently changing menu might include a cylinder of seared tuna with a rice cracker crust, steamed black bass with a basil vinaigrette, black pepper crab dumplings with sugar snap peas, or rack of lamb with a crunchy coat.

## PHO BANG                                                           $

157 Mott St (at Grand), Little Italy

☎ 212.966.3797 ☒ No Website

**VIETNAMESE**                                          MAP L1 #73

3 Pike St (at Division), Chinatown

☎ 212.233.3947                                          MAP L1 #74

This Vietnamese noodle house is a step up from the common Chinatown grunge spot. It only makes a stab at comfort and décor with its tile floor, classic French café chairs and Vietnamese prints. But it kills when it comes to food. The house specialties are a dozen or so versions of pho, a traditional beef soup with rice noodles, along with a few vermicelli rice dishes studded with everything from grilled pork and beef to marinated grilled shrimp.

## POP BURGER                                                         $

58 Ninth Ave (at 15th), Chelsea

☎ 212.414.8686 ☒ popburger.com

**AMERICAN | OPEN LATE**                                 MAP G2 #75

Hamburgers get hip at this fashionable lounge with good little burgers, thick shakes, mood lighting, Basquiat prints, low-slung seating and a full bar. It's a popular place, though somewhat Bridge and Tunnel, with a lively atmosphere that seems to get more crowded as the night goes on. Served in pairs and slathered with Russian dressing, the miniature burgers are delicious. At lunch, you can get them for about

half the price at a less formal take-out counter. And because Pop Burger stays open late, it's a great place to relieve post-drink munchies.

## PUBLIC                                                          $$$

210 Elizabeth St (at Prince), Nolita

☎ 212.343.7011 ☒ public-nyc.com

**GLOBAL**                                              MAP L1 #76

Post offices, libraries and other public institutions are the inspiration for this stylish restaurant created and managed by the New York-based design firm AvroKo (**Odea**, **Stanton Social**). Sleek wood and glass dining rooms abound with whimsical details that include a library of periodicals and dozens of wooden mailboxes which you can actually rent. And there's nothing institutional about the classy cooking; freestyle global cuisine with an Australian bent that ranges from juicy grilled scallops with sweet chili sauce to seared kangaroo with coriander falafel, and includes chorizo mashed potatoes and onion-licorice chutney. Even the friendly and informal service has a Down Under attitude. There's a good bar in back (peach margaritas!) and it's a good place for brunch too.

## PURE FOOD AND WINE                                              $$$

54 Irving Pl (at 17th), Gramercy

☎ 212.477.1010 ☒ purefoodandwine.com

**RAW VEGAN**                                           MAP I2 #77

While most high-end restaurants grudgingly accommodate healthists, PF&W goes the whole hog so to speak, with a meat-, egg- and milk-free kitchen that borders on *haute*. From appetizers to dessert, everything is strictly vegan and nothing is heated above 118-degrees Fahrenheit. Exceptionally creative meals might include butternut squash "raw-violi," black bean mole torte with caramelized plantains and cashew sour cream, pecan crusted portobello in a syrah reduction, and truffled white bean cassoulet. Portions are small, but flavors are big and beg for analytical deconstruction with each bite. True to its name, the restaurant also has a good organic wine selection, as well as excellent cocktails. During warm weather, the best seats are outside in the garden.

## PYLOS                                                            $$

128 East 7th St (at Ave A), East Village

☎ 212.473.0220 ☒ pylosrestaurant.com

**GREEK**                                               MAP I2 #78

Stylishness now pervades restaurants the world over, but the word "trendy" rarely precedes "Greek." In this regard, Pylos

Pop Burger

is a vanguard: a top-notch Hellenic restaurant with an edgy East Village atmosphere hard by Tompkins Square Park. The room is small and handsome and meals are at once classic and contemporary, and include perfectly charred grilled octopus, mint-infused meatballs, whole baked fish, and lamb with orzo cooked in a clay pot. Only gruff service mars what is otherwise a meal worthy of the gods.

## RED CAT                                          $$$

227 Tenth Ave (at 23rd), Chelsea

☎ 212.242.1122  🌐 theredcat.com

MEDITERRANEAN AMERICAN                    🗺 G1 #79

This Chelsea hotspot gets going early in the evening with a boisterous artsy cocktail crowd from the neighborhood and continues through the night with diners who come from afar. All are attracted by the warm welcome, the stylish, narrow crimson room lit by oversize Moroccan lanterns, the lack of any bogus attitude and the bold-flavored and reasonably priced Mediterranean-American cuisine by chef

Jimmy Bradley (**The Harrison**). You might begin with a warm grilled endive salad with blue cheese and balsamic vinegar, or roasted Manila clams with red pepper, smoked ham and sherry. Mains run the gamut from mustard-crusted trout, to sliced baby lamb with grilled red onions and sour cherries. And Red Cat caters to solo diners at the long and lively stone-topped bar.

## REPUBLIC                                           $

37 Union Square West (at 16th), Union Square

☎ 212.627.7172  🌐 thinknoodles.com

ASIAN                                        🗺 H2 #80

This quick and cheap nouvelle noodle warehouse offers hip dining on trendy Union Square. A high-tech "slurpateria," Republic is intensively designed to serve as many light-and-healthy meals as they can in as short a time as possible. Diners are seated at communal tables on uncomfortable benches, and model-cum-waiters relay orders to the kitchen via handheld computers. Very good, fresh food makes the

Public

industrial atmosphere palatable. The best of the Asian-inspired meals-in-a-bowl are spicy chicken in coconut milk; Malaysian chicken with coconut, lime and lemongrass; and a pseudo-Vietnamese grilled beef with rice noodles. There's also a good long bar for solitary dining.

## Rice                                                   $

227 Mott St (at Prince), Nolita

☎ 212.226.5775 ☲ riceny.com

ASIAN                                             **MAP** L1 #81

115 Lexington Ave (at 28th), Midtown

☎ 212.686.5400                                    **MAP** I1 #82

Still one of the busiest restaurants in Nolita, Rice is a cheap-and-trendy tip of the toque to nouvelle Asian cuisine. Small, dark and handsome, the restaurant offers a short menu of simplistic rice-based treats like vegetarian sushi rolls, Thai beef salad, and Indian chicken curry. Stylish surroundings, good people watching and competent food (in that order) make for long waits almost every night of the week.

## Rosa Mexicano                                        $$$

1063 First Ave (at 58th), Midtown

☎ 212.753.7407 ☲ rosamexicano.com

MEXICAN                                           **MAP** F2 #83

61 Columbus Ave (at 62nd), Upper West Side

☎ 212.977.7700                                    **MAP** D1 #84

9 East 18th St (at Fifth), Union Square

☎ 212.533.3350                                    **MAP** H2 #104

Rosa's is real Mexican cuisine: large plates of delicately prepared meats and fishes without a burrito in sight. Most every table begins with a round of fresh pomegranate margaritas and an order of guacamole. Prepared tableside, the avocados are peeled into a large volcanic-stone mortar and blended using perfect proportions of tomatoes, onions, chilies, cilantro and lime juice. Sautéed bay shrimp, marinated in a zesty mustard-and-chili vinaigrette is the second most-popular starter, followed by red snapper ceviche flavored with spearmint, basil, parsley and green olives. Regulars come here for one of two entrees: *mixiote*

Sush Samba

de Cordero, an amazingly tender three-chili- and garlic-infused lamb shank steamed in parchment paper, or the chicken enchiladas with mole sauce. Created by David Rockwell, the decor is best at the new Union Square location.

## SAMMY'S ROUMANIAN $$$

157 Chrystie St (at Delancey), Lower East Side

☎ 212.673.0330 🖵 No Website

JEWISH                                        MAP L1 #85

Artery-clogging Jewish comfort food and a rollicking, decidedly non-kosher dining room make unlikely bedfellows in this famous, divvy Lower Eastsider. The crowd can be hit or miss, but when it's on there's not a more amusing party in the city. On our last visit, there was a strolling fiddler serenading a birthdaying Mafia don, a quiet Chinese family and several large tables of black-clad hipsters who spent most of the night dancing around the room. None of which would be particularly odd, but for the menu, which is filled with cardiovascular no-no's like kishka (herb-stuffed intestinal casing), sweetbreads (thymus glands), fertilized chicken eggs and chopped liver mixed with heavy doses of schmaltz (rendered chicken fat), which sits on the table in a little pitcher. The Romanian hanger tenderloin alone, is enough to drop you into an eater's coma. Vodka, frozen in a block of ice, is the drink of choice along with egg creams.

## SCHILLER'S LIQUOR BAR $$

131 Rivington St (at Norfolk), Lower East Side

☎ 212.260.4555 🖵 schillersny.com

AMERICAN                                      MAP L1 #86

Schiller's is one of the latest offerings from Keith McNally (**Balthazar**, **Lucky Strike**, **Pastis**), the godfather of hip dining in New York. His admirable trademark is in creating energetic and transporting dining rooms that impart a distinctive sense of place. And they get better as they grow older. At this tight, loud and usually crowded bistro, the scene is set

with white-tiled walls, antique mirrors and busboys wearing T-shirts printed with Heimlich maneuver instructions. House wine is served in plain bottles stenciled "cheap," "decent" and "good." The very likable and fairly priced menu ranges from penne arrabiata and garlic shrimp served in a sizzling iron skillet, to meat loaf with mashed potatoes, and very good steak frites. They do very good weekend brunches too.

## Second Avenue Deli                                    $$

156 Second Ave (at 10th), East Village

☎ 212.677.0606  ◻ 2ndavedeli.com

DELICATESSEN                                     ᴍᴀᴘ I2 #87

A venerable New York institution, Second Avenue Deli is situated in the center of what was once the Yiddish language theater district, as evidenced by the sidewalk, a Jewish walk of fame etched with the names of bygone stars. Inside is more restaurant than deli, with wisecracking waiters serving an encyclopedic menu of Jewish soul food that includes chicken-in-the-pot (boiled lifeless with vegetables and noodles), and kasha varnishkas (bowtie noodles with buckwheat). Of course, they have matzoh ball soup, knishes, chopped liver and huge sandwiches too.

## SobaKoh                                              $

309 East 5th St (at Second), East Village

☎ 212.254.2244  ◻ No Website

JAPANESE                                         ᴍᴀᴘ I2 #88

A dead ringer for any number of noodle shops in Tokyo, SobaKoh attracts a loyal clientele who fill the small dining room with noodle slurps and chopstick clacks. Udon (thick wheat noodles) or soba (narrow buckwheat linguine) are the main choices here. Both are served either hot or cold in a variety of soups and sauces and once they sell out they close up shop. It all seems so authentically Japanese—except the prices.

## Spice Market                                        $$$

403 West 13th St (at Ninth), Meatpacking District

☎ 212.675.2322  ◻ jean-georges.com

SOUTHEAST ASIAN                                  ᴍᴀᴘ G2 #89

Vietnamese street food gets a sybaritic spin at this white-hot concept restaurant collaboration between superchefs Jean-Georges Vongerichten (**66**, **Mercer Kitchen**, **Perry Street**, **Vong**) and Gray Kunz. Once past the velvet rope (yes, there's a rope), diners enter an extravagant Jacques Garcia–designed two-story space with golden-lit teak pagodas and

a buzzy atmosphere that often includes boldface names. And there's lots of great places to sit. Groups are catered to in semi-private alcoves, singles and duos should choose seats at the bar in front of the exhibition kitchen (for which reservations are not accepted) and everyone else should reserve upstairs, in the liveliest part of the restaurant. The small plates that emerge from the kitchen range from average to ethereal. The best combine the chef's trademarks of heat and sweet and include tuna with coconut and kaffir lime juice, pork vindaloo, and tender short ribs with chilies and onion. Vietnamese coffee, served with condensed milk ice cream, is a terrific finish.

## Spotted Pig, The                                     $$

314 West 11th St (at Greenwich), Greenwich Village

☎ 212.620.0393  ◻ thespottedpig.com

ENGLISH MODERN                                   ᴍᴀᴘ H2 #90

It's basically a tiny London-style gastropub, but for New York, it's something unique. Uniquer still, is the friendly and casual neighborhood atmosphere, solid cooking and decent prices. British comfort foods are well made from quality ingredients, and include meaty shepherd's pie, charred skirt steak with horseradish cream, and wild bass in a spicy anchovy sauce. All of which are meant to be washed down with perfectly poured pints. They do weekend brunches too. Reservations are not accepted: Cross your fingers, put your name on the list and head to the bar.

## SushiSamba                                          $$$

245 Park Ave South (at 20th), Gramercy

☎ 212.475.9377  ◻ sushisamba.com

SOUTH AMERICAN, JAPANESE                         ᴍᴀᴘ I2 #91

87 Seventh Ave South (at Barrow), Greenwich Village

☎ 212.691.7885                                   ᴍᴀᴘ H2 #92

It's all about the energetic scene at SushiSamba, colorful places for twentysomething trendies to pick up on each other while eating very good sushi and ceviche and getting soused on inventive Latin-based cocktails. Other Asian-South American combinations are served too, like fried snapper with coconut-scented rice, and shitake mushroom empanadas. There's even a five-course tasting menu. One part restaurant and two parts bar, the newer Village location boasts a wonderful rooftop garden in which DJs (and occasional live bands) spin revelers into a frenzy. Yeah, it's kind of Bridge and Tunnel, but with tongue firmly in cheek, these places can be fun.

Vento

## Tabla Bread Bar $$$$

11 Madison Ave (at 25th), Midtown

☎ 212.889.0667 🖰 tablany.com

**INDIAN NEW** 〔MAP〕 H1 #93

"New Indian" doesn't do justice to Danny Meyer's (**Blue Smoke**, Gramercy Tavern, Union Square Cafe) exquisite two-story restaurant and bar in which the décor and the flavors are exotic indeed. Forget any Indian food you've ever tasted when you order the duck samosa sparked by pumpkin-and-orange chutney and almonds. And you've probably never had a curry as beguiling as the taro-crusted wild striped bass with sides of baby bok choy and wild mushrooms. Wines are good too, with a emphasis on the Rieslings and gewürztraminers that can stand up to spices. A grand staircase leads to the main dining room overlooking Madison Square Park. It's extraordinarily comfortable, set with large, generously spaced tables and rich coral and jade decor. At the Bread Bar on the first floor, a limited à la carte menu (and lower prices) attracts a younger more boisterous crowd.

## Tal Bagels $

333 East 86th St (at Second), Upper East Side

☎ 212.427.6811 🖰 No Website

**BAGELS** 〔MAP〕 B2 #94

1228 Lexington Ave (at 83rd), Upper East Side

☎ 212.717.2080 〔MAP〕 B2 #95

Who makes the best bagels in Manhattan? By our estimation it's Tal, a terrific mini-chain known for crusty and chewy bread rings that are state-of-the art. And toppings here are terrific. From a schmeer of butter, to smoked whitefish, to lox and cream cheese, this is classic New York eating.

## Tao $$$

42 East 58th St (at Madison), Midtown

☎ 212.888.2288 🖰 taorestaurant.com

**ASIAN** 〔MAP〕 E2 #96

If you've been to Buddha Bar in Paris then you know the sexy and trendy vibe that this cacophonous high-style clone recreates (complete with homemade CDs). Lorded over by an enormous seated Buddha sculpture and dotted with bamboo and reflecting pools, the swanky triple-height dining room is a former movie palace that's nothing if not dramatic. A temple to cuisine this is not, as the food is mediocre: large plates, designed for sharing, that hop around Asia from crunchy spring rolls and creative sushi rolls, to garlic lobster dumplings, pad Thai, and Chilean sea bass satay. At its heart, Tao is about cocktails and camaraderie and almost guarantees a spirited night of fun.

## TAVERN ON THE GREEN $$$$
**Central Park West (at 67th), Upper West Side**
☎ 212.873.3200 🌐 tavernonthegreen.com
AMERICAN                                            🗺 D1 #97

As wonderful and magical as it is kitschy and tourist-mobbed, Tavern on the Green is a once in a lifetime experience because that's exactly how many times you should go. But go you should, especially in winter, seated in the totally over-the-top Crystal Room. Despite crowds, both service and food are quite good, at times even excellent. Drink a little too much and you'll have a blast.

## TOWN $$$$
**Chambers Hotel, 15 West 56th St (at Fifth), Midtown**
☎ 212.582.4445 🌐 townnyc.com
AMERICAN NEW                                        🗺 E2 #98

A dazzling destination place in the depths of the trendy Chambers Hotel, Town is a tony restaurant at the top of the food chain with service, atmosphere and prices to match. Chef-owner Geoffrey Zakarian has created a sophisticated place to sign contracts, celebrate anniversaries and generally toast to each other's success. Food here is intense and intricate, using lots of time consuming glazes and stock reductions to create meals ranging from escargot risotto and Basque-style veal tongue, to duck steak and roasted venison loin. And, yes, do order the chocolate soufflé dessert. Come here for lunch, or to snack on an abbreviated menu between regular meal hours—the back door to what can otherwise be a very pricey experience.

## VENTO $$$
**675 Hudson St (at 14th), Meatpacking District**
☎ 212.699.2400 🌐 brguestrestaurants.com
ITALIAN                                             🗺 G2 #99

Warm woods and exposed brick in a triangle, window-wrapped dining room create a inviting atmosphere at this solid Italian-ish restaurant by Steve Hanson's B.R. Guest Restaurants Group (**Atlantic Grill**, **Blue Fin**). There's a happening subterranean lounge (**Level V**) too, and in warm weather lots the best seats

spill onto a sidewalk full with activity. The extensive menu is full of crowd-pleasing hits, and very few misses, and includes grilled meats, sturdy house-made pastas and thin-crust wood-fired pizzas topped with extravagant things like seared wild mushrooms, pancetta and truffle oil. They serve a good weekend brunch too.

## VESELKA $
**144 Second Ave (at 9th), East Village**
☎ 212.228.9682 🌐 veselka.com
UKRAINIAN | OPEN **NONSTOP**                        🗺 I2 #100

When we were kids, we used to visit Veselka at 4am for cheap late-night plates of super-heavy Eastern European uncomfort food like borscht, blintzes, pierogis, potato pancakes and kielbasa. Now we're all grown up, but Veselka, which hasn't budged an inch, still serves the same purpose in our lives. Service is grumpy, the lighting is all wrong and you probably wouldn't want to visit when the sun is shining. In sum, this place is a New York classic.

## VONG $$$$
**200 East 54th St (at Third), Midtown**
☎ 212.486.9592 🌐 jean-georges.com
THAI                                                🗺 E2 #101

Now with outposts in Chicago and Hong Kong, Vong lets diners taste Jean-Georges Vongerichten (**66**, **Mercer Kitchen**, **Perry Street**, **Spice Market**) at his best, without the expense of his eponymous restaurant on Columbus Circle. A striking bamboo and gold leaf dining room designed by David Rockwell is the setting for Asian-fusion of the highest order that might include crab spring rolls, foie gras with ginger and mango, duck breast with tamarind sauce, and galangal-infused salmon. Service is exceptional. There's a relatively low priced pre-theater *prix fixe* too.

## WD-50 $$$$
**50 Clinton St (at Stanton), Lower East Side**
☎ 212.477.2900 🌐 wd-50.com
ECLECTIC                                            🗺 L1 #102

Chef Wylie Dufresne's WD-50 is the only restaurant in New York showcasing envelope-pushing cuisine in the style of Ferran Adrià's El Bulli restaurant in Spain. It's culinary creativity taken to the edge, with meals that ride the fence between food, art and humor—though not necessarily in that order. Think chocolate truffled foie gras, venison tartare with edamame ice cream, shrimp noodles made without flour or

Vong

eggs (or perhaps even shrimp), and pickled beef tongue with deep-fried cubes of mayonnaise. In short, it's a place for pricey gastroporn and the antithesis of hearty comfort food.

## 'WICHCRAFT $

397 Greenwich St (at Beach), Tribeca

☎ 212.780.0577  ◆ wichcraftnyc.com

SANDWICHES                    MAP K1 #103

Chef Tom Colicchio's super high-end lunch bar with mezzanine seating elevates the sandwich to gourmet status with fillings like grilled Gruyère with caramelized onions, tuna with shaved fennel and lemon, and fried egg and bacon with Gorgonzola. There are also zingy soups and salads, and good ice cream'wiches for dessert. The light-filled dining room is minimalist, futuristic and exceedingly casual, making this a excellent choice for a quick neighborhood lunch. And if you can't get to Tribeca, look for their kiosks in Union Square and Bryant Park.

AUREOLE
CHARLIE PALMER

## CHARLIE PALMER

*One of America's most highly regarded chefs,*
*Charlie Palmer first won critical acclaim in*
*1988 with the opening of Aureole in New York,*
*when he was only 28 years old. His empire now*
*extends to almost a dozen top restaurants in*
*New York, California and Las Vegas. Over the*
*years, Chef Palmer has trained and inspired a*
*legion of young cooks who have gone on to be*
*some of America's leading chefs, including Diane*
*Forley of Verbena and Michael Mina of Aqua in*
*San Francisco. Charlie is the author of three*
*cookbooks and is a frequent guest on NBCs*
*Today Show. And he still lives in New York City.*

**Avant-Guide:** What can you get in New York that you can't get anywhere else?

**Charlie Palmer:** Great Chinese food within minutes. It's just a phone call away — delivered strikingly hot, miraculously consistent. The place to get it: Tang Tang.

**=∧=** Where is your favorite place in New York to shop?

**CP:** Barneys, Citarella supermarket [424 Sixth Ave, at 9th] and JB Prince [36 East 31st St]: Great clothes, great food and one of the best places to get all of those hard-to-find cooking utensils!

**=∧=** What five non-essential items do you never travel without?

**CP:** Portable DVD Player (when not flying Jet Blue), black V-ball Pilot pens, plenty of food reads, The New York Times and a picture of my wife and boys.

**=∧=** Describe your perfect hotel room. What kind of architecture, furniture, facilities and services would you like it to have?

**CP:** A King size bed, which includes a feather bed, down comforter and six to eight large pillows. A Large shower where the showerhead is at 7 feet. Oh yeah, quick room service!

**=∧=** What aspect of your profession do you most enjoy, and why?

**CP:** The intensity of the kitchen. It takes real teamwork to work in a kitchen and at times it can get very intense. Watching cooks interact in my kitchens puts a smile on my face. It makes me think this is what life's all about.

**=∧=** What is your fallback job, and why?

**CP:** Making wine. Because even if I was stone broke I would still have something to drink!

**=∧=** What is your favorite motto or catch phrase?

**CP:** A clean kitchen is a happy kitchen.

| Map | # | Price | Cuisine | Restaurant | Address | Phone | Design Driven | Bar Scene | Celebrity Chef | Classic New York | Dining Alone | Date Place | Business Power | Kid Friendly | Outdoor Seating | Breakfast/Brunch | Dessert | After Midnight |
|---|---|---|---|---|---|---|---|---|---|---|---|---|---|---|---|---|---|---|
| **Chelsea** | | | | | | | | | | | | | | | | | | |
| G2 | 75 | $ | American | Pop Burger | 58 Ninth Ave | 212.414.8686 | ★ | ★ | | | | ★ | | | | | | ★ |
| H2 | 67 | $ | Pan Asian | Nooch | 143 Eighth Ave | 212.691.8600 | ★ | | ★ | ★ | | | | ★ | | | | |
| G1 | 8 | $$$ | American New | BED New York | 530 West 27th St | 212.594.4109 | ★ | ★ | | | | ★ | | | ★ | | | |
| G2 | 48 | $$$ | Italian | La Bottega | Maritime Hotel | 212.243.8400 | ★ | ★ | | | | ★ | | | | | | |
| G1 | 15 | $$$ | Italian Northern | Bottino | 246 Tenth Ave | 212.206.6766 | | | | | | | ★ | | ★ | | | |
| G2 | 59 | $$$ | Japanese | Matsuri | Maritime Hotel | 212.243.6400 | ★ | ★ | | | ★ | ★ | | | | | | |
| G1 | 79 | $$$ | Med-American | Red Cat | 227 Tenth Ave | 212.242.1122 | | ★ | ★ | | ★ | ★ | | | | | | |
| H1 | 9 | $$$$ | Asian New | Biltmore Room | 290 Eighth Ave | 212.807.0111 | ★ | | | | | ★ | | | | | | |
| **Chinatown** | | | | | | | | | | | | | | | | | | |
| L1 | 74 | $ | Vietnamese | Pho Bang | 3 Pike St | 212.233.3947 | | | | | | | ★ | | ★ | | | |
| L1 | 32 | $$ | Dim Sum | Golden Unicorn | 18 East Broadway | 212.941.0911 | | | | ★ | | | | ★ | ★ | | | |
| **East Harlem** | | | | | | | | | | | | | | | | | | |
| B1 | 49 | $ | Mexican | La Casa De Los Tacos | 2277 First Ave | 212.860.6858 | | | | | ★ | ★ | | | | | | |
| **East Village** | | | | | | | | | | | | | | | | | | |
| I2 | 88 | $ | Japanese | SobaKoh | 309 East 5th St | 212.254.2244 | | | | | ★ | | | | | | | |
| I2 | 100 | $ | Ukrainian | Veselka | 144 Second Ave | 212.228.9682 | | | | | ★ | ★ | | | ★ | ★ | | ★ |
| I2 | 18 | $ | Venezuelan | Caracas Arepa Bar | 91 East 7th St | 212.228.5062 | | | | | ★ | | | | | | | |
| I2 | 87 | $$ | Delicatessen | Second Avenue Deli | 156 Second Ave | 212.677.0606 | | | | | ★ | ★ | | | ★ | ★ | | |
| I2 | 21 | $$ | Dessert | ChikaLicious | 203 East 10th St | 212.995.9511 | | | | | | ★ | | | | | | ★ |
| I2 | 78 | $$ | Greek | Pylos | 128 East 7th St | 212.473.0220 | | | | | | ★ | | | ★ | | | |
| I2 | 26 | $$ | Korean | Dok Suni's | 119 First Ave | 212.477.9506 | | | | | | ★ | | | | | | |
| I2 | 38 | $$ | Thai | Holy Basil | 2nd Fl, 149 Second Ave | 212.460.5557 | | | | | | ★ | | | ★ | | | |
| I2 | 41 | $$$ | Vietnamese | Indochine | 430 Lafayette St | 212.505.5111 | | | | | | ★ | | | | | | |
| J2 | 6 | $$$ | Vietnamese New | Bao 111 | 111 Ave C | 212.254.7773 | ★ | | | | | ★ | | | | | | ★ |
| **Financial District** | | | | | | | | | | | | | | | | | | |
| K2 | 54 | $ | Pizza | Little Italy Pizza | 11 Park Pl | 212.227.7077 | | | | | ★ | ★ | | ★ | | | | |
| **Gramercy** | | | | | | | | | | | | | | | | | | |
| H2 | 23 | $$ | American | Coffee Shop | 29 Union Sq. West | 212.243.7969 | ★ | | | | ★ | ★ | | | | ★ | ★ | ★ |
| I2 | 20 | $$ | Spanish Nuevo | Bar Jamón | 125 East 17th St | 212.253.2773 | | ★ | | | | ★ | | | | | | |
| I2 | 77 | $$$ | Raw Vegan | Pure Food and Wine | 54 Irving Pl | 212.477.1010 | | | | | | ★ | | | | | | |
| I2 | 91 | $$$ | S. American, Japanese | SushiSamba | 245 Park Ave South | 212.475.9377 | ★ | ★ | | | | ★ | | | | | | |
| I2 | 19 | $$$ | Spanish Nuevo | Casa Mono | 52 Irving Pl | 212.253.2773 | | ★ | | | | ★ | | | | | | |

| Map | # | Price | Cuisine | Restaurant | Address | Phone | Design Driven | Bar Scene | Celebrity Chef | Classic New York | Dining Alone | Date Place | Business Power | Kid Friendly | Outdoor Seating | Breakfast/Brunch | Dessert | After Midnight |
|---|---|---|---|---|---|---|---|---|---|---|---|---|---|---|---|---|---|---|
| **Greenwich Village** | | | | | | | | | | | | | | | | | | |
| H2 | 33 | $ | American | Gray's Papaya | 402 Sixth Ave | 212.260.3532 | | | ★ | ★ | | | | ★ | | | | ★ |
| H2 | 43 | $ | Pizza | John's Pizzeria | 278 Bleecker St | 212.243.1680 | | | ★ | | ★ | | ★ | | | | | |
| H2 | 22 | $$ | Asian | Chow Bar | 230 West 4th St | 212.633.2212 | ★ | | | | ★ | | | | | | | |
| H2 | 90 | $$ | English Modern | Spotted Pig, The | 314 West 11th St | 212.620.0393 | ★ | | ★ | ★ | ★ | | | | | ★ | | |
| H2 | 25 | $$ | Mexican | Diablo Royale | 189 West 10th St | 212.620.0223 | ★ | | | | | ★ | ★ | | | | | |
| H2 | 71 | $$ | Seafood | Pearl Oyster Bar | 18 Cornelia St | 212.691.8211 | | | | | | ★ | ★ | | | | | |
| G2 | 70 | $$$ | French Bistro | Pastis | 9 Ninth Ave | 212.929.4844 | ★ | ★ | | | | ★ | | | | | | |
| G2 | 72 | $$$ | French New | Perry Street | 176 Perry St | 212.352.1900 | ★ | | ★ | | | ★ | ★ | ★ | | | | |
| K1 | 57 | $$$ | Italian | Lupa | 170 Thompson St | 212.982.5089 | | | ★ | | | ★ | | | | | | |
| H2 | 92 | $$$ | S. American, Japanese | SushiSamba | 87 Seventh Ave South | 212.691.7885 | ★ | ★ | | | | ★ | | | ★ | | | |
| H2 | 4 | $$$$ | Italian | Babbo | 110 Waverly Pl | 212.777.0303 | | | ★ | | | ★ | ★ | | | | | |
| **Little Italy** | | | | | | | | | | | | | | | | | | |
| L1 | 29 | $ | Dessert Italian | Ferrara | 195 Grand St | 212.226.6150 | | | | ★ | | | | | | | | ★ |
| L1 | 73 | $ | Vietnamese | Pho Bang | 157 Mott St | 212.966.3797 | | | | | ★ | | | ★ | | | | |
| L1 | 50 | $$ | Mexican | La Esquina | 106 Kenmare St | 646.613.7100 | ★ | | ★ | ★ | | | | | | | | |
| **Lower East Side** | | | | | | | | | | | | | | | | | | |
| L1 | 55 | $ | American | LoSide Diner | 157 East Houston St | 212.254.2080 | | | | ★ | | | | ★ | | | ★ | ★ |
| L1 | 40 | $ | Dessert | Il Laboratorio Del Gelato | 95 Orchard St | 212.343.9922 | | | | | ★ | ★ | | | | | | ★ |
| L1 | 86 | $$ | American | Schiller's Liquor Bar | 131 Rivington St | 212.260.4555 | ★ | | | | | ★ | | | | | | |
| L1 | 31 | $$ | American New | Freemans | Freeman Alley | 212.420.0012 | ★ | | | | | ★ | | | | | | |
| L1 | 42 | $$ | Italian | 'inoteca | 98 Rivington St | 212.614.0473 | ★ | | | | | | | | | | | |
| L1 | 85 | $$$ | Jewish | Sammy's Roumanian | 157 Chrystie St | 212.673.0330 | | | | | | ★ | ★ | ★ | | | | |
| L1 | 102 | $$$$ | Eclectic | WD-50 | 50 Clinton St | 212.477.2900 | | | | ★ | | | ★ | | | | | |
| **Meatpacking District** | | | | | | | | | | | | | | | | | | |
| G2 | 30 | $$ | French Bistro | Florent | 69 Gansevoort St | 212.989.5779 | | | | | | ★ | ★ | | | ★ | ★ | ★ |
| G2 | 58 | $$$ | Belgian | Markt | 401 West 14th St | 212.727.3314 | ★ | | | | | ★ | | | ★ | ★ | | |
| G2 | 99 | $$$ | Italian | Vento | 675 Hudson St | 212.699.2400 | ★ | | | | | ★ | ★ | ★ | ★ | | | |
| G2 | 89 | $$$ | Southeast Asian | Spice Market | 403 West 13th St | 212.675.2322 | ★ | ★ | ★ | | | | ★ | | | | | |
| **Midtown** | | | | | | | | | | | | | | | | | | |
| H1 | 35 | $ | American | Gray's Papaya | 539 Eighth Ave | 212.904.1588 | | | ★ | ★ | | | | ★ | | | | ★ |
| C2 | 24 | $ | American Regional | Daisy May's BBQ USA | 623 Eleventh Ave | 212.977.1500 | | | | | | | | ★ | | | | |
| I1 | 82 | $ | Asian | Rice | 115 Lexington Ave | 212.686.5400 | | | | | | | | ★ | | | | |

| Map | # | Price | Cuisine | Restaurant | Address | Phone | Design Driven | Bar Scene | Celebrity Chef | Classic New York | Dining Alone | Date Place | Business Power | Kid Friendly | Outdoor Seating | Breakfast/Brunch | Dessert | After Midnight |
|---|---|---|---|---|---|---|---|---|---|---|---|---|---|---|---|---|---|---|
| D2 | 45 | $ | Pizza | John's Pizzeria | 260 West 44th St | 212.391.7560 | | | | | | ★ | | ★ | | | | |
| D2 | 51 | $ | Pizza | Little Italy Pizza | 55 West 45th St | 212.730.7575 | | | | ★ | ★ | | | ★ | | | | |
| E2 | 52 | $ | Pizza | Little Italy Pizza | 1 East 43rd St | 212.687.3660 | | | | ★ | ★ | | | ★ | | | | |
| I1 | 13 | $$ | American Regional | Blue Smoke | 116 East 27th St | 212.447.7733 | ★ | | | | | | | ★ | | | | |
| H1 | 47 | $$ | Korean | Kum Gang San | 49 West 32nd St | 212.967.0909 | | | | | | ★ | ★ | ★ | | | | |
| D2 | 7 | $$$ | American New | Bar Americain | 152 West 52nd St | 212.265.9700 | ★ | ★ | ★ | | | ★ | ★ | ★ | ★ | | | |
| E2 | 96 | $$$ | Asian | Tao | 42 East 58th St | 212.888.2288 | ★ | ★ | | | | ★ | ★ | | | | | |
| E2 | 16 | $$$ | French Brasserie | Brasserie | 100 East 53rd St | 212.751.4840 | ★ | | | | | ★ | ★ | ★ | ★ | | | ★ |
| H1 | 93 | $$$ | Indian New | Bread Bar at Tabla | 11 Madison Ave | 212.889.0667 | ★ | | | | | ★ | ★ | ★ | | | | |
| I1 | 28 | $$$ | Italian | English Is Italian | 622 Third Ave | 212.404.1700 | | | | | ★ | | | ★ | | | | |
| D2 | 37 | $$$ | Latin New | Hell's Kitchen | 679 Ninth Ave | 212.977.1588 | ★ | | | | | ★ | | ★ | | | | |
| F2 | 83 | $$$ | Mexican | Rosa Mexicano | 1063 First Ave | 212.753.7407 | | | | | | ★ | | ★ | | | | |
| D2 | 11 | $$$ | Seafood | Blue Fin | W Times Square | 212.918.1400 | ★ | | | | | ★ | ★ | ★ | | | | |
| E2 | 69 | $$$ | Seafood | Oyster Bar, The | Grand Central Terminal | 212.490.6650 | | | | ★ | ★ | | | ★ | | | | |
| H1 | 46 | $$$ | Steakhouse | Keens Steakhouse | 72 West 36th St | 212.947.3636 | | | | ★ | | | ★ | ★ | | | | |
| E2 | 98 | $$$$ | American New | Town | Chambers Hotel | 212.582.4445 | ★ | | | | | | ★ | ★ | | | | |
| E2 | 63 | $$$$ | Chinese | Mr. Chow | 324 East 57th St | 212.751.9030 | | | | | | ★ | ★ | ★ | | | | |
| H1 | 93 | $$$$ | Indian New | Tabla | 11 Madison Ave | 212.889.0667 | ★ | | ★ | | | | ★ | ★ | | | | |
| E2 | 66 | $$$$ | Japanese Peruvian | Nobu 57 | 40 West 57th St | 212.757.3000 | ★ | | ★ | | | ★ | ★ | ★ | | | | |
| E2 | 101 | $$$$ | Thai | Vong | 200 East 54th St | 212.486.9592 | | | ★ | | | | ★ | ★ | | | | |
| | | | | **Nolita** | | | | | | | | | | | | | | |
| L1 | 81 | $ | Asian | Rice | 227 Mott St | 212.226.5775 | | | | | | | | ★ | | | | |
| L1 | 76 | $$$ | Global | Public | 210 Elizabeth St | 212.343.7011 | ★ | ★ | | | | | | ★ | ★ | | | |
| | | | | **Soho** | | | | | | | | | | | | | | |
| K1 | 53 | $ | Pizza | Little Italy Pizza | 180 Varick St | 212.366.5566 | | | | ★ | ★ | | | ★ | | | | |
| K1 | 39 | $$ | Caribbean | Ideya | 349 West Broadway | 212.625.1441 | ★ | ★ | | | | ★ | | ★ | | | | |
| K1 | 56 | $$ | French Bistro | Lucky Strike | 59 Grand St | 212.941.0479 | | | | | | | | | | | | ★ |
| K1 | 12 | $$$ | American New | Blue Ribbon | 97 Sullivan St | 212.274.0404 | | | | | | | ★ | | | | | ★ |
| K1 | 5 | $$$ | French Brasserie | Balthazar | 80 Spring St | 212.965.1414 | ★ | ★ | | | | | ★ | | | | | ★ |
| K1 | 61 | $$$ | French, American New | Mercer Kitchen | Mercer Hotel | 212.966.5454 | ★ | ★ | ★ | | | | ★ | | | | | |
| K1 | 2 | $$$ | Seafood | Aquagrill | 210 Spring St | 212.274.0505 | ★ | | | | | | ★ | ★ | | ★ | | |
| | | | | **Tribeca** | | | | | | | | | | | | | | |
| K1 | 103 | $ | Sandwiches | 'Wichcraft | 397 Greenwich St | 212.780.0577 | ★ | | ★ | | ★ | | | ★ | | ★ | | |

| Map | # | Price | Cuisine | Restaurant | Address | Phone | Design Driven | Bar Scene | Celebrity Chef | Classic New York | Dining Alone | Date Place | Business Power | Kid Friendly | Outdoor Seating | Breakfast/Brunch | Dessert | After Midnight |
|---|---|---|---|---|---|---|---|---|---|---|---|---|---|---|---|---|---|---|
| **Tribeca** | | | | | | | | | | | | | | | | | | |
| K1 | 1 | $$$ | Chinese | 66 | 241 Church St | 212.925.0202 | ★ | ★ | ★ | | | ★ | ★ | | | | | |
| K1 | 68 | $$$ | French Bistro | Odeon | 145 West Broadway | 212.233.0507 | | | ★ | | | ★ | ★ | | ★ | ★ | | ★ |
| K1 | 36 | $$$ | Med-American | Harrison, The | 355 Greenwich St | 212.274.9310 | | | | ★ | | ★ | ★ | ★ | | | | |
| K1 | 27 | $$$ | Steakhouse | Dylan Prime | 62 Laight St | 212.334.4783 | ★ | | | | | | ★ | | | | | |
| K1 | 60 | $$$$ | Japanese | Megu | 62 Thomas St | 212.964.7777 | ★ | ★ | | | | ★ | ★ | | | | | |
| K1 | 64 | $$$$ | Japanese Peruvian | Nobu | 105 Hudson St | 212.219.0500 | ★ | | ★ | | | ★ | ★ | ★ | | | | |
| K1 | 65 | $$$$ | Japanese Peruvian | Nobu, Next Door | 105 Hudson St | 212.334.4445 | ★ | | ★ | | | ★ | ★ | ★ | | | | |
| **Union Square** | | | | | | | | | | | | | | | | | | |
| H2 | 80 | $ | Asian | Republic | 37 Union Square West | 212.627.7172 | ★ | | | | | | | | ★ | | | |
| H2 | 62 | $$$ | American Regional | Mesa Grill | 102 Fifth Ave | 212.807.7400 | | ★ | ★ | | | ★ | ★ | ★ | ★ | | | |
| H2 | 104 | $$$ | Mexican | Rosa Mexicano | 9 East 18th St | 212.533.3350 | ★ | ★ | | | | ★ | ★ | | ★ | | | |
| H2 | 10 | $$$ | Seafood | BLT Fish | 21 West 17th St | 212.691.8888 | | | | ★ | | | ★ | | | | | |
| **Upper East Side** | | | | | | | | | | | | | | | | | | |
| B2 | 94 | $ | Bagels | Tal Bagels | 333 East 86th St | 212.427.6811 | | | | | ★ | ★ | | ★ | | ★ | | |
| B2 | 95 | $ | Bagels | Tal Bagels | 1228 Lexington Ave | 212.717.2080 | | | | | ★ | ★ | | ★ | | ★ | | |
| F1 | 44 | $ | Pizza | John's Pizzeria | 408 East 64th St | 212.935.2895 | | | | | | | ★ | ★ | | | | |
| D1 | 14 | $$$ | American New | Boat House | in Central Park | 212.517.2233 | | | | | | | ★ | | ★ | ★ | | |
| E1 | 3 | $$$ | Seafood | Atlantic Grill | 1341 Third Ave | 212.988.9200 | ★ | | | | | | ★ | ★ | | | | |
| **Upper West Side** | | | | | | | | | | | | | | | | | | |
| D1 | 34 | $ | American | Gray's Papaya | 2090 Broadway | 212.799.0243 | | | | | ★ | ★ | | ★ | | | | ★ |
| A2 | 17 | $$$ | Latin Nuevo | Calle Ocho | 446 Columbus Ave | 212.873.5025 | ★ | ★ | | | | | ★ | | | | | |
| D1 | 84 | $$$ | Mexican | Rosa Mexicano | 61 Columbus Ave | 212.977.7700 | | | | | | | ★ | ★ | | | | |
| D1 | 97 | $$$$ | American | Tavern on the Green | Central Park West | 212.873.3200 | ★ | | | ★ | | | ★ | ★ | ★ | ★ | ★ | |

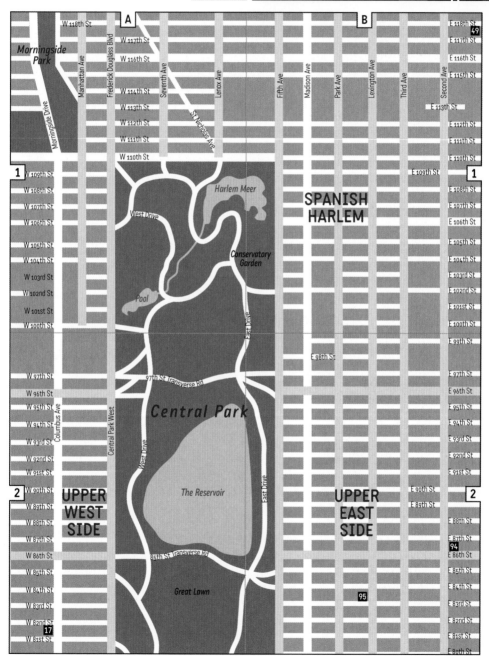

Morningside Park

W 118th St
W 117th St
W 116th St
W 114th St
W 113th St
W 112th St
W 111th St
W 110th St

Manhattan Ave
Frederick Douglass Blvd
Morningside Drive
Seventh Ave
St Nicholas Ave
Lenox Ave

**A**

E 118th St **49**
E 117th St
E 116th St
E 115th St

Fifth Ave
Madison Ave
Park Ave
Lexington Ave
Third Ave
Second Ave

**B**

E 113th St

E 112th St
E 111th St
E 110th St

**1**

W 109th St
W 108th St
W 107th St
W 106th St
W 105th St
W 104th St
W 103rd St
W 102nd St
W 101st St
W 100th St

Harlem Meer
West Drive
Conservatory Garden
Pool

**SPANISH HARLEM**

E 109th St
E 108th St
E 107th St
E 106th St
E 105th St
E 104th St
E 103rd St
E 102nd St
E 101st St
E 100th St
E 99th St

**1**

W 97th St
W 96th St
W 95th St
W 94th St
W 93rd St
W 92nd St
W 91st St

Columbus Ave
Central Park West

97th St Transverse Rd

*Central Park*

East Drive

E 98th St

E 97th St
E 96th St
E 95th St
E 94th St
E 93rd St
E 92nd St
E 91st St

**2**

W 90th St
W 89th St
W 88th St
W 87th St
W 86th St
W 85th St
W 84th St
W 83rd St
W 82nd St **17**
W 81st St

**UPPER WEST SIDE**

West Drive

*The Reservoir*

85th St Transverse Rd

*Great Lawn*

East Drive

**UPPER EAST SIDE**

E 90th St
E 89th St

**95**

E 88th St
E 87th St **94**
E 86th St
E 85th St
E 84th St
E 83rd St
E 82nd St
E 81st St
E 80th St

**2**

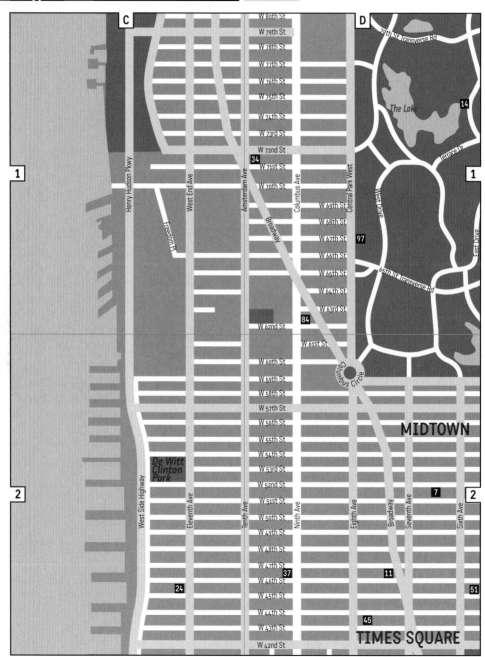

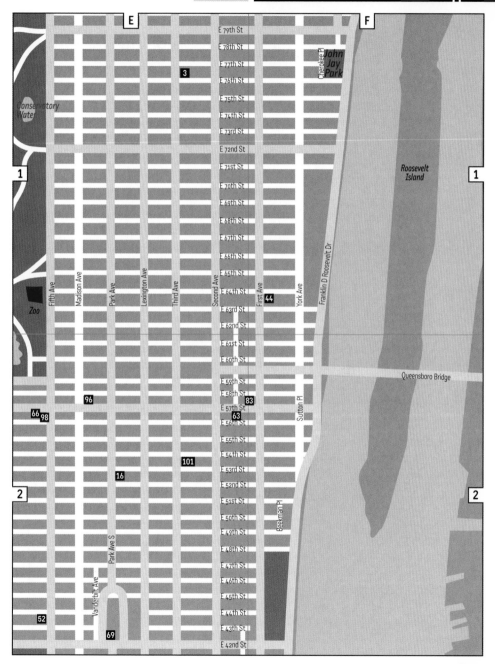

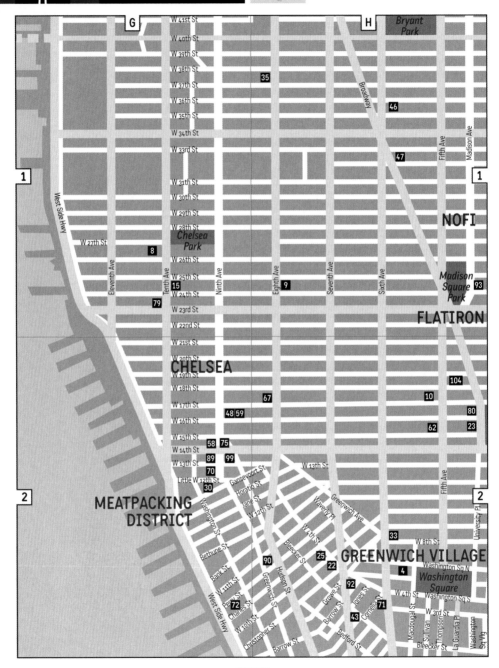

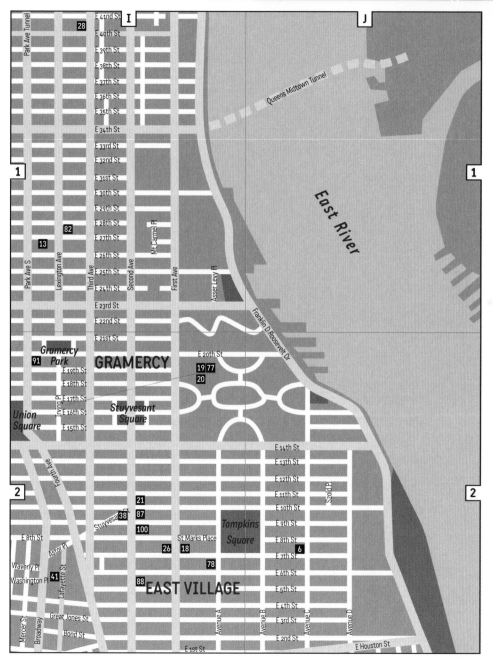

# SHOP
# 3

As every dedicated clothes-hound knows, shopping isn't just about saving money. It's a holistic, sensual experience that you just can't put a price on—especially if you're using someone else's credit card. For the sheer pleasure of urban hunting-and-gathering, New York remains one of the best places on the planet. Affluent urban hippie is the New York look, and there are tons of stores offering unique styles to moneyed bohemians. With few exceptions, the city has resisted the global trend toward urban mall-ification, allowing shoppers to floss in and out of independent boutiques while strolling around some of the city's most exciting streets. And, for better or worse, globalization has made it possible to find almost anything you want in New York, at lower prices than London or Paris. If you're only looking for the biggest names in corporate fashion, simply phone 411 and crawl Madison Avenue. If you're looking for the best independent shops in the city, then Avant-Guide has your number.

# WHERE TO SHOP

**MADISON AVENUE** | This rarefied avenue, from the high 50's to the low 80's, is New York's most legendary shopping strip, packed shoulder to shoulder with the biggest names in fashion.

**FIFTH AVENUE** | From 42nd to 59th streets, this heavily-touristed strip has gone from high- to low-brow, and back again, and is now a good mix of luxury designers and pop-shops like Disney and H&M.

**UPPER WEST SIDE** | Columbus Avenue in the 70's, in particular, is full of mid-priced fashion shops aimed squarely at young professionals who live in the neighborhood.

**CHELSEA** | The finest art galleries are colonized on the streets between 20th and 26th west of Ninth Avenue. There are lots of good, independent men's clothing shops in the neighborhood too.

**GREENWICH VILLAGE** | The Village remains the city's top destination for urban streetwear, especially on Broadway and (for shoes) along 8th Street (between Sixth Avenue and Broadway). Meanwhile, the East Village, especially between Second Avenue and Avenue A, is honeycombed with lots of little vintage shops.

**SOHO** | The art gallery edge has moved elsewhere—primarily to Chelsea—but for upscale, downtown fashion, Soho remains tops.

**NOLITA** | Packed with independent boutiques, the area north of Little Italy is hottest for the boho-chic blend of funkiness and sophistication that New York is known for.

**LOWER EAST SIDE** | Orchard Street, between Houston and Canal streets, is where bargains were invented. Come to this former wholesale neighborhood for designer fashions and family apparel at about 25% off the retail price—all in no-nonsense surroundings.

**MEATPACKING DISTRICT** | Super-high-end downtown shops cluster in the vicinity of Ninth Avenue and 14th Street.

**CANAL STREET** | There's nothing in America quite like Canal Street between Broadway and the Bowery for designer knock-offs at dirt-cheap prices. "Rolex" watches "Cartier" sunglasses and "Kate Spade" bags are specialties.

# MARKETS

**CHELSEA MARKET** | 75 Ninth Ave (at 16th), Chelsea, **T** No phone **W** chelseamarket.com **MAP** G2 #1 There's so much abundance, it's practically food porn at this huge, over-the-top market in an old Nabisco cookie factory featuring about two dozen high-end vendors. The scent of freshly baked bread at Amy's; sausages, cheeses and regional olive oils from Buon Italia; wine, fish, meat and, of course, lots of luxury produce. And you can snack at on-site tables. Fittingly, the Food Network has TV studios upstairs. It's open daily 8am-8pm.

**GREENMARKET AT UNION SQUARE** | Broadway (at 17th), Union Square, **T** 212.788.7476 **W** cenyc.org **MAP** I2 #2, Honest-to-God farmers haul their best produce to the center of the city from as far away as New Hampshire. Cider, fish, flowers and other natural products are also sold. It's open Monday, Wednesday, Friday and Saturday.

Spa at the Mandarin Oriental

## THE BEST DAY SPAS

**BLISS 57** | 19 East 57th St (at Fifth), Midtown, ☎ 212.219.8970 🌐 blissworld.com 🅼🅰🅿 **E2 #3**
**BLISS SOHO** | 568 Broadway (at Prince), Soho, ☎ 212.219.8970 🅼🅰🅿 **E2 #4**, Bliss is a hyper-contemporary space offering the company's trademark oxygen treatments and ginger rubs, along with more traditional indulgencies. Phone early and you can probably get a same-day appointment.

**CORNELIA DAY RESORT** | 663 Fifth Ave (at 52nd), Midtown, ☎ 212.871.3050 🌐 cornelia.com 🅼🅰🅿 **E2 #5**, Situated on two floors above the Salvatore Ferragamo flagship store, Cornelia is both wonderful and huge. Founder Cornelia Zicu's amazing body ritual is based on concoctions her grandmother made while growing up in Romania. And the treatments are strictly VIP, including a floating massage in warm water, an indoor watsu pool, a rooftop garden and snacks by star caterer Abigail Kirsch.

**JUVENEX** | 25 West 32nd St (at Fifth), Midtown, ☎ 646.733.1330 🌐 juvenexspa.com 🅼🅰🅿 **H1 #6**, If you needed even more proof that New York is the city that never sleeps, Juvenex offers jade saunas and bamboo-wrapped steam rooms open 24/seven. Situated in the heart of Koreatown, the spa plays primarily to local late-night workers. It's women-only from 8am-9pm, and coed at all other times.

**RUSSIAN AND TURKISH BATHS** | 268 East 10th St (at First), East Village, ☎ 212.473.8806 🌐 russianturkishbaths.com 🅼🅰🅿 **I2 #7**, Not for the faint of heart, this old-style, budget-priced *shvitz* is a genuine classic: an off-beat favorite of fashion models and film types that shuttles you from the sauna to the steam room and into the icy cold plunge. And the brawny, bald masseur is a dead ringer for Mr. Clean. Phone for hours.

**SPA AT THE MANDARIN ORIENTAL** | 35th Fl., Time Warner Center, 80 Columbus Circle (at 59th), Upper West Side, ☎ 212.805.8800 🌐 mandarinoriental.com 🅼🅰🅿 **D2 #8**, The city's most avant spa is a suitably calm, minimalist space with snazzy bamboo floors, an Oriental Tea Room, a tinkling waterfall, bubbling pools of hot water and a wonderful raft of pamperings from scalp rubs and mud wraps, to aloe-spearmint scrubs.

## 10 THINGS TO BUY

*What:* INDIVIDUALLY CUSTOMIZED JEANS — Pick a style, then choose the color of the thread, adjust pockets and buttons, and be on your way in just a couple of hours.
*Where:* AN EARNEST CUT & SEW

*What:* A SERIOUSLY COOL UMBRELLA — Why walk around with a little toy umbrella that's sure to blow apart with the next gust of wind when you can carry the Rolls Royce of rain deflection?
*Where:* BRELLA BAR

*What:* D&G AT H&M PRICES — Helmut Lang, Dolce & Gabbana, Jil Sander and others, priced 50% and more off original retail. High-end bargains are New York's strongest suits.
*Where:* CENTURY 21

*What:* HAUTE DOG DRESSING — Super-high-end caninewear that includes customized doggy tees, leather coats and monogrammed blankets.
*Where:* DOGGYSTYLE

*What:* REAL NEW YORK CHEESECAKE — The tart sour creamy flavor of real New York cheesecake is one of the great tastes of this city.
*Where:* EILEEN'S SPECIAL CHEESECAKE

*What:* MADE-TO-MEASURE SANDALS — Fine tune your bespoke hippie look with hand-cut, nailed and stitched leather sandals from a trendy bohemian cobbler.
*Where:* JUTTA NEUMANN

*What:* REALLY USEFUL KITCHEN KNIVES — Forget the Ginsu, every home chef needs at least one perfect knife and there are few places in the world with a greater selection of high-carbon steel blades.
*Where:* KORIN JAPANESE TRADING CORP.

*What:* ANTIQUE PUBLIC LIGHT FIXTURES — Chandeliers that once hung in schools and libraries are made from original molds and have a great retro look.
*Where:* SCHOOLHOUSE ELECTRIC CO.

*What:* CHINESE DRESSES AND MAO SUITS — Spend some time in one of the largest Chinatowns in North America and you'll discover all kinds of cool clothes and gifts that you just can't find elsewhere.
*Where:* PEARL RIVER

*What:* BAR TRICKS AND LEVITATION DEVICES — Win friends and influence people when you pick up the secrets that will make objects float in front of you and make others disappear.
*Where:* TANNEN'S MAGIC SHOP

## ABC CARPET & HOME

**888 Broadway (at 19th), Flatiron District**

☎ 212.473.3000 ☐ abchome.com     MAP H2 #9

ABC is a large and amazing high-end home store filled with eight floors of wonderful flat fillers. In addition to lots of great rugs, the "home" holds up its half of the ampersand with amazing selections of things both time-honored and new-fangled, from Victorian-era garden furniture to vintage lamps to mod bath fittings. There's a great deli and cheese department too.

## ADD

**461 West Broadway (at Prince), Soho**

☎ 212.539.1439 ☐ No website     MAP K1 #10

Accessories galore at this shop packed with colorful and imaginative finds from stone-studded belts to cowboy hats with faux fur and everything in-between. Lots of gift-worthy jewelry and bags too.

## A DETACHER

**262 Mott St (at Prince), Nolita**

☎ 212.625.3380 ☐ No website     MAP L1 #11

A small and unusual selection of slightly abstract feminine fashions are sold alongside more concrete items like modern, modular ceramic trays and bowls, beautiful books, handbags, hairpins and lots of other great gift items.

## AGENT PROVOCATEUR

**133 Mercer St (at Prince), Soho**

☎ 212.965.0229 ☐ agentprovocateur.com     MAP K1 #12

Designed in pink and black with crystal chandeliers, this London-based shop for sexy underthings would make Victoria blush. Designed by Serena Rees and Joe Corré, the son of Vivienne Westwood and Malcolm McLaren, AP's classic ranges include sexy bras and knickers, augmented by fishnet stockings, leather goods and high-heeled footwear. Bellybutton chains, ankle bracelets, candles, soaps and perfumes too.

## ALIFE

**158 Rivington St (at Clinton), Lower East Side**

☎ 212.375.8128 ☐ rivingtonclub.com     MAP L1 #13

It's mostly super stylish shoes and sneakers at this artsy store for phat hip-hopish footwear. Alife often gets new styles before they open nationwide. Look for hard-to-find styles from 6876, Duffer of St. George, Gola, Nike and Tsubo, as well as cool styles from the shop's house brand, T-shirts, clothing, jewelry and more.

## ALLAN & SUZI

**416 Amsterdam Ave (at 80th), Upper West Side**

☎ 212.724.7445 ☐ allanandsuzi.net     MAP C1 #14

Disco never dies at this wonderful shop full of marvelous dead stock that includes decades old couture gowns, Studio 54-worthy halter tops from Versace, Kansai Yamamoto sweaters and so much more retro fashion, all ticketed at significant markdowns.

## AN EARNEST CUT & SEW

**821 Washington St (at Gansevoort), Meatpacking District**

☎ 212.242.3414 ☐ earnestsewn.com     MAP G2 #15

In-store customization is the main reason to shop at this posh jeans store. Sure you can buy them straight off the rack, but you can also fine-tune cuts, choose the color of the thread, adjust pockets and buttons, and be on your way in just a couple of hours.

## ANIK

**1355 Third Ave (at 77th), Upper East Side**

☎ 212.861.9840 ☐ No website     MAP E1 #16

**1122 Madison Ave (at 83rd), Upper East Side**

☎ 212.249.2417     MAP B2 #17

Shop here for basic tops and bottoms from brands like Diesel, Juicy Couture and Theory. They've got a very well chosen stock of both casual- and cocktail-wear, along with related accessories.

## ANNA

**150 East 3rd St (at Ave A), East Village**

☎ 212.358.0195 ☐ annanyc.com     MAP I2 #18

There are lots of wonderful women's clothes here that we're hard pressed to find anywhere else, including hand-stitched frocks, sexy constructivist tops and lots of other original things that ride the chic fashion fence between East Village and Soho. There's a rack of vintage clothes and prices are good too.

## ANNA SUI

**113 Greene St (at Prince), Soho**

☎ 212.941.8406 ☐ annasui.com     MAP K1 #19

Anna Sui has the uncanny ability to simultaneously appeal to both LA and NYC with collections that are a little bit high-fashion and a little bit rock 'n' roll. Think sequined skirts, leather pants and other flashy female fashions. We like the pink-and-black shop too.

*An Earnest Cut & Sew*

## A.P.C.

**131 Mercer St (at Prince), Soho**

☎ 212.966.9685 🖥 apc.fr     MAP **K1 #20**

Parisian basics for men and women include top-quality cotton T-shirts, great turtleneck sweaters, black leather jackets and oiled motorcycle jeans in a variety of colors. The initials stand for Atelier Production and Creation. You get the idea.

## BABELAND

**43 Mercer St (at Grand), Soho**

☎ 212.966.2120 🖥 babeland.com     MAP **K1 #21**

**94 Rivington St (at Ludlow), Lower East Side**

☎ 212.375.1701     MAP **L1 #22**

This trio of friendly sex toy stores offer an upscale setting, knowledgeable staff and products that will almost literally knock your sox off. Hits for traveling "jetrosexuals" include toys that can get past airport security, vibrators in the shape of lipstick and hairbrushes, and a Mile High Kit, stocked with a mini vibrator, condoms and lube.

## BANG BANG

**53 East 8th St (at Mercer), Greenwich Village**

☎ 212.475.8220 🖥 bangbang.com     MAP **I2 #23**

**147 Eighth Ave (at 17th), Chelsea**

☎ 212.807.8457     MAP **H2 #24**

Club clothes galore at this amazing shop that seems to anticipate trends long before they hit the catwalks. Colorful racks under disco lights groan with a cool selection that includes diaphanous shirts, tiny tops, sequined halters, glitter jeans and the like. They play equally to both men and women.

## BARBARA BUI

**115 Wooster St (at Prince), Soho**

☎ 212.625.1938 🖥 barbarabui.com     MAP **K1 #25**

This Parisian designer's only American shop is a huge space stocked with the full line of Bui's classic women's designs, each beautifully tailored and containing some playful surprises. Find everything from slacks and shrink-wrapped T-shirts to spectacular vented vest-dresses that ride the fence between traditional and trendy.

## BARNES & NOBLE

**33 East 17th St (at Broadway), Union Square**

☎ 212.253.0810 🖥 barnesandnoble.com     MAP **I2 #26**

**1280 Lexington Ave (at 86th), Upper East Side**

☎ 212.423.9900     MAP **B2 #27**

**600 Fifth Ave (at 48th), Midtown**

☎ 212.765.0590     MAP **E2 #28**

**and other locations**

Manhattan, the birthplace of Barnes & Noble, contains several well-stocked superstores. The Union Square shop, in a beautiful four-story 1881 building, is a particularly wonderful place to browse. In addition to books, you'll find music, software, a newsstand, cafe and lots of comfortable chairs for lounging.

Babeland

## BARNEYS

660 Madison Ave (at 60th), Upper East Side

☎ 212.826.8900 🌐 barneys.com  MAP E2 #29

The flagship of the Barneys fashion empire is stocked with top-quality brands for both sexes and maintains the best selection of leading-edge designers. Look for good prices on casual wear on the top floor and their always-fabulous windows designed by creative director Simon Doonan.

## BARNEYS CO-OP

236 West 18th St (at Seventh), Chelsea

☎ 212.593.7800 🌐 barneys.com  MAP H2 #30

2151 Broadway (at 76th), Upper West Side

☎ 646.335.0978  MAP C1 #31

116 Wooster St (at Prince), Soho

☎ 212.965.9964  MAP K1 #32

Shoppers hunting for Marc Jacobs flats, Dries van Noten dresses and Seven jeans no longer have to trek over to Barneys main store. But the Co-op's cheeky selection extends to clothes by Diane Von Furstenberg, Rebecca Taylor and Juicy Couture, and includes plenty for men as well.

## BEBE

100 Fifth Ave (at 15th), Union Square

☎ 212.675.2323 🌐 bebe.com  MAP H2 #33

805 Third Ave (at 49th), Midtown

☎ 212.588.9060  MAP E2 #34

1127 Third Ave (at 66th), Upper East Side

☎ 212.935.2444  MAP E1 #35

Up-to-the-moment derivatives translate into moderately priced knockoffs of top designer styles. Look for well-tailored dresses, suits, tops and other feminine wearables that will get you past the velvet ropes.

## BERGDORF GOODMAN

754 Fifth Ave (at 58th), Midtown

☎ 212.753.7300 🌐 bergdorfgoodman.com  MAP E2 #36

This queen of department stores is beautiful, like walking into a lively museum. People dress up to shop here, and the selling floors are laid out like a collection of boutiques. Although the store is a favorite with ladies who lunch (quite literally, eating chopped Gotham salads at their fifth-floor cafe), Bergdorf has worked hard in recent years to attract younger shoppers.

## Betsey Johnson

138 Wooster St (at Prince), Soho
☎ 212.995.5048  W betseyjohnson.com          MAP K1 #37
248 Columbus Ave (at 72nd), Upper West Side
☎ 212.362.3364                                MAP D1 #38
251 East 60th St (at Second), Upper East Side
☎ 212.319.7699                                MAP E2 #39
1060 Madison Ave (at 80th), Upper East Side
☎ 212.734.1257                                MAP B2 #40

In addition to Johnson's trademark skintight flesh-wrappers, you'll find plenty of feminine urban trashwear made with leather, lace and fishnet. Check out her line of peek-a-boo lingerie too.

## B&H Photo

420 Ninth Ave (at 33rd), Midtown
☎ 212.444.6615  W bhphotovideo.com            MAP G1 #41

This is where the city's professional photographers come to purchase their equipment. It is a vast store which sells almost every brand of digital and 35mm camera, plus a full range of video and other filmmaking equipment, from lighting to color processors. This is the place to buy film in bulk at very low prices.

## Big Drop

174 Spring St (at Thompson), Soho
☎ 212.966.4299  W bigdropnyc.com              MAP K1 #42
1321 Third Ave (at 76th), Upper East Side
☎ 212.988.3344                                MAP E1 #43
and other locations

The New York look is codified at these wonderful basics boutiques, each of which stocks upscale streetwear and accessories, most of which is arranged by color. Styles from dozens of designers almost guarantee you'll find something you love, from a structured jacket to a fuchsia mini-tote.

## Bloomingdale's

1000 Third Ave (at 59th), Upper East Side
☎ 212.705.2000  W bloomingdales.com           MAP E2 #44

## Bloomingdale's Soho

504 Broadway (at Broome), Soho
☎ 212.729.5900                                MAP K1 #45

Open since 1879, Bloomingdale's on Lex is as venerable as Grand Central Station, and almost as crowded. The upper decks (except for the shoe departments) are more sedate and staffed with responsive help. True to its surroundings, the newer Soho store is hipper, containing counters for M.A.C and Chanel as well as for Bliss and Bumble & Bumble. Plus, there's a good cafe on the fifth floor. Others can't figure out what all the excitement is about: Andy Warhol once said "Death is like going to Bloomingdale's. It's nothing."

## Bond 07

7 Bond St (at Broadway), East Village
☎ 212.677.8487  W selimaoptique.com           MAP I2 #46

Beyond being one of the most fabulous optical boutiques anywhere, Selima Salaun's shop is full of avant fashions, enchanting vintage and contemporary jewelry and furnishings, and the French owner's own line of botanical lipsticks and glosses.

## Books of Wonder

18 West 18th St (at Fifth), Union Square
☎ 212.989.3270  W booksofwonder.net           MAP H2 #47

BoW is the best, largest and oldest children's bookstore in the city. This is the place to go for interactive learning books, terrific picture books and even old, rare and antiquarian children's books.

## Bra Smyth

905 Madison Ave (at 73rd), Upper East Side
☎ 212.772.9400  W brasmyth.com                MAP E1 #48

Everything you've ever wanted to know about bras (and panties) can be found in this Upper East Side shop stocking some 1,500 styles from around the world. One lucky on-site tailor customizes shoppers' selections for a perfect fit.

## Breakbeat Science

181 Orchard St (at Stanton), Lower East Side
☎ 212.995.2592  W breakbeatscience.com        MAP L1 #49

All jungle all the time, Breakbeat Science is the vinyl-only headquarters for an unmatched selection of drum 'n' bass. Obscure albums and pre-releases are their specialty.

## Brella Bar

1043 Third Ave (at 62nd), Upper East Side
☎ 212.813.9530  W brellabar.com               MAP E1 #50

A seriously cool umbrella is the latest must-have accessory and Brella Bar stocks the best from serious brands like Flann Lippincott and Francesco Maglia. Silk canopies and handmade wooden handles are what you're looking for, priced from about $100. There are some cool antique umbrellas and parasols too.

Betsey Johnson

## Built By Wendy

7 Centre Market Pl (at Grand), Little Italy

☎ 212.925.6538 🖩 builtbywendy.com          MAP L1 #51

Best known for designing shiny colored vinyl guitar straps and other indie-rock gear, Wendy Mullen has branched out and looked south for inspiration on an entire line of amusing and reasonably priced clothes created for the urban cowgirl.

## Calypso

935 Madison Ave (at 74th), Upper East Side

☎ 212.535.4100 🖩 calypso-celle.com          MAP E1 #52

654 Hudson St (at Gansevoort), Meatpacking District

☎ 646.638.3000          MAP G2 #53

280 Mott St (at Houston), Nolita

☎ 212.965.0990          MAP L1 #54

424 Broome St (at Crosby), Soho

☎ 212.274.0449          MAP K1 #55

Imbued with the cheerful character of the Caribbean, Calypso is the place to find frilly girlie things that make us happy. Things like iridescent silk shirts by Dosa, rich beaded tops, bustle skirts, vivid sarongs and ruffled suede coats. Even their winterwear is colorful and lively.

## Carlos Miele

408 West 14th St (at Ninth), Meatpacking District

☎ 646.336.6642 🖩 No website          MAP G2 #56

Some of the hippest fashions in South America are created by Carlos Miele. Here, at Miele's first boutique outside of Brazil, you'll find the eponymous designer's Technicolor separates and dresses, adorned with lots of surprises and shining brightly against the shops space-age white walls and furnishings. Leave practical to The Gap.

## Catherine Malandrino

468 Broome St (at Greene), Soho

☎ 212.925.6765 🖩 catherinemalandrino.com          MAP K1 #57

652 Hudson St (at Gansevoort), Meatpacking District

☎ 212.929.8710          MAP G2 #58

The former design director for Diane Von Furstenberg, now creates her own colorful hippie-meets-French Riviera look, sold from a clean, white Soho shop. Look for sequined party gowns, hip-hugger leather pants and other shabby-chic wear that's ready for a close-up in Cannes.

## Century 21

22 Cortlandt St (at Broadway), Financial District

☎ 212.227.9092 🖩 c21stores.com          MAP K2 #59

A fashion zoo if ever there was one, Century 21 is famous with bargainistas for last season's designer collections at massively reduced rates. Intrepid shoppers elbow their way through unorganized racks and bins of Romeo Gigli, Helmut Lang, D&G, Jil Sander and others, priced 50% and more off original retail. Dressing rooms are scarce (and non-existent for men). The trick here is to arrive without a jacket or any other bulky clothing so you can try things on over what you are wearing.

## Christopher Totman

262 Mott St (at Prince), Nolita

☎ 212.925.7495 🖩 No website          MAP L1 #60

Men and women are equally catered to at this very urban store selling wonderfully original separates with a Latin American flair. The look covers the continent, with bold, hand-knit Peruvian sweaters, breezy flo-through shirts and flouncy party dresses in tropical palettes.

## Comme des Garçons

520 West 22nd St (at Tenth), Chelsea

☎ 212.604.9200 🖩 No website          MAP G1 #61

Comme des Garçons is so remarkable and cerebral that their bridge line looks like other designers' haute couture. The shop's

Carlos Miele

unusual interior is wonderful, the designs are breathtaking and so are the price tags.

## CRAFT CARAVAN

**63 Greene St (at Broome), Soho**

☎ 212.431.6669 🌐 craftcaravannewyork.com     MAP **K1 #62**

A Soho vanguard, Craft Caravan has been selling pan-African homeware and handicrafts since the early 1970's. The ethnic applied art here spans thousands of strange items, from Ethiopian ceramics and carved Tanzanian bar stools to fertility dolls from Togo. If you like what you see, ask to visit the basement, where a whole other world of merchandise awaits.

## CYNTHIA ROWLEY

**376 Bleecker St (at Perry), Greenwich Village**

☎ 212.242.3803 🌐 cynthiarowley.com     MAP **H2 #63**

Both sophisticated and sensible, Rowley's patterns are ceaselessly creative and the fabrics are always comfortable. Sexy dresses are often embroidered or beaded. And wonderful, whimsical accessories include purses, lipstick bags, totes and shoes. There are plenty of stylish goodies for men too. We love this shop.

## DARLING

**1 Horatio St (at Eighth), Meatpacking District**

☎ 646.336.6966 🌐 darlingny.com     MAP **H2 #64**

Here's the back-story: Ann French Emonts was a Brooklyn school teacher and Broadway costume designer before opening this whitewashed shop to sell her own feminine fashions alongside lingerie by Mary Green and pretty dresses by Tara Jarmon, Cynthia Steeffe and others. It's a pretty neighborhood space with a bucolic back garden that doubles as a waiting room for boyfriends.

## DARYL K

**21 Bond St (at Lafayette), East Village**

☎ 212.529.8790 🌐 darylk.com     MAP **I2 #65**

Twiggy ankle-braceleted girls look fabulous in Daryl Kerrigan's slim fit low-rider pants, still the must-have apparel for rough girls with a bit of cash to spare. The rest of the offerings are informed by the same rock 'n' roll sensibility: velvet slacks, luxuriant dresses and jackets that will confirm your street cred.

## Dean & DeLuca

560 Broadway (at Prince), Soho

☎ 212.226.6800 Ⓦ deandeluca.com  MAP K1 #66

1150 Madison Ave (at 85th), Upper East Side

☎ 212.717.0800  MAP B2 #67

As big and bright as a Soho art gallery, D&D is especially known for cheese, chocolates, pastries and fresh produce, all at stratospheric prices. A foodie's dream, there's no better place in the city to lick the windows.

## DeMask

135 West 22nd St (at Sixth), Chelsea

☎ 212.352.2850 Ⓦ demask.com  MAP H1 #68

The Amsterdam-based fetish shop is the best in the world for PVC and other plastic playwear. Some of the best items are downstairs, including not one, but an entire selection of rubber tuxedos. And there's even a bargain bin.

## Design Within Reach

408 West 14th St (at Ninth), Meatpacking District

☎ 212.242.9449 Ⓦ dwr.com  MAP G2 #69

142 Wooster St (at Prince), Soho

☎ 212.475.0001  MAP K1 #70

and other locations

Displayed in a retail-friendly environment, furniture and houseware by classic mid-century designers like Eames, Le Corbusier and van der Rohe are taken from trade-only showrooms and made accessible to the public. Look for everything from seating and dining tables, to shelving, mirrors and outdoor furnishings. There's lots from contemporary stylists too in the mode of Philippe Starck.

## Diesel

770 Lexington Ave (at 60th), Upper East Side

☎ 212.308.0055 Ⓦ diesel.com  MAP E2 #71

1 Union Square West (at 14th), Union Square

☎ 646.336.8552  MAP H2 #72

135 Spring St (at Wooster), Soho

☎ 212.625.1555  MAP K1 #73

Situated across from Bloomingdale's, the awesome Upper East Side flagship for the Italian clothes house is one of the greatest shopping emporia in the city. The brand's trademark jeans, underwear and even eyewear spreads across two ample floors that include a cafe and DJ booth.

## DKNY

655 Madison Ave (at 60th), Upper East Side

☎ 212.223.3569 Ⓦ dkny.com  MAP E2 #74

420 West Broadway (at Spring), Soho

☎ 646.613.1100  MAP K1 #75

There was no DKNY shop in NYC until late 1998; the designer was sold exclusively by department stores and other retailers. These bright and beautiful spaces right that wrong, offering the complete line of Donna Karan goods.

## DoggyStyle

100 Thompson St (at Spring), Soho

☎ 212.431.9200 Ⓦ doggystylenyc.com  MAP K1 #76

A great name for a great shop selling super-high-end caninewear that pampers pooches better than most people we know. Designer collars and leashes from names like Ella Dish and Wagwear are sold alongside customized doggy tees, leather coats, monogrammed blankets and pet portraits by owner Andy Schulman.

## Dosa

107 Thompson St (at Prince), Soho

☎ 212.431.1733 Ⓦ No website  MAP K1 #77

Uptown girls with downtown tastes shop at this wonderful store for timeless basics with an Asian flair. Separates and dresses are created from distinctive materials like silk in wonderfully unconventional colors.

## Dylan's Candy Bar

1011 Third Ave (at 60th), Upper East Side

☎ 646.735.0078 Ⓦ dylanscandybar.com  MAP E2 #78

Dylan's has turned a fairly mundane retail category into an experience. Huge in both size and assortment, it's a candy world that would make Willy Wonka proud. In addition to tons of candy by the pound, look for giant lollypops, vintage Pez dispensers ($2,000) and candy-scented spa items that include chocolate bar soaps and bubble gum bath fizz. Dylan, by the way, is Ralph Lauren's daughter.

## EdgeNY

65 Bleecker St (at Broadway), Greenwich Village

☎ 212.358.0255 Ⓦ edgeny.com  MAP I2 #79

Dozens of young, New York-based designers run their own independent stalls or mini-boutiques in this huge warehouse for fresh clothes, bags and other accessories. Demand for selling space is high, so the owners of the space are able to do some heavy curating and select the newest and most unique.

## Eileen's Special Cheesecake

**17 Cleveland Pl (at Kenmare), Nolita**

☎ 212.966.5585 W eileenscheesecake.com   MAP L1 #80

Cheesecake, of course, is the iconic New York dessert, but not all are created equal. The best are created by Eileen Avezzano based on a recipe passed down from her mother and sold at her cloyingly cute Nolita shop. It's the very zenith of extraordinary New York cheesecake: rich, sweet, tart, and ethereally light.

## Elizabeth Charles

**639 1/2 Hudson St (at Horatio), Meatpacking District**

☎ 212.243.3201 W elizabeth-charles.com   MAP G2 #81

The best of Australian and New Zealand design is spotlighted in this small shop selling distinctive clothing for women. The South Pacific style includes everything from lingerie and jewelry to jeans, dresses and suede skirts.

## Eugenia Kim

**203 East 4th St (at Ave A), Lower East Side**

☎ 212.673.9787 W eugeniakim.com   MAP I2 #82

Eugenia Kim is New York's young milliner to the stars, creating a huge variety of avant toppers that span the spectrum from feathered fedoras, wool newsboys and cowboy hats to patchwork beavers, veiled pillboxes and crocheted head wrappers for both men and women.

## FAO Schwarz

**767 Fifth Ave (at 58th), Midtown**

☎ 212.644.9400 W fao.com   MAP E2 #83

This play palace is so awesome that most young aristobrats believe it when their parents tell them they're actually in a toy museum. Three floors full of frivolity include house-sized stuffed animals, mini-Porsche automobiles that actually work, a wall of M&M chocolate candies sorted by color and all manner of toys and games.

## Fat Beats

**406 Sixth Ave (at 8th), Greenwich Village**

☎ 212.673.3883 W fatbeats.com   MAP H2 #84

Hip-hop here is so phat it's obese. There's also an excellent selection of reggae, acid jazz and trip-hop. Look in the "used" bins for good prices on hard-to-find classics.

## Find Outlet

**361 West 17th St (at Ninth), Chelsea**

☎ 212.243.3177 W findoutlet.com   MAP G2 #85

**229 Mott St (at Prince), Nolita**

☎ 212.226.5167   MAP L1 #86

For a limited selection of off-price brand-name clothes, Find is, well, a place to discover. Formerly trendy women's fashions, mostly from closeouts and samples, are sold in a white, gallery-like space, sometimes at 50% off.

## Flou

**42 Greene St (at Grand), Soho**

☎ 212.941.9101 W flou.it   MAP K1 #87

Designer beds and bedding are what you'll find at this super stylish Italian shop that sells modern mix-and-match sleep sets with an excellent price-quality ratio. And there are few other places we know in which you can buy a complete bed and bedding, ready for sleep.

## Flying A

**169 Spring St (at Thompson), Soho**

☎ 212.965.9090 W flyinga.net   MAP K1 #88

Big shoes and sneakers at small prices is the trademark of Flying A, an offshoot of Buffalo Boots in London. No major brands here. Instead you will find a huge selection of fabulously fun and flashy footwear for stylish men, women and kids. They've got some very downtown clothing and accessories too, including vintage rabbit-fur jackets and socks emblazoned with Japanese anime.

## Gabay's

**225 First Ave (at 13th), East Village**

☎ 212.254.3180 W gabaysoutlet.com   MAP I2 #89

Where does merchandise from Bergdorf Goodman go to die? To Gabay's, that's where, New York's oldest discount designer store, selling top names for up to 50% off. Some of the best deals are on accessories, including handbags and shoes.

## Ghost

**28 Bond St (at Lafayette), East Village**

☎ 646.602.2891 W ghost.co.uk   MAP I2 #90

London style is all the rage at this shop selling Tanya Sarne's feminine boho-urban fashions along with Erickson Beamon jewelry. The look is a mix of historical and up-to-the-moment: flowy, lacy and delicate. There are a few men's pieces as well.

## Henri Bendel

712 Fifth Ave (at 56th), Midtown

☎ 212.247.1100 🖳 No website     **MAP** E2 #91

The epitome of elegance, with a 1920s-Paris-meets-the-new-millennium atmosphere created with rich woods, magnificent Lalique windows and fabulous oval staircases in lieu of escalators. There's a Tiffany's boutique selling vintage jewelry and handbags, and the store stays relevant by stocking up-to-date designs by the likes of Shoshanna and Sophia Kokosalaki.

## Hotel Venus

382 West Broadway (at Broome), Soho

☎ 212.966.4066 🖳 patriciafield.com     **MAP** K1 #92

Patricia Field's shop is club kid central, filled with glamourpuss-sleazy garments for clubbing. Untraditional materials run the gamut from plastic and fur to spandex and feathers, and most of the dresses and heels are also available in men's sizes.

## Housing Works Thrift Shop

143 West 17th St (at Sixth), Chelsea

☎ 212.366.0820 🖳 housingworks.org     **MAP** H2 #93

157 East 23rd St (at Lexington), Midtown

☎ 212.529.5955     **MAP** I1 #94

202 East 77th St (at Third), Upper East Side

☎ 212.772.8461     **MAP** E1 #95

306 Columbus Ave (at 74th), Upper West Side

☎ 212.579.7566     **MAP** D1 #96

There is some seriously good thrifting in New York and Housing Works often seems to have the best furniture, clothes and collectables. This is where New York's most affluential residents donate their unwanted tuxedos and taffetas, and designers sometimes send their overstock here. Proceeds benefit people living with AIDS.

## If

94 Grand St (at Greene), Soho

☎ 212.334.4964 🖳 No website     **MAP** K1 #97

If you're already on the fashion edge, you probably know this place. If you want to find out the latest in experimental clothing, this is your museum. Avant Dries Van Noten and Comme des Garcons have pride of place here, surrounded by only marginally lesser lights like Veronique Branquinho, Martin Margiela and Marc Le Bihan. Both men's and women's lines are here, along with accessories.

## Ina

101 Thompson St (at Prince), Soho

☎ 212.941.4757 🖳 inanyc.com     **MAP** K1 #98

21 Prince St (at Elizabeth), Nolita

☎ 212.334.9048     **MAP** L1 #99

208 East 73rd St (at Third), Upper East Side

☎ 212.249.0014     **MAP** E1 #100

Men's Store, 262 Mott St (at Prince), Nolita

☎ 212.334.2210     **MAP** L1 #101

Designer resale shops can be found almost everywhere these days, but Ina remains one of the best for Gucci, Helmut Lang, Prada and others for both men and women. It's a particularly good place for high-end, off-price shoes from Miu Miu, Sigerson Morrison, Manolo Blahnik and other passion brands.

## Ingo Maurer

89 Grand St (at Greene), Soho

☎ 212.965.8817 🖳 ingo-maurer.com     **MAP** K1 #102

German-born Ingo Maurer emigrated to the USA and worked as a designer before turning to lamp and lighting design. His designs are now included the collection of the Museum of Modern Art. This store, too, feels like it doubles as a museum, featuring production pieces and one-of-a-kind lightings that are basically art objects.

## Intermix

1003 Madison Ave (at 77th), Upper East Side

☎ 212.249.7858 🖳 intermixonline.com     **MAP** E1 #103

125 Fifth Ave (at 19th), Flatiron District

☎ 212.533.9720     **MAP** H2 #104

210 Columbus Ave (at 70th), Upper West Side

☎ 212.769.9116     **MAP** D1 #105

365 Bleecker St (at Charles), Greenwich Village

☎ 212.929.7180     **MAP** H2 #106

Intermix doesn't follow trends, it anticipates them with an avalanche of avant design created by dozens of young and established designers from around the world. The stock plays to society types with subscriptions to W and platinum in their purses. Other designers certainly browse these racks for inspiration.

## Jack Spade

56 Greene St (at Broome), Soho

☎ 212.625.1820 🖳 jackspade.com     **MAP** K1 #107

Everything comes up spades at this preppy-themed manly man's luggage store developed by Andy Spade, husband

Ingo Maurer

of handbag queen Kate Spade. Designed with taxidermied animals, model cars and locker room trophies, the shop is stocked with portage items that are tough and functional, built from canvas, nylon and waxwear.

## Jacques Torres Chocolate Haven

**350 Hudson St (at Charlton), Soho**
**☎ 212.414.2462 W mrchocolate.com**            **MAP K1 #108**

Former Le Cirque pastry chef Jacques Torres' place is equal parts retail store and chocolate factory, in which visitors are treated to unobstructed views of the bean-to-bar process, all while enjoying a cup of hot chocolate. Enveloped by the factory, the glass-enclosed, cacao-pod shaped cafe and shop was designed by Pierre Court with a statue of the Aztec cacao god.

## Jeffrey

**449 West 14th St (at Ninth), Chelsea**
**☎ 212.206.1272 W jeffreynewyork.com**          **MAP G2 #109**

Former Barneys shoe buyer Jeffrey Kalinsky was one of the first high-end retailers to colonize the Meatpacking District with this mini department store. Power outfits from Gucci, Prada, Jil Sander and the like are matched by a stellar shoe department filled with a foot fetishist's dream of Manolo Blahniks, Christian Louboutins and other beauties by Fendi, Celine and Dolce & Gabbana. Prices of course are sky high.

## J. Lindeberg

**126 Spring St (at Greene), Soho**
**☎ 212.625.9403 W jlindeberg.com**             **MAP K1 #110**

Stockholm-based J. Lindeberg is the designer behind this bi-level shop for men selling super-hip casualwear and very fashionable sportswear, all cut straight and tight. In a single stroke Lindeberg proves that golfers can look cool.

## John Fluevog

**250 Mulberry St (at Prince), Nolita**
**☎ 212.431.4484 W fluevog.com**               **MAP L1 #111**

The flagship of the Fluevog empire offers very cool shoes for the urban jungle: Funky men's and women's styles for the club and street. There always seem to be a lot of Japanese tourists here, so it must be stylish.

*Kirna Zabete*

## JONATHAN ADLER

47 Greene St (at Broome), Soho

☎ 212.941.8950 🌐 jonathanadler.com　　　MAP K1 #112

1097 Madison Ave (at 83rd), Upper East Side

☎ 212.772.2410　　　MAP B2 #113

Adler's spectacular couture pottery is now augmented by a "Pot a Porter" collection and an increasing number of lifestyle choices, ranging from groovy textiles to glamorous furniture. There's a lot to like here, including colorful bedding, towels, stationery and even handbags. We love this store.

## JUTTA NEUMANN

158 Allen St (at Rivington), East Village

☎ 212.982.7048 🌐 juttaneumann-newyork.com　　　MAP L1 #114

Very enticing made-to-measure sandals are hand-cut, nailed and stitched at this trendy bohemian cobbler. The bespoke hippie look comes in a range of styles, skins and shades and will set you back about $200.

## KATE'S PAPERIE

561 Broadway (at Prince), Soho

☎ 212.941.9816 🌐 katespaperie.com　　　MAP K1 #115

8 West 13th St (at Fifth), Greenwich Village

☎ 212.633.0570　　　MAP H2 #116

1282 Third Ave (at 74th), Upper East Side

☎ 212.396.3670　　　MAP E1 #117

140 West 57th St (at Sixth), Midtown

☎ 212.459.0700　　　MAP D2 #118

The most celebrated stationery store in the city stocks everything from hand-made papyrus art paper to silly printed toilet wipe. Look for beautiful rice papers, seductively bound journals and even kites and hatboxes.

## KAZUYO NAKANO

117 Crosby St (at Prince), Soho

☎ 212.941.7093 🌐 kazuyonakano.com　　　MAP K1 #119

Designer Kazuyo Nakano creates some of the most creative and up-to-the-moment leather bags, purses and leather accessories in town. You can find her work at other stylish shops in the city, but this teeny boutique stocks the entire collection.

## KIDROBOT

126 Prince St (at Wooster), Soho

☎ 212.966.6688 🌐 kidrobot.com　　　MAP K1 #120

A paradise of Asian popaganda, Kidrobot is chock full of vinyl toy action figures from Japan and elsewhere. Enthusiasts will go wild over this store's stock, custom-made in limited quantities. Other wildly popular toys you've probably never heard of include Gloomy Bears, Murakami DOB dolls, and Kubricks plastic miniatures.

## KIEHL'S

109 Third Ave (at 13th), East Village

☎ 212.677.3171 🌐 kiehls.com　　　MAP I2 #121

150 Columbus Ave (at 67th), Upper West Side

☎ 212.799.3438　　　MAP D1 #122

Founded in the East Village in 1851 as a homeopathic pharmacy, the first Kiehl's shop gradually grew into a natural-cosmetics store, selling herbal-based moisturizers, shampoos, eye creams, masques, facial cleansers, talcs, lipsticks and toners—packaged in trademark no-frills containers and sold at Lancôme prices. It's a quirky place that's great fun to browse. And free samples are generously thrust upon customers.

## Kirna Zabete

96 Greene St (at Spring), Soho

☎ 212.941.9656 🌐 kirnazabete.com     **MAP** K1 #123

If you're a gallery owner, or a fashion industry executive or some other clockless worker, then Kirna Zabete is your store. Basically, this is a super-fashion shop for stylish girls with jobs; a place selling hot fashions from the likes of Alice Roi, Balenciaga and Sonia Rykiel in one of the most playful environments in Soho.

## Korin Japanese Trading Corp.

57 Warren St (at West Broadway), Financial District

☎ 212.587.7021 🌐 korin.com     **MAP** K2 #124

Formerly a to-the-trade only kitchen supply store, Korin has now made their unmatched selection of Japanese kitchen knives available to the public; some 500 models at last count. Most are high-carbon steel, forged in ancient family-run factories and sharpened Japanese style, on only one side of the blade. We love this place.

## Label

265 Lafayette St (at Prince), Nolita

☎ 212.966.7736 🌐 labelnyc.com     **MAP** K1 #125

Unique streetwear for feminine skate rats doesn't get more fashionable than the offerings at this cool and slender Soho shop. Sexy separates and dresses are emblazoned with pop culture silk screens and other urban motifs. There is some boywear too, and all are priced to move.

## Le Corset

80 Thompson St (at Spring), Soho

☎ 212.334.4936 🌐 selimaoptique.com     **MAP** K1 #126

The finest lingerie from the US, Europe and Asia is sold alongside sexy things from the store's own designer, Ellen Berkenbilt. All the top brands are here, including Andre Sarda, Aubade, Colette Dinnigan and Fifi Chachnil. Of course, prices are tops too.

## Love Saves The Day

119 Second Ave (at 7th), East Village

☎ 212.228.3802 🌐 No website     **MAP** I2 #127

New York's best novelty store is chock full of oddball gifts and kitschy vintage clothing. From blacklight Elvis wall art, "antique" Pez dispensers and retro Kiss figurines, to Playboy mags and pinball machines from yesterdecade, goods are piled all the way to the ceiling. In the middle are lots of racks crammed with leather and denim clothing guaranteed to punk up your life.

## Lucy Barnes

320 West 14th St (at Eighth), Meatpacking District

☎ 212.255.9148 🌐 lucybarnes.biz     **MAP** H2 #128

There's a lot to like about this Scottish designer's boutique, including great shapes on sexy separates, at prices that seem far lower than they should be. Both haute and diffusion lines are sold in this clean and welcoming space, along with bikinis, vintage scarves, tons of kitschy bangles and hair accessories.

## Malia Mills

199 Mulberry St (at Kenmare), Nolita

☎ 212.625.2311 🌐 maliamills.com     **MAP** L1 #129

1031 Lexington Ave (at 74th), Upper East Side

☎ 212.517.7485     **MAP** E1 #130

220 Columbus Ave (at 70th), Upper West Side

☎ 212.874.7200     **MAP** D1 #131

Swimwear meets art at Malia Mills, the creator of some of the finest garments for bathing beauties anywhere. Whether your "kini" is bi or mono, they've got you covered with a mix-and-match selection that pleases us. They've got tees, hats and bags too.

## Manny's

156 West 48th St (at Seventh), Midtown

☎ 212.819.0576 🌐 No website     **MAP** D2 #132

Forty-Eighth Street between Sixth and Seventh avenues is electric guitar heaven. It's also one of the best places in the nation for keyboards, drums, woodwinds and other instruments. If you're a hardcore musician you probably already know about this strip. If you're not, it's worth coming here and to **Sam Ash** to discover what all the fuss is about.

## Marc Jacobs

403-405 Bleecker St (at 11th), Greenwich Village

☎ 212.924.0026 🌐 marcjacobs.com     **MAP** H2 #133

163 Mercer St (at Houston), Soho

☎ 212.343.1490     **MAP** K1 #134

Jacobs' Bleecker Street shop is a vanguard of name-brand retailing on a block that has never been associated with high-end retail. Adjacent stores offer the savvy designer's complete lines for both men and women, including the bridge line, Marc by Marc Jacobs, plus a shop dedicated to accessories. The Mercer Street shop is far more unassuming.

## ME&RO

241 Elizabeth St (at Prince), Nolita

**T** 917.237.9215 **W** meandrojewelry.com **MAP** L1 #135

Me (Michele Quan) and Ro (Robin Renzi) are the pair behind this celebrity-magnate of a jewelry store offering Eastern-inspired baubles in a laid-back Nolita salesroom. Many of the sensual designs are inscribed with Asian lettering, including pearl earrings and circular pendants hanging from leather strings.

## MISS SIXTY

386 West Broadway (at Broome), Soho

**T** 212.334.9772 **W** misssixty.com **MAP** K1 #136

This Soho shop whets our whistle, a retro-cool and colorful space designed with white plastic pillars, spherical sofas and crimson cubicle displays that feel like they stepped out of the pages of Wallpaper magazine. Supertight embroidered jeans are Miss Sixty's main sellers, along with ruffle shirts, miniskirts and even tinier graphic T-shirts.

## MORGANE LE FAY

67 Wooster St (at Broome), Soho

**T** 212.219.7672 **W** morganelefay.com **MAP** K1 #137

746 Madison Ave (at 65th), Upper East Side

**T** 212.879.9700 **MAP** E1 #138

Known for flowing, floor-length evening dresses that could be worn as bridal gowns, Morgane Le Fay is the home store of designer Liliana Casabal, a creator of elegant, modern, feminine clothing that includes everything from simple pajamas to artistically structured winter coats.

## MOSS

146 Greene St (at Prince), Soho

**T** 212.204.7100 **W** mossonline.com **MAP** K1 #139

Murray Moss' amazing white-box shop is a contender for one of the best industrial design stores anywhere. From Nymphenburg figurines, reproductions of 18th-century busts and giant majolica garden statues, to Cindy Sherman-designed plates and Claudy Jongstra bedding, you never know what gems you'll find. Homeware includes decorative, tabletop and accessories as well as furniture and lighting, all with extensive product information.

## MUJI AT MOMA

81 Spring St (at Crosby), Soho

**T** 646.613.1367 **W** No website **MAP** K1 #140

Mujirushi Ryohin's first North American shop full of stylish, minimalist "no-brand goods" is set to become as iconic as their stores in Europe and Japan. Set within the MoMA Design Store, Muji sells cool, design heavy items like cardboard speakers, aluminum business-card cases and even fold-up bicycles—all at very affordable prices. We love this store.

## NOM DE GUERRE

640 Broadway (at Bleecker), Greenwich Village

**T** 212.253.2891 **W** nomdeguerre.net **MAP** K1 #141

Along with **Alife**, this multi-level, subterranean shop endeavors to sell some of the hardest-to-find sneakers in the world. If vintage Nikes or red-and-white Supreme Dunks are your fetish, then Nom de Guerre is your place. They've got a menswear collection too, featuring cashmere knits, Japanese denim and button-front shirts.

## OLDE GOOD THINGS

124 West 24th St (at Sixth), Chelsea

**T** 212.989.8401 **W** oldegoodthings.com **MAP** H1 #142

19 Greenwich Ave (at 10th), Greenwich Village

**T** 212.229.0850 **MAP** H2 #143

Before the wrecking ball strikes, Old Good Things moves in to salvage what otherwise might have been hauled off. From a glass door knob to an Art Nouveau stained-glass window, most of the treasures are ornamental, and can be as large as an entire marble facade from a monumental building. The selection is largest at the Chelsea location.

## OTHER MUSIC

15 East 4th St (at Lafayette), Greenwich Village

**T** 212.477.8150 **W** othermusic.com **MAP** I2 #144

A one-stop shop for great, hard-to-find dub and underground CDs, as well as house, techno, jungle, trip-hop and other club styles. Plus, the staff are helpful and enthusiastic.

## PEARL RIVER

477 Broadway (at Broome), Soho

**T** 212.431.4770 **W** pearlriver.com **MAP** K1 #145

Of all the kitschy trinket shops in the city, this sprawling Chinese bazaar comes up trumps for bamboo parasols, porcelain vases, waving kitty statues, Mao suits, bone carvings, chopstick sets, lacquered boxes, colorful kimonos and even furniture.

## PETIT PETON

27 West 8th St (at Fifth), Greenwich Village

**T** 212.677.3730 **W** petitpeton.com **MAP** H2 #146

Eighth Street on a Saturday is always a blast for Technicolor shoes, people watching, and blang (cheap

bling). The strip's best shoe store is right in the middle of it all, selling some of the coolest, sexiest, high-priced, no-brand footwear we've seen anywhere. It's for both men and women.

## Polo/Ralph Lauren

| 867 Madison Ave (at 71st), Upper East Side | |
|---|---|
| ☎ 212.606.2100 🖥 polo.com | MAP E1 #147 |
| 888 Madison Ave (at 72nd), Upper East Side | |
| ☎ 212.434.8000 | MAP E1 #148 |
| 379 West Broadway (at Broome), Soho | |
| ☎ 212.625.1660 | MAP K1 #149 |
| 31 Prince Street (at Mott), Nolita | |
| ☎ 212.680.0181 | MAP L1 #150 |

Lauren's $14 million reconstruction of the Upper East Side Rhinelander mansion has given rise to one of the most incredible store/museums in Manhattan. The wood paneled sales rooms, dressed with gentlemen's club-meets-safari decor, mimics a vintage British hunting lodge.

## Porthault

| 18 East 69th St (at Madison), Upper East Side | |
|---|---|
| ☎ 212.688.1660 🖥 No website | MAP E1 #151 |

When you've figured out that Frette is passé, head to this fine French white-goods store, offering some of the most luxurious bedding, towels and bathrobes anywhere. The shop is suitably handsome and prices are as high as you'd expect.

## Prada

| 575 Broadway (at Prince), Soho | |
|---|---|
| ☎ 212.334.8888 🖥 prada.com | MAP K1 #152 |
| 45 East 57th St (at Madison), Midtown | |
| ☎ 212.308.2332 | MAP E2 #153 |
| 724 Fifth Ave (at 56th), Midtown | |
| ☎ 212.664.0010 | MAP E2 #154 |

The massive, swanky and super-high-tech Soho shop gets the Avant-Guide nod for its stunning design by Rem Koolhaas; a temple of clothes, shoes and leather goods. A cross between art installation and retailtainment makes this a store that shouldn't be missed. Oh yeah, all the complete Prada lines are here too, including housewear.

## Quiksilver

| 3 Times Square (at 42nd & Seventh), Midtown | |
|---|---|
| ☎ 212.840.8534 🖥 quiksilver.com | MAP D2 #155 |

Quiksilver's Times Square megashop earns mention for creating a full-on retail experience that includes tons of flat screens, gaming systems and more. From logo caps to board shorts, all the Quicksilver and Roxy clothes are here, for both dudes and dudettes.

## R 20TH CENTURY DESIGN

82 Franklin St (at Church), Tribeca

☎ 212.343.7979 🌐 r20thcentury.com          MAP K1 #156

Antique, furniture and design shops stand cheek-to-jowl on this street, and R is the best. Make this your destination for mid-20th-century furnishings by name-brand designers like Dunbar and Knoll.

## REISS

387 West Broadway (at Spring), Soho

☎ 212.925.5707 🌐 reiss.co.uk          MAP K1 #157

British-based Reiss aims to create own-brand fashions for both men and women that bridge between cheap chain stores and name-brand designers. They have over 30 stores in the UK and this is their first US flagship boutique. Think of it as aspirational, and affordable for those twenty- and thirty-somethings.

## ROBERT MARC

436 West Broadway (at Prince), Soho

☎ 212.343.8300 🌐 robertmarc.com          MAP K1 #158

551 Madison Ave (at 55th), Midtown

☎ 212.319.2000          MAP E2 #159

190 Columbus Ave (at 69th), Upper West Side

☎ 212.799.4600          MAP D1 #160

and other locations

Robert Marc has shops all over town because he's one of the best. House styles are sold here alongside other avant brands that you just can't get elsewhere so easily. The Retrospecs line interprets vintage styles made from precious metals.

## RUE ST. DENIS

170 Ave B (at 11th), East Village

☎ 212.260.3388 🌐 vintagenyc.com          MAP J2 #161

Excellent condition vintage can outfit any aspiring hipster from top to toe. Nothing here is cheap, but it's all far less than buying it new—if you could even find this stuff anymore.

## SAM ASH

155 West 48th St (at Seventh), Midtown

☎ 212.719.2625 🌐 samashmusic.com          MAP D2 #162

Along with **Manny's**, this string of mega-shops carry everything for the musician from guitar picks to MIDI systems. Their selection of acoustic instruments is unparalleled, and their DJ tables, lighting packages and software selections aren't too shabby either.

## SCHOOLHOUSE ELECTRIC CO.

27 Vestry St (at Hudson), Tribeca

☎ 212.226.6113 🌐 schoolhouseelectric.com          MAP K1 #163

We love it when undervalued old furnishings are resurrected and given new lives in contemporary settings. That's why we're hot on this shop specializing in light fixtures that once hung in schools and libraries a century ago. The reproductions sold here are made from original molds, have a great retro look and are priced to move.

## SCOOP

1275 Third Ave (at 73rd), Upper East Side

☎ 212.535.5577 🌐 scoopnyc.com          MAP E1 #164

532 Broadway (at Spring), Soho

☎ 212.925.2886          MAP K1 #165

430 West 14th St (at Washington), Meatpacking District

☎ 212.929.1244          MAP G2 #166

This New York fashion sensation for It girls and boys created the "ultimate closet" concept for must-have staples: low-rise cords, luxe velvet fitted jackets, pencil skirts, Fair Isle sweaters, embroidered velvet scarves and the latest Jimmy Choos.

## SCREAMING MIMI'S

382 Lafayette St (at 4th), East Village

☎ 212.677.6464 🌐 screamingmimis.com          MAP I2 #167

Vintage so classic and in such good condition, you'll swear it's new. And they certainly don't make those funky sequined dresses anymore, do they? Good selection of vintage shoes, too.

## SELIA YANG BRIDAL

328 East 9th St (at Second), East Village

☎ 212.254.9073 🌐 seliayang.com          MAP I2 #168

## SELIA YANG READY TO WEAR

324 East 9th St (at Second), East Village

☎ 212.254.8980          MAP I2 #169

If we ever get married (again), we're definitely wearing Selia Yang. Luckily, you don't have to tie the knot to cozy up to her fantastic cocktail and evening dresses. Her lace beaded bustier gown with bias cut silk crepe bottom is sexy and delicious. And the drop waist drawstring mini in beaded silk chiffon is to die for.

## SSUR PLUS

7 Spring St (at Elizabeth), Nolita

☎ 212.431.3152 🌐 ssurempirestate.com          MAP L1 #170

When you're looking for the perfect gift for the super-stylish skate rat on your list, look no further than SSUR Plus

Petit Peton

(pronounced "surplus," get it?!), a homegrown boarder-clothes paradise in the mold of **Triple-Five Soul**. Pop imagery finds its way onto everything from T-shirts to pillow cases, with particular fondness for all things Planet of the Apes and Che Guevara.

## STRAND BOOKSTORE

828 Broadway (at 12th), East Village

☎ 212.473.1452 ⊞ strandbooks.com     **MAP** I2 #171

95 Fulton St (at William), Financial District

☎ 212.732.6070     **MAP** K2 #172

The Strand is one of the largest second-hand bookshops anywhere. The selection is absolutely enormous; groaning bookshelves that extend down rickety stairs into a cluttered firetrap of a basement. Although it can at first seem rather overwhelming, the store's stock is helpfully organized by subject.

## STELLA MCCARTNEY

429 West 14th St (at Ninth), Chelsea

☎ 212.255.1556 ⊞ stellamccartney.com     **MAP** G2 #173

Stella Mac's first freestanding store contains the designer's complete collection of girly-tough outfits. Following in her mother's animal-welfare footsteps, everything here is made without animal products, including shoes, which

are made from a leather-like plant derivative. Of course, nothing's cheap, so bring lots of sugar.

## STEVEN ALAN

103 Franklin St (at Church), Tribeca

☎ 212.343.0692 ⊞ stevenalan.com     **MAP** K1 #174

229 Elizabeth St (at Prince), Nolita

☎ 212.226.7482     **MAP** L1 #175

465 Amsterdam Ave (at 82nd), Upper West Side

☎ 212.595.8451     **MAP** A2 #176

A star of Casual Friday New York fashion for over a decade, Steven Alan is a master of urban separates for avant boys and girls. His shops are friendly, downscale places for ear-to-the-ground brands like Katayone Adeli, Rogan and even pajamas by Cabane de Zucca.

## SWATCH

1528 Broadway (at 45th), Midtown

☎ 212.764.5541 ⊞ swatch.com     **MAP** D2 #177

You know the brand: innovative and inexpensive watches that you can change as often as you change your mind. It's said that the company produces more than 400 styles per year, and at this colorful Times Square flagship shop you can probably see more variety than just about anywhere else.

Quiksilver

Reiss

## Tannen's Magic Shop

45 West 34th St (at Fifth), Midtown

☎ 212.929.4500 ⓦ tannens.com　　　　　　MAP H1 #178

One of the largest and most respected magic shops in the world, Tannen's sells everything from thumb tips and reels to levitation devices, plus plenty of unique items created for exclusive sale in this store. Get a copy of their catalogue.

## T. Anthony

445 Park Ave (at 56th), Midtown

☎ 212.750.9797 ⓦ tanthony.com　　　　　　MAP E2 #179

T. Anthony creates some of the world's finest luggage: stylish and rugged canvas bags in the label's trademark colors of ruby and sapphire. They've got handsome, Cunard-ready hard sided sets too, along with copious leather goods, jewelry boxes and briefcases all united by chic-simple designs and free monogramming while you wait.

## TG-170

170 Ludlow St (at Stanton), Lower East Side

☎ 212.995.8660 ⓦ tg170.com　　　　　　MAP L1 #180

Owner Terri Gillis has a nose for discovering designers on their way up so it's not unusual to see offerings from unknowns here long before they start to appear in other stores around town. Her spacious shop is filled with desirable clothes, along with bags, accessories and some gift items. Definitely add this one to your Ludlow Street crawl.

## Tokio7

64 East 7th St (at Second), East Village

☎ 212.353.8443 ⓦ No website　　　　　　MAP I2 #181

Couture consignment shops have been popping up all over the city, but for low prices on high fashions, Tokio7 may be tops. From Dior and Gucci, to Fendi and Prada, all the big names are here, often for pennies on the dollar.

## Trash & Vaudeville

4 St Mark's Pl (at Third), East Village

☎ 212.982.3590 ⓦ No website　　　　　　MAP I2 #182

Punk lives at this St. Mark's Place pioneer; a second-floor shop that's been here since the heyday of CBGBs and now looks like it will far outlast it. Concert tees, bondage pants, fishnets, steel-toe boots and anything with safety pins are the stock in trade, making this place either a cultural museum or a good place for a Halloween costume.

## Triple Five Soul

290 Lafayette St (at Prince), Soho

☎ 212.431.2404 ⓦ triple5soul.com　　　　　　MAP K1 #183

One of the coolest names in skatewear, TFS is the place to get baggier-than-thou, in the form of giant pants, aphorism tees, tube hats, messenger bags and sweats with the 555 logo.

Selia Yang

Swatch

## Universal News

676 Lexington Ave (at 56th), Midtown

☎ 212.750.1855 🌐 universalnewsusa.com    MAP E2 #184

977 Eighth Ave (at 57th), Midtown

☎ 212.459.0932    MAP D2 #185

1586 Broadway (at 48th), Midtown

☎ 212.586.7205    MAP D2 #186

270 Park Ave South (at 21st), Flatiron District

☎ 212.674.6595    MAP I2 #187

484 Broadway (at Broome), Soho

☎ 212.965.9042    MAP K1 #188

These amazing magazine malls stock over 7,000 international and domestic newspaper and magazine titles, conveniently arranged by subject. And they're open until midnight.

## Urban Outfitters

374 Sixth Ave (at Waverly), Greenwich Village

☎ 212.677.9350 🌐 urbanoutfitters.com    MAP H2 #189

162 Second Ave (at 10th), East Village

☎ 212.375.1277    MAP I2 #190

2081 Broadway (at 72nd), Upper West Side

☎ 212.579.3912    MAP C1 #191

999 Third Ave (at 60th), Midtown

☎ 212.308.1518    MAP E2 #192

Clothier to college types across America, Urban Outfitters is known for trend-setting basic wear at fair prices. They've got funky candles, funny books and a huge variety of playful gift items too.

## Village Chess Shop

230 Thompson St (at 3rd), Greenwich Village

☎ 212.475.9580 🌐 chess-shop.com    MAP H2 #193

Knights, bishops, pawns and eggheads come together in this cramped Village landmark. They sell boards, mats, clocks and accessories, and an opponent seems to always be on hand for quality in-shop play.

## Zabar's

2245 Broadway (at 80th), Upper West Side

☎ 212.787.2000 🌐 zabars.com    MAP A2 #194

Zabar's is the quintessential New York gourmet shop for Jewish delicacies; most notably smoked salmon and other kippered fish. There are at least half a dozen varieties of the first, sliced so thin that it practically takes several slices to register on the scale. Great cheeses and gourmet cookware as well.

## SIMON DOONAN

*Born in 1952 in Reading, England, Simon Doonan began trimming windows on London's Savile Row before emigrating to Southern California in the late seventies. A job at Maxfield, the avant-garde Los Angeles clothing store, soon established his reputation as an arbiter of style and image in the fashion world. After working under the legendary Diana Vreeland at the Costume Institute of the Metropolitan Museum of Art, Doonan joined Barneys New York in 1986, where he is now creative director. He has also written three books,* Confessions of a Window Dresser, Wacky Chicks **and** Nasty.

**Avant-Guide:** Where do you take out-of-towners when you want to show them a one-of-a-kind New York City experience?

**Simon Doonan:** I take them to L'Escualita, which is a Puerto Rican transvestite bar on Ninth Avenue. It's a gay-Latin-transvestite place where they have these cabaret shows that are really funny... Again, there's an amazing mixture of people; regulars, plus people just checking it out. Once I saw Andree Putman there with Azzedine Alaia.

**=∧=** What is it about New York City that you dream about when you're away?

**SD:** When I'm away I dream about the windows at Barneys, I dream about what the hell we're going to do next. And I have those weird dreams where you're standing in the window with no clothes on and everyone is staring at you.

**=∧=** Where is your favorite place in New York City to shop?

**SD:** Well I have two favorites... One is Barneys and so I have a lot of loyalty there, I have so much fun, with the windows and advertising, and the other place is my boyfriend's shop, Jonathan Adler, at 43 Greene Street. He makes ceramics and textiles. If I didn't mention him he'd probably whack me when I got home!

**=∧=** What five non-essential items do you never travel without, and why?

**SD:** My doggie, Liberace, he's a Norwich terrier; My computer, because I write a lot. Along with Barneys, I have the writing career that I'm trying to keep going. I write for the New York Observer on a bimonthly basis; Comme Des Garcons Shiso perfume. It has a weird smell, but it makes me feel at home; My running shoes, because I like to go jogging so I don't get fat; And, the other thing... if possible, I try to travel with my boyfriend, Jonathan Adler. I hate going anywhere without him.

**=∧=** What is your fallback job, and why?

**SD:** I'd love to be a stripper. I think that it would be really funny, getting loads of cash and have everyone ogling you and telling you how fabulous you are. But I'm getting a bit old for that... you'd have to pay for everything in dollar bills though which could be a bit embarrassing.

| Map | # | Area | Shop | Address | Phone | Design Driven | Celebrity Clientele | Legendary | Only in New York |
|---|---|---|---|---|---|---|---|---|---|
| | | | **FASHION & BEAUTY** | | | | | | |
| | | | **Accessories** | | | | | | |
| I2 | 82 | Lower East Side | Eugenia Kim | 203 East 4th St | 212.673.9787 | ★ | ★ | | ★ |
| D2 | 177 | Midtown | Swatch | 1528 Broadway | 212.764.5541 | ★ | | | |
| K1 | 10 | Soho | Add | 461 West Broadway | 212.539.1439 | | | | ★ |
| K1 | 12 | Soho | Agent Provocateur | 133 Mercer St | 212.965.0229 | | ★ | | |
| K1 | 107 | Soho | Jack Spade | 56 Greene St | 212.625.1820 | | ★ | | |
| K1 | 119 | Soho | Kazuyo Nakano | 117 Crosby St | 212.941.7093 | ★ | ★ | | ★ |
| E1 | 50 | Upper East Side | Brella Bar | 1043 Third Ave | 212.813.9530 | ★ | ★ | | ★ |
| | | | **Clothing—Basics** | | | | | | |
| G2 | 166 | Meatpacking District | Scoop | 430 West 14th St | 212.929.1244 | ★ | ★ | | |
| E2 | 34 | Midtown | Bebe | 805 Third Ave | 212.588.9060 | ★ | | | |
| D2 | 155 | Midtown | Quiksilver | 3 Times Square | 212.840.8534 | ★ | | | |
| K1 | 42 | Soho | Big Drop | 174 Spring St | 212.966.4299 | ★ | | | ★ |
| K1 | 165 | Soho | Scoop | 532 Broadway | 212.925.2886 | ★ | ★ | | |
| H2 | 33 | Union Square | Bebe | 100 Fifth Ave | 212.675.2323 | ★ | | | |
| E1 | 35 | Upper East Side | Bebe | 1127 Third Ave | 212.935.2444 | ★ | | | |
| E1 | 43 | Upper East Side | Big Drop | 1321 Third Ave | 212.988.3344 | ★ | | | ★ |
| E1 | 164 | Upper East Side | Scoop | 1275 Third Ave | 212.535.5577 | ★ | ★ | | |
| | | | **Clothing—Designer** | | | | | | |
| G1 | 61 | Chelsea | Comme des Garçons | 520 West 22nd St | 212.604.9200 | ★ | ★ | | |
| G2 | 173 | Chelsea | Stella McCartney | 429 West 14th St | 212.255.1556 | ★ | ★ | | |
| I2 | 65 | East Village | Daryl K | 21 Bond St | 212.529.8790 | ★ | ★ | | |
| I2 | 90 | East Village | Ghost | 28 Bond St | 646.602.2891 | ★ | | | |
| I2 | 168 | East Village | Selia Yang Bridal | 328 East 9th St | 212.254.9073 | ★ | ★ | | ★ |
| I2 | 169 | East Village | Selia Yang Ready to Wear | 324 East 9th St | 212.254.8980 | ★ | | | ★ |
| H2 | 63 | Greenwich Village | Cynthia Rowley | 376 Bleecker St | 212.242.3803 | ★ | ★ | | |
| H2 | 133 | Greenwich Village | Marc Jacobs | 403–405 Bleecker St | 212.924.0026 | ★ | | | |
| L1 | 51 | Little Italy | Built By Wendy | 7 Centre Market Pl | 212.925.6538 | ★ | ★ | | ★ |
| G2 | 15 | Meatpacking District | An Earnest Cut & Sew | 821 Washington St | 212.242.3414 | | ★ | | ★ |
| G2 | 53 | Meatpacking District | Calypso | 654 Hudson St | 646.638.3000 | ★ | | | |
| G2 | 56 | Meatpacking District | Carlos Miele | 408 West 14th St | 646.336.6642 | ★ | ★ | | |
| G2 | 58 | Meatpacking District | Catherine Malandrino | 652 Hudson St | 212.929.8710 | ★ | | | ★ |
| H2 | 64 | Meatpacking District | Darling | 1 Horatio St | 646.336.6966 | ★ | | | ★ |
| G2 | 81 | Meatpacking District | Elizabeth Charles | 639 1/2 Hudson St | 212.243.3201 | | | | ★ |
| H2 | 128 | Meatpacking District | Lucy Barnes | 320 West 14th St | 212.255.9148 | ★ | | | ★ |
| E2 | 153 | Midtown | Prada | 45 East 57th St | 212.308.2332 | ★ | ★ | | |
| E2 | 154 | Midtown | Prada | 724 Fifth Ave | 212.664.0010 | ★ | ★ | | |
| E2 | 159 | Midtown | Robert Marc | 551 Madison Ave | 212.319.2000 | ★ | | | ★ |
| L1 | 11 | Nolita | A Detacher | 262 Mott St | 212.625.3380 | | | | ★ |
| L1 | 54 | Nolita | Calypso | 280 Mott St | 212.965.0990 | ★ | | | |
| L1 | 60 | Nolita | Christopher Totman | 262 Mott St | 212.925.7495 | | | | ★ |
| L1 | 129 | Nolita | Malia Mills | 199 Mulberry St | 212.625.2311 | ★ | ★ | | ★ |

**3** | DIRECTORY
**SHOP**

| Map | # | Area | Shop | Address | Phone | Design Driven | Celebrity Clientele | Legendary | Only in New York |
|---|---|---|---|---|---|---|---|---|---|
| | | | **Clothing—Designer** | | | | | | |
| L1 | 150 | Nolita | Polo/Ralph Lauren | 31 Prince Street | 212.680.0181 | ★ | | | |
| K1 | 19 | Soho | Anna Sui | 113 Greene St | 212.941.8406 | ★ | | | |
| K1 | 20 | Soho | A.P.C. | 131 Mercer St | 212.966.9685 | ★ | | | |
| K1 | 25 | Soho | Barbara Bui | 115 Wooster St | 212.625.1938 | | ★ | | |
| K1 | 37 | Soho | Betsey Johnson | 138 Wooster St | 212.995.5048 | ★ | | | |
| K1 | 55 | Soho | Calypso | 424 Broome St | 212.274.0449 | ★ | | | |
| K1 | 57 | Soho | Catherine Malandrino | 468 Broome St | 212.925.6765 | | ★ | | ★ |
| K1 | 73 | Soho | Diesel | 135 Spring St | 212.625.1555 | ★ | | | |
| K1 | 75 | Soho | DKNY | 420 West Broadway | 646.613.1100 | ★ | | | |
| K1 | 77 | Soho | Dosa | 107 Thompson St | 212.431.1733 | | ★ | | ★ |
| K1 | 92 | Soho | Hotel Venus | 382 West Broadway | 212.966.4066 | | ★ | | ★ |
| K1 | 110 | Soho | J. Lindeberg | 126 Spring St | 212.625.9403 | | ★ | | |
| K1 | 134 | Soho | Marc Jacobs | 163 Mercer St | 212.343.1490 | ★ | | | |
| K1 | 136 | Soho | Miss Sixty | 386 West Broadway | 212.334.9772 | ★ | | | |
| K1 | 137 | Soho | Morgane Le Fay | 67 Wooster St | 212.219.7672 | | ★ | | ★ |
| K1 | 149 | Soho | Polo/Ralph Lauren | 379 West Broadway | 212.625.1660 | ★ | | | |
| K1 | 152 | Soho | Prada | 575 Broadway | 212.334.8888 | ★ | ★ | | |
| K1 | 157 | Soho | Reiss | 387 West Broadway | 212.925.5707 | ★ | | | |
| K1 | 158 | Soho | Robert Marc | 436 West Broadway | 212.343.8300 | ★ | | | ★ |
| H2 | 72 | Union Square | Diesel | 1 Union Square West | 646.336.8552 | ★ | | | |
| E2 | 39 | Upper East Side | Betsey Johnson | 251 East 60th St | 212.319.7699 | ★ | | | |
| B2 | 40 | Upper East Side | Betsey Johnson | 1060 Madison Ave | 212.734.1257 | ★ | | | |
| E1 | 52 | Upper East Side | Calypso | 935 Madison Ave | 212.535.4100 | ★ | | | ★ |
| E2 | 71 | Upper East Side | Diesel | 770 Lexington Ave | 212.308.0055 | ★ | | | |
| E2 | 74 | Upper East Side | DKNY | 655 Madison Ave | 212.223.3569 | ★ | | | |
| E1 | 130 | Upper East Side | Malia Mills | 1031 Lexington Ave | 212.517.7485 | ★ | ★ | | ★ |
| E1 | 138 | Upper East Side | Morgane Le Fay | 746 Madison Ave | 212.879.9700 | | ★ | | ★ |
| E1 | 147 | Upper East Side | Polo/Ralph Lauren | 867 Madison Ave | 212.606.2100 | ★ | | ★ | |
| E1 | 148 | Upper East Side | Polo/Ralph Lauren | 888 Madison Ave | 212.434.8000 | ★ | | | |
| D1 | 38 | Upper West Side | Betsey Johnson | 248 Columbus Ave | 212.362.3364 | ★ | | | |
| D1 | 131 | Upper West Side | Malia Mills | 220 Columbus Ave | 212.874.7200 | ★ | ★ | | ★ |
| D1 | 160 | Upper West Side | Robert Marc | 190 Columbus Ave | 212.799.4600 | ★ | | | ★ |
| | | | **Clothing—Multilabel Stores** | | | | | | |
| H2 | 24 | Chelsea | Bang Bang | 147 Eighth Ave | 212.807.8457 | | | | ★ |
| G2 | 109 | Chelsea | Jeffrey | 449 West 14th St | 212.206.1272 | ★ | ★ | | ★ |
| I2 | 18 | East Village | Anna | 150 East 3rd St | 212.358.0195 | | | | ★ |
| I2 | 182 | East Village | Trash & Vaudeville | 4 St Mark's Pl | 212.982.3590 | | | ★ | ★ |
| I2 | 190 | East Village | Urban Outfitters | 162 Second Ave | 212.375.1277 | ★ | | | |
| H2 | 104 | Flatiron District | Intermix | 125 Fifth Ave | 212.533.9720 | ★ | ★ | | ★ |
| I2 | 23 | Greenwich Village | Bang Bang | 53 East 8th St | 212.475.8220 | | | | ★ |
| I2 | 79 | Greenwich Village | EdgeNY | 65 Bleecker St | 212.358.0255 | ★ | | | ★ |
| H2 | 106 | Greenwich Village | Intermix | 365 Bleecker St | 212.929.7180 | ★ | ★ | | ★ |

| Map | # | Area | Shop | Address | Phone | Design Driven | Celebrity Clientele | Legendary | Only in New York |
|---|---|---|---|---|---|:-:|:-:|:-:|:-:|
| K1 | 141 | Greenwich Village | Nom de Guerre | 640 Broadway | 212.253.2891 | | ★ | | ★ |
| H2 | 146 | Greenwich Village | Petit Peton | 27 West 8th St | 212.677.3730 | | ★ | | ★ |
| H2 | 189 | Greenwich Village | Urban Outfitters | 374 Sixth Ave | 212.677.9350 | ★ | | | |
| L1 | 180 | Lower East Side | TG-170 | 170 Ludlow St | 212.995.8660 | ★ | ★ | | ★ |
| E2 | 192 | Midtown | Urban Outfitters | 999 Third Ave | 212.308.1518 | ★ | | | |
| K1 | 125 | Nolita | Label | 265 Lafayette St | 212.966.7736 | | | | ★ |
| L1 | 170 | Nolita | SSUR Plus | 7 Spring St | 212.431.3152 | | | | ★ |
| L1 | 175 | Nolita | Steven Alan | 229 Elizabeth St | 212.226.7482 | ★ | ★ | | |
| K1 | 97 | Soho | If | 94 Grand St | 212.334.4964 | ★ | ★ | | ★ |
| K1 | 123 | Soho | Kirna Zabete | 96 Greene St | 212.941.9656 | ★ | ★ | | ★ |
| K1 | 183 | Soho | Triple Five Soul | 290 Lafayette St | 212.431.2404 | | ★ | | |
| K1 | 174 | Tribeca | Steven Alan | 103 Franklin St | 212.343.0692 | ★ | ★ | | |
| E1 | 16 | Upper East Side | Anik | 1355 Third Ave | 212.861.9840 | ★ | | | |
| B2 | 17 | Upper East Side | Anik | 1122 Madison Ave | 212.249.2417 | ★ | | | |
| E1 | 103 | Upper East Side | Intermix | 1003 Madison Ave | 212.249.7858 | ★ | ★ | | ★ |
| D1 | 105 | Upper West Side | Intermix | 210 Columbus Ave | 212.769.9116 | ★ | ★ | | ★ |
| A2 | 176 | Upper West Side | Steven Alan | 465 Amsterdam Ave | 212.595.8451 | ★ | ★ | | |
| C1 | 191 | Upper West Side | Urban Outfitters | 2081 Broadway | 212.579.3912 | ★ | | | |
| | | | **Clothing—Vintage & Thrift** | | | | | | |
| H2 | 93 | Chelsea | Housing Works Thrift Shop | 143 West 17th St | 212.366.0820 | | | | ★ |
| I2 | 18 | East Village | Anna | 150 East 3rd St | 212.358.0195 | | | | ★ |
| J2 | 161 | East Village | Rue St. Denis | 170 Ave B | 212.260.3388 | | | | ★ |
| I2 | 167 | East Village | Screaming Mimi's | 382 Lafayette St | 212.677.6464 | | | | ★ |
| I2 | 181 | East Village | Tokio7 | 64 East 7th St | 212.353.8443 | ★ | | | ★ |
| I1 | 94 | Midtown | Housing Works Thrift Shop | 157 East 23rd St | 212.529.5955 | | | | ★ |
| E1 | 95 | Upper East Side | Housing Works Thrift Shop | 202 East 77th St | 212.772.8461 | | | | ★ |
| C1 | 14 | Upper West Side | Allan & Suzi | 416 Amsterdam Ave | 212.724.7445 | | | | ★ |
| D1 | 96 | Upper West Side | Housing Works Thrift Shop | 306 Columbus Ave | 212.579.7566 | | | | ★ |
| | | | **Clothing—Designer Outlet** | | | | | | |
| G2 | 85 | Chelsea | Find Outlet | 361 West 17th St | 212.243.3177 | | | | ★ |
| I2 | 89 | East Village | Gabay's | 225 First Ave | 212.254.3180 | | | | ★ |
| K2 | 59 | Financial District | Century 21 | 22 Cortlandt St | 212.227.9092 | | | ★ | ★ |
| L1 | 86 | Nolita | Find Outlet | 229 Mott St | 212.226.5167 | | | | ★ |
| L1 | 99 | Nolita | Ina | 21 Prince St | 212.334.9048 | | | | ★ |
| L1 | 101 | Nolita | Ina Men's Store | 262 Mott St | 212.334.2210 | | | | ★ |
| K1 | 98 | Soho | Ina | 101 Thompson St | 212.941.4757 | | | | ★ |
| E1 | 100 | Upper East Side | Ina | 208 East 73rd St | 212.249.0014 | | | | ★ |
| | | | **Cosmetics, Fragrance & Grooming** | | | | | | |
| I2 | 121 | East Village | Kiehl's | 109 Third Ave | 212.677.3171 | | | ★ | ★ |
| K1 | 12 | Soho | Agent Provocateur | 133 Mercer St | 212.965.0229 | ★ | | | |
| D1 | 122 | Upper West Side | Kiehl's | 150 Columbus Ave | 212.799.3438 | | | ★ | |
| | | | **Eyewear** | | | | | | |
| I2 | 46 | East Village | Bond 07 | 7 Bond St | 212.677.8487 | ★ | ★ | | ★ |

| Map | # | Area | Shop | Address | Phone | Design Driven | Celebrity Clientele | Legendary | Only in New York |
|---|---|---|---|---|---|---|---|---|---|
| | | | **Department Stores** | | | | | | |
| H2 | 30 | Chelsea | Barneys Co-Op | 236 West 18th St | 212.593.7800 | ★ | | | |
| E2 | 36 | Midtown | Bergdorf Goodman | 754 Fifth Ave | 212.753.7300 | | | ★ | ★ |
| E2 | 91 | Midtown | Henri Bendel | 712 Fifth Ave | 212.247.1100 | | | ★ | |
| K1 | 32 | Soho | Barneys Co-Op | 116 Wooster St | 212.965.9964 | ★ | | | |
| K1 | 45 | Soho | Bloomingdale's Soho | 504 Broadway | 212.729.5900 | | ★ | | |
| E2 | 29 | Upper East Side | Barneys | 660 Madison Ave | 212.826.8900 | ★ | | | |
| E2 | 44 | Upper East Side | Bloomingdale's | 1000 Third Ave | 212.705.2000 | | ★ | | |
| C1 | 31 | Upper West Side | Barneys Co-Op | 2151 Broadway | 646.335.0978 | ★ | | | |
| | | | **Handbags & Luggage** | | | | | | |
| E2 | 179 | Midtown | T. Anthony | 445 Park Ave | 212.750.9797 | ★ | ★ | | |
| L1 | 11 | Nolita | A Detacher | 262 Mott St | 212.625.3380 | | | | ★ |
| K1 | 10 | Soho | Add | 461 West Broadway | 212.539.1439 | | | | ★ |
| K1 | 107 | Soho | Jack Spade | 56 Greene St | 212.625.1820 | | | ★ | |
| K1 | 119 | Soho | Kazuyo Nakano | 117 Crosby St | 212.941.7093 | ★ | ★ | | ★ |
| | | | **Jewelry** | | | | | | |
| I2 | 46 | East Village | Bond 07 | 7 Bond St | 212.677.8487 | ★ | ★ | | ★ |
| I2 | 90 | East Village | Ghost | 28 Bond St | 646.602.2891 | | ★ | | |
| G2 | 81 | Meatpacking District | Elizabeth Charles | 639 1/2 Hudson St | 212.243.3201 | | | | ★ |
| L1 | 135 | Nolita | Me&Ro | 241 Elizabeth St | 917.237.9215 | ★ | ★ | | ★ |
| K1 | 10 | Soho | Add | 461 West Broadway | 212.539.1439 | | | | ★ |
| K1 | 12 | Soho | Agent Provocateur | 133 Mercer St | 212.965.0229 | | ★ | | |
| | | | **Lingerie** | | | | | | |
| G2 | 81 | Meatpacking District | Elizabeth Charles | 639 1/2 Hudson St | 212.243.3201 | | | | ★ |
| K1 | 12 | Soho | Agent Provocateur | 133 Mercer St | 212.965.0229 | ★ | | | |
| K1 | 126 | Soho | Le Corset | 80 Thompson St | 212.334.4936 | ★ | | | ★ |
| E1 | 48 | Upper East Side | Bra Smyth | 905 Madison Ave | 212.772.9400 | ★ | | | ★ |
| | | | **Shoes** | | | | | | |
| G2 | 109 | Chelsea | Jeffrey | 449 West 14th St | 212.206.1272 | ★ | ★ | | ★ |
| L1 | 114 | East Village | Jutta Neumann | 158 Allen St | 212.982.7048 | ★ | | | ★ |
| K1 | 141 | Greenwich Village | Nom de Guerre | 640 Broadway | 212.253.2891 | ★ | | | ★ |
| L1 | 13 | Lower East Side | Alife | 158 Rivington St | 212.375.8128 | | | | ★ |
| L1 | 111 | Nolita | John Fluevog | 250 Mulberry St | 212.431.4484 | ★ | | | |
| K1 | 88 | Soho | Flying A | 169 Spring St | 212.965.9090 | ★ | | | |
| | | | **HOME** | | | | | | |
| | | | **Antiques & Auction Houses** | | | | | | |
| H1 | 142 | Chelsea | Olde Good Things | 124 West 24th St | 212.989.8401 | | | ★ | ★ |
| H2 | 9 | Flatiron District | ABC Carpet & Home | 888 Broadway | 212.473.3000 | | ★ | ★ | ★ |
| H2 | 143 | Greenwich Village | Olde Good Things | 19 Greenwich Ave | 212.229.0850 | | | ★ | ★ |
| K1 | 156 | Tribeca | R 20th Century Design | 82 Franklin St | 212.343.7979 | ★ | ★ | | ★ |
| | | | **Home Furnishings** | | | | | | |
| H1 | 142 | Chelsea | Olde Good Things | 124 West 24th St | 212.989.8401 | | | ★ | ★ |
| H2 | 9 | Flatiron District | ABC Carpet & Home | 888 Broadway | 212.473.3000 | | ★ | ★ | ★ |

| Map | # | Area | Shop | Address | Phone | Design Driven | Celebrity Clientele | Legendary | Only in New York |
|---|---|---|---|---|---|---|---|---|---|
| H2 | 143 | Greenwich Village | Olde Good Things | 19 Greenwich Ave | 212.229.0850 | | | ★ | ★ |
| G2 | 69 | Meatpacking District | Design Within Reach | 408 West 14th St | 212.242.9449 | ★ | | | ★ |
| K1 | 62 | Soho | Craft Caravan | 63 Greene St | 212.431.6669 | | | ★ | ★ |
| K1 | 70 | Soho | Design Within Reach | 142 Wooster St | 212.475.0001 | ★ | | | ★ |
| K1 | 87 | Soho | Flou | 42 Greene St | 212.941.9101 | ★ | | | |
| K1 | 112 | Soho | Jonathan Adler | 47 Greene St | 212.941.8950 | ★ | ★ | | |
| K1 | 139 | Soho | Moss | 146 Greene St | 212.204.7100 | ★ | ★ | | ★ |
| K1 | 140 | Soho | Muji at MoMA | 81 Spring St | 646.613.1367 | ★ | | | |
| K1 | 145 | Soho | Pearl River | 477 Broadway | 212.431.4770 | | | | ★ |
| K1 | 156 | Tribeca | R 20th Century Design | 82 Franklin St | 212.343.7979 | ★ | ★ | | ★ |
| B2 | 113 | Upper East Side | Jonathan Adler | 1097 Madison Ave | 212.772.2410 | ★ | ★ | | |
| E1 | 151 | Upper East Side | Porthault | 18 East 69th St | 212.688.1660 | ★ | ★ | | |
| | | | **Lighting** | | | | | | |
| H2 | 9 | Flatiron District | ABC Carpet & Home | 888 Broadway | 212.473.3000 | ★ | | ★ | ★ |
| G2 | 69 | Meatpacking District | Design Within Reach | 408 West 14th St | 212.242.9449 | ★ | | | ★ |
| K1 | 70 | Soho | Design Within Reach | 142 Wooster St | 212.475.0001 | ★ | | | ★ |
| K1 | 102 | Soho | Ingo Maurer | 89 Grand St | 212.965.8817 | ★ | ★ | | ★ |
| K1 | 139 | Soho | Moss | 146 Greene St | 212.204.7100 | ★ | ★ | | ★ |
| K1 | 163 | Tribeca | Schoolhouse Electric Co. | 27 Vestry St | 212.226.6113 | ★ | | | ★ |
| | | | **Kitchen & Tableware** | | | | | | |
| K2 | 124 | Flatiron District | Korin Japanese Trading Corp. | 57 Warren St | 212.587.7021 | | | | ★ |
| K1 | 145 | Soho | Pearl River | 477 Broadway | 212.431.4770 | | | | ★ |
| | | | **LIFESTYLE** | | | | | | |
| | | | **Books & Magazines** | | | | | | |
| I2 | 171 | East Village | Strand Bookstore | 828 Broadway | 212.473.1452 | | | ★ | |
| K2 | 172 | Financial District | Strand Bookstore | 95 Fulton St | 212.732.6070 | | | ★ | |
| I2 | 187 | Flatiron District | Universal News | 270 Park Ave South | 212.674.6595 | | | | ★ |
| E2 | 28 | Midtown | Barnes & Noble | 600 Fifth Ave | 212.765.0590 | | | ★ | |
| E2 | 184 | Midtown | Universal News | 676 Lexington Ave | 212.750.1855 | | | | ★ |
| D2 | 185 | Midtown | Universal News | 977 Eighth Ave | 212.459.0932 | | | | ★ |
| D2 | 186 | Midtown | Universal News | 1586 Broadway | 212.586.7205 | | | | ★ |
| K1 | 188 | Soho | Universal News | 484 Broadway | 212.965.9042 | | | | ★ |
| I2 | 26 | Union Square | Barnes & Noble | 33 East 17th St | 212.253.0810 | | | ★ | |
| H2 | 47 | Union Square | Books of Wonder | 18 West 18th St | 212.989.3270 | | | | ★ |
| B2 | 27 | Upper East Side | Barnes & Noble | 1280 Lexington Ave | 212.423.9900 | | | ★ | |
| | | | **Cameras & Electronics** | | | | | | |
| G1 | 41 | Midtown | B&H Photo | 420 Ninth Ave | 212.444.6615 | | | | ★ |
| | | | **Food & Drink** | | | | | | |
| G2 | 1 | Chelsea | Chelsea Market | 75 Ninth Ave | No phone | ★ | | | |
| L1 | 80 | Nolita | Eileen's Special Cheesecake | 17 Cleveland Pl | 212.966.5585 | | | ★ | ★ |
| K1 | 66 | Soho | Dean & DeLuca | 560 Broadway | 212.226.6800 | ★ | | ★ | ★ |
| K1 | 108 | Soho | Jacques Torres Chocolate | 350 Hudson St | 212.414.2462 | ★ | | | ★ |
| I2 | 2 | Union Square | Greenmarket at Union Square | Broadway | 212.788.7476 | | | | ★ |

| Map | # | Area | Shop | Address | Phone | Design Driven | Celebrity Clientele | Legendary | Only in New York |
|-----|---|------|------|---------|-------|---|---|---|---|
| | | | **Food & Drink** | | | | | | |
| B2 | 67 | Upper East Side | Dean & DeLuca | 1150 Madison Ave | 212.717.0800 | | ★ | ★ | ★ |
| E2 | 78 | Upper East Side | Dylan's Candy Bar | 1011 Third Ave | 646.735.0078 | ★ | ★ | | |
| A2 | 194 | Upper West Side | Zabar's | 2245 Broadway | 212.787.2000 | | ★ | ★ | ★ |
| | | | **Gifts, Novelties & Museum Stores** | | | | | | |
| I2 | 127 | East Village | Love Saves The Day | 119 Second Ave | 212.228.3802 | ★ | | | ★ |
| H1 | 178 | Midtown | Tannen's Magic Shop | 45 West 34th St | 212.929.4500 | | | ★ | ★ |
| K1 | 120 | Soho | Kidrobot | 126 Prince St | 212.966.6688 | ★ | | | |
| K1 | 140 | Soho | Muji at MoMA | 81 Spring St | 646.613.1367 | ★ | | | |
| | | | **Music & Video** | | | | | | |
| H2 | 84 | Greenwich Village | Fat Beats | 406 Sixth Ave | 212.673.3883 | | | | ★ |
| I2 | 144 | Greenwich Village | Other Music | 15 East 4th St | 212.477.8150 | ★ | | | |
| L1 | 49 | Lower East Side | Breakbeat Science | 181 Orchard St | 212.995.2592 | ★ | | | ★ |
| | | | **Musical Instruments** | | | | | | |
| D2 | 132 | Midtown | Manny's | 156 West 48th St | 212.819.0576 | ★ | | | ★ |
| D2 | 162 | Midtown | Sam Ash | 155 West 48th St | 212.719.2625 | ★ | ★ | | |
| | | | **Pet Supply** | | | | | | |
| K1 | 76 | Soho | DoggyStyle | 100 Thompson St | 212.431.9200 | ★ | | | ★ |
| | | | **Sex Shops** | | | | | | |
| H1 | 68 | Chelsea | DeMask | 135 West 22nd St | 212.352.2850 | ★ | | | |
| L1 | 22 | Lower East Side | Babeland | 94 Rivington St | 212.375.1701 | ★ | | | |
| K1 | 21 | Soho | Babeland | 43 Mercer St | 212.966.2120 | ★ | | | |
| | | | **Spas** | | | | | | |
| I2 | 7 | East Village | Russian and Turkish Baths | 268 East 10th St | 212.473.8806 | | ★ | ★ | ★ |
| E2 | 3 | Midtown | Bliss 57 | 19 East 57th St | 212.219.8970 | ★ | | | |
| E2 | 5 | Midtown | Cornelia Day Resort | 663 Fifth Ave | 212.871.3050 | ★ | | | ★ |
| H1 | 6 | Midtown | Juvenex | 25 West 32nd St | 646.733.1330 | | | | ★ |
| E2 | 4 | Soho | Bliss Soho | 568 Broadway | 212.219.8970 | ★ | | | |
| D2 | 8 | Upper West Side | Spa at the Mandarin Oriental | 80 Columbus Circle | 212.805.8800 | ★ | | | |
| | | | **Stationery** | | | | | | |
| H2 | 116 | Greenwich Village | Kate's Paperie | 8 West 13th St | 212.633.0570 | ★ | | | ★ |
| D2 | 118 | Midtown | Kate's Paperie | 140 West 57th St | 212.459.0700 | ★ | | | ★ |
| K1 | 115 | Soho | Kate's Paperie | 561 Broadway | 212.941.9816 | ★ | | | ★ |
| E1 | 117 | Upper East Side | Kate's Paperie | 1282 Third Ave | 212.396.3670 | ★ | | | ★ |
| | | | **Toys** | | | | | | |
| H2 | 193 | Greenwich Village | Village Chess Shop | 230 Thompson St | 212.475.9580 | | | | ★ |
| E2 | 83 | Midtown | FAO Schwarz | 767 Fifth Ave | 212.644.9400 | ★ | ★ | | |
| H1 | 178 | Midtown | Tannen's Magic Shop | 45 West 34th St | 212.929.4500 | | | ★ | ★ |
| K1 | 120 | Soho | Kidrobot | 126 Prince St | 212.966.6688 | ★ | | | |

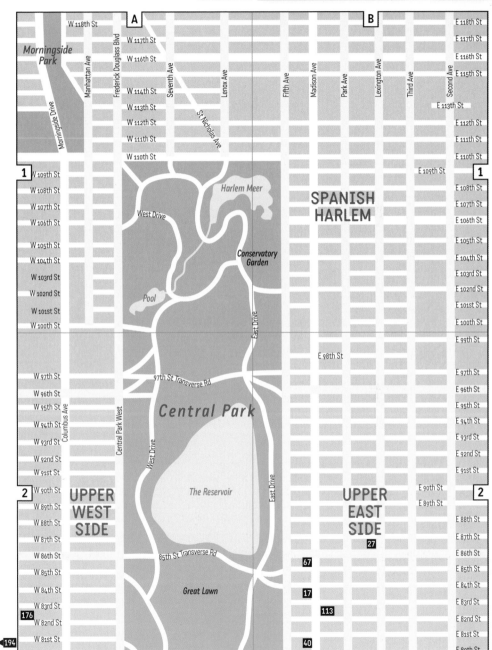

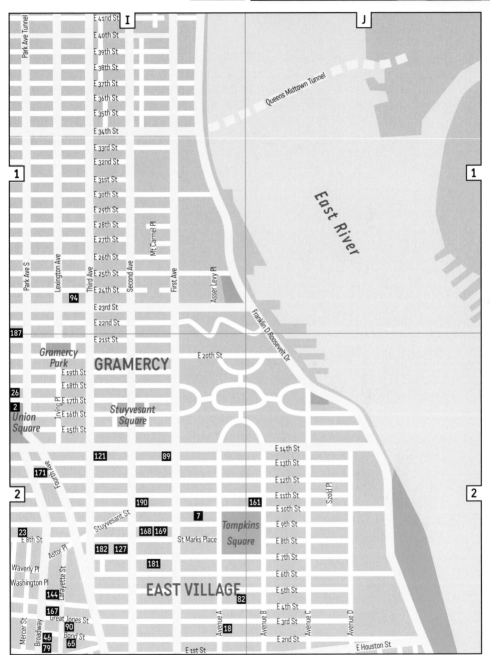

# 3 K|L
## SHOP

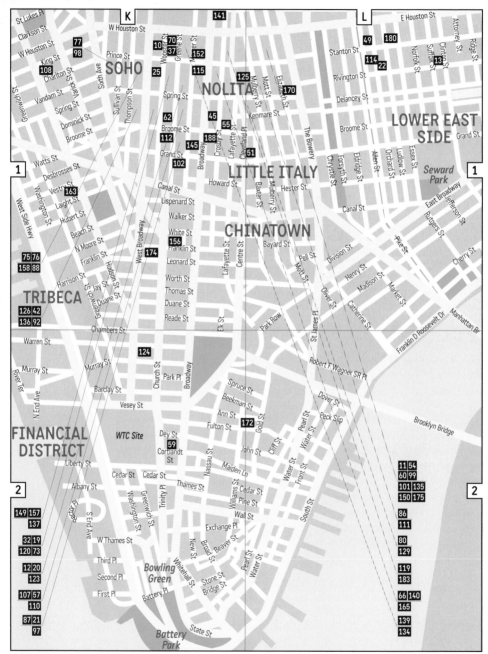

# PLAY

# 4

It's an exciting time for nightlife in New York with several distinctive, competing entertainment trends: an abundance of speakeasy-like places with discreet entrances and serious cocktail lists; super-extravagant ultralounges offering expensive bottle service; velvet rope places in which the season's latest shoes are required to get in the door; and rooftop lounges with terrific views. And if that's not enough, Pimm's Cups have made a comeback and big dance clubs have too. From Harlem to the Meatpacking District, whatever thin line there was between nightclub, lounge and restaurant has dissolved, with the former offering full dinner menus and many restaurants devolving into door goon-fronted style scenes.

# Best Bars To...

### Bring A Date
Angel's Share
Barrio Chino
Chibitini
Cibar
Royalton Lounge & Round Bar
Russian Vodka Room
Single Room Occupancy
Stanton Social, The

### Channel Old New York
Campbell Apartment, The
Chumley's
Lenox Lounge
McSorley's Old Ale House
Monkey Bar
Old Town Bar
White Horse Tavern

### Colonize A Couch
Bungalow 8
Church Lounge
Duvet
Happy Ending
Movida
Odea
PM

### Dance All Night
Aer
Cain
Cielo
Crobar

### Eat, Drink & Be Very
Bar 89
Calle Ocho
Hiro
Level V
Pravda
Stone Rose Lounge
Suba
Temple Bar

### Enjoy The View
Ava Lounge
Delancey, The
Luna Park
Metropolitan Museum Roof Garden
Rare View

### Find Mr. Right-now
APT
G
Latitude
Son Cubano
Starlight Lounge
Uncle Ming's
XL

### Obsess About Cocktails
East Side Company Bar
Employees Only
Flatiron Lounge
Milk and Honey

### Order Beers & Shots
Dark Room
Hogs & Heifers
Sakagura
Trailer Park
Whiskey Ward

### Pretend You're An A&R Executive
Arlene's Grocery
Living Room
Nuyorican Poets Cafe
Pianos
Rififi
Rothko

### Spot Celebrities
40/40
Cabanas, The
Marquee
MO Bar & Lobby Lounge

# 4 | A—Z PLAY

## 40/40

**6 West 25th St (at Broadway), Flatiron District**

☎ 212.832.4040 🌐 the4040club.com     **MAP H1 #1**

Hip hop meets basketball meets ultralounge at Jay-Zs upscale DJ-driven sports bar in which bona fide celebrities and plenty of very good looking fans of Jay and Beyoncé pull out the platinum for Absolut Vanilla cocktails, fried chicken wings and flat-panel TVs projecting the latest game. And it's the only sports bar we know in which sneakers and baseball caps are banned.

## AER

**409 West 13th St (at Ninth), Meatpacking District**

☎ 212.989.0100 🌐 aerlounge.com     **MAP G2 #2**

A huge dance club with lots of chillout space and a good restaurant to boot, Aer is a great place to have fun without too much snobbery. It's ultramodern and perfectly lit, the sound system is excellent and there are plenty of seductive places to dance. The bottle service and VIP areas are not places for the faint of wallet. Like other velvet rope joints, clubocenti know call ahead, tell them who you are and get on the list.

## ANGEL'S SHARE

**2nd Fl., 8 Stuyvesant St (at Third), East Village**

☎ 212.777.5415 🌐 No website     **MAP I2 #3**

This small upstairs bar takes a bit of finding: Climb the stairs into a sushi restaurant and then go through a door to the left that opens into a pint-size room with a long bar and a handful of tables overlooking the street. It's a hidden gem with a great vibe and serious Japanese bartenders mixing good cocktails with scientific precision. Note the rules: no standing, no shouting and no groups larger than four.

## APT

**419 West 13th St (at Washington), Meatpacking District**

☎ 212.414.4245 🌐 aptwebsite.com     **MAP G2 #4**

Metrosexual bachelor pad is the theme at this homey velvet-rope lounge hidden in what looks like an unmarked apartment building. Downstairs, DJs spin in a wood-paneled environment in which snacks and light meals are served and mixologists at twin bars specialize in Pimm's Cups, complete with a slice of cucumber. Upstairs, where the decor is sexier and more intimate and even includes a bed, often requires reservations.

## ARLENE'S GROCERY

**95 Stanton St (at Ludlow), Lower East Side**

☎ 212.995.1652 🌐 arlenesgrocery.net     **MAP L1 #5**

One of the edgiest live-rock venues in town, Arlene's Grocery is a small post-punk dive in which no-name thrasher bands are served up nightly. It's a good place to hear up-and-comers, along with an occasional came-and-wenter debuting a new project. Few audience members stay an entire night, unless they're "with the band." But there's no cover during the week and it's only a few bucks on weekends.

Cielo

## AVA LOUNGE

**Dream Hotel, 210 West 55th St (at Broadway), Midtown**

☎ 212.956.7020 Ⓦ avaloungenyc.com        MAP D2 #6

On the 14th floor and rooftop deck of the stylish Dream Hotel, everything about Ava is dazzling: the beautiful singles, the outdoor bed, the Midtown views, the insufferable attitude of the employees and even the prices of the drinks. Set with black banquettes and Lucite tables atop sparkling black-and-white floors, it's a swanky place to drink house martinis, and it only improves in warm weather when the party extends to the DJ terrace. There are lots of private parties here, so phone in advance to avoid disappointment.

## BAR 89

**89 Mercer St (at Spring), Soho**

☎ 212.274.0989 Ⓦ No Website        MAP K1 #7

A nightly soiree of corporate card-carrying members of G8, Bar 89 is the place to go in Soho when looking to mingle with what used to be known as the "jet set." That's the bait. The hooks are monster Ketel One martinis that really pack power, and supercool conversation-worthy bathrooms with clear glass toilet stalls that turn opaque when you latch them.

## BARRIO CHINO

**253 Broome St (at Orchard), Lower East Side**

☎ 212.228.6710 Ⓦ barriochinonyc.com        MAP L1 #8

Mexican partying in Chinatown is the eclectic attraction of this supersexy space featuring trendy music, a tapas menu (fish tacos!), fifty fine t'kill'yas and killer jalapeño martinis. It's a comfortable place behind a nondescript entrance, in which resident bartenders really know what they're doing and forty is a crowd.

## BUNGALOW 8

**515 West 27th St (at Tenth), Chelsea**

☎ 212.629.3333 Ⓦ No Website        MAP G1 #9

It certainly helps to grace the cover of the New York Times Magazine because ever since owner Amy Sacco appeared there several years ago, her club has been suffereing from hipatitis: white-hot with boroughbreds and bunga-hos who like to rub shoulders (and other body parts) with similarly pedigreed others. Champagne cocktails are the drinks of choice here, along with light snacks. And the party gets going around 2am. Be sure to phone ahead to get on the list.

## CABANAS, THE

**Maritime Hotel, 88 Ninth Ave (at 16th), Chelsea**

☎ 212.835.5537 Ⓦ themaritimehotel.com        MAP G2 #10

There are several excellent bars at the very trendy Maritime Hotel, but these twin rooftop lounges rule the roost in warm weather. Situated atop **La Bottega** and run by Amy Sacco (**Bungalow 8**), the Cabanas is a beach-themed velvet rope place (read: make reservations) with a split personality. North Cabana offers waitress service and reserved seating. South Cabana is more about mingling.

*Boom Boom Room*

# 4 | A—Z PLAY

## CAIN

544 West 27th St (at Tenth), Chelsea

☎ 212.947.8000 🌐 cainnyc.com     MAP G1 #11

Colonial Africa is the theme at this intimate (capacity 400) dance club/safari lounge created by Jamie Mulholland, the former bar manager of Lotus and PM. Dressed with faux zebra skins and a DJ booth carved from a giant boulder, it's one of the best, and best-looking, spaces of its kind. Seats are reserved for bottle service and the door goons can be exasperating, but if this is your scene than Cain is a must-see.

## CALLE OCHO

446 Columbus Ave (at 81st), Upper West Side

☎ 212.873.5025 🌐 calleochonyc.com     MAP A2 #12

Although it's primarily a Nuevo Latino restaurant, we like to visit the beautiful and energetic lounge area in front to enjoy excellent snacks (lobster empanadas!) and specialty mojitos (watermelon!), either with or without a date. As close as you can get to Miami in Manhattan, Calle Ocho enchants with tropical colors, high curving ceilings and professional meringue dancers who encourage everyone to get up and swivel their hips.

## CAMPBELL APARTMENT, THE

Grand Central Terminal, 15 Vanderbilt Ave (at 43rd), Midtown

☎ 212.953.0409 🌐 hospitalityholdings.com     MAP E2 #13

Secreted in a small room just above the main floor of Grand Central, The Campbell Apartment is a polished, sophisticated and transporting place for a well-made drink. Set with club chairs and tapestry-upholstered sofas under tall painted ceilings and heavy chandeliers, it packs-in the after work crowd, then mellows into one of the finest places in the neighborhood. And because of a loophole in the anti-smoking law, this is one of the few bars in the city in which you're allowed to light up. No jeans or sneakers.

## CHIBITINI

63 Clinton St (at Rivington), Lower East Side

☎ 212.674.7300 🌐 chibitini.com     MAP L1 #14

## CHIBI'S SAKE BAR

238 Mott St (at Prince), Nolita

☎ 212.274.0054 🌐 chibisbar.com     MAP L1 #15

These tiny, twin, low-key sake bars are united by wonderful cocktails and amiable service in romantic, beautifully lit surroundings. Some two dozen hot and cold sakes (also available as flights) are served along with tasty snacks. Arrive early to secure a table, and don't forget to bring a date.

## CHUMLEY'S

86 Bedford St (at Barrow), Greenwich Village

☎ 212.675.4449 🌐 No Website     MAP H2 #16

Walk under an unmarked brick portal on Bedford Street and through a small courtyard to an unmarked door that is lit at night. The concealed entrance hasn't changed since this was a speakeasy during Prohibition and to this day kegs of beer still come up from the cellar via trick floorboards. These days, Chumley's attracts college-aged slackademics who carve their names in the tables and the vibe is bookish and bohemian.

## CHURCH LOUNGE

Tribeca Grand Hotel, 2 Sixth Ave (at White), Tribeca

☎ 212.519.6664 🖥 tribecagrand.com     🗺 K1 #17

Beneath a towering eight-story atrium, the dramatic lobby lounge of the stylish Tribeca Grand is the sceney setting for a laid-back parade of beautiful people; some from out of town, some from the neighborhood, and many of whom are working as servers. Cool electric "candles" impart a sexy glow over the luxurious banquettes and aerodynamic bar. In warm weather, tables spill onto the sidewalk.

## CIBAR

Inn at Irving Place, 56 Irving Pl (at 17th), Gramercy

☎ 212.460.5656 🖥 cibarlounge.com     🗺 I2 #18

Set in a stately townhouse hotel on one of the city's prettiest tree-lined blocks, Cibar is the ultimate date lounge. The interior is warm and sexy, designed with ceiling fans, swoony lighting, love seats in front of a fireplace that's perfect for snogging. And there's a wonderful bamboo garden out back. A raft of single malts plus a long selection of drinks ending in "ini" play perfectly to both sexes. Avoid weekends, when it can be a Bridge and Tunnel traffic jam.

## CIELO

18 Little West 12th St (at Ninth), Meatpacking District

☎ 212.645.5700 🖥 cieloclub.com     🗺 G2 #19

A wonderful little microclub in the heart of the Meatpacking District, Cielo can be a terrifically fun place to dance, provided, of course, that you can get past the velvet ropes. Music-loving people really take to the central dance floor here because the sound is great and the DJs are world class, due to the influence of the club's owner, Nicolas Matar, the former resident DJ at Ibiza's Pacha. As always, it's important to phone ahead and let them know you're coming.

## CROBAR

530 West 28th St (at Tenth), Chelsea

☎ 212.629.9000 🖥 crobar.com     🗺 G1 #20

If you're looking to dance in a New York City megaclub, then Crobar is your place. It's a HUGE hangar-like space, packed with all the sweaty colors of Benetton dancing to big DJs like

Sasha, Sander Kleinenberg and Paul van Dyk. And with more nooks and crannies than an English muffin, there are plenty of little alcoves to explore. Expect to pay $10 and more for a poorly made drink and party until 5am.

## DARK ROOM

165 Ludlow St (at Stanton), Lower East Side

☎ 212.353.0536 🖥 No Website     🗺 L1 #21

Situated right in the middle of bar-studded Ludlow Street, Dark Room is actually a pair of boisterous basement bars known for its great modern-rock jukebox and pop-DJs, along with a late-night crowd and well-made, well-priced drinks. They've got a decent tap beer selection too. It's a cozy place with comfortable pleather banquette seating and, as the name would have it, sensuous low lighting. Weekends here are for amateurs.

## DELANCEY, THE

168 Delancey St (at Clinton), Lower East Side

☎ 212.254.9920 🖥 thedelancey.com     🗺 L1 #22

The tri-level Delancey is as laidback and trendy as its Lower East Side digs at the foot of the Williamsburg Bridge. A straightforward DJ bar/lounge is sandwiched between a live-music performance space in the cellar and a happening, island-theme roof deck, both of which usually have a cover on weekends. It's best early in the night, starting at 5pm.

## DUVET

45 West 21st St (at Fifth), Flatiron District

☎ 212.989.2121 🖥 duvetny.com     🗺 H2 #23

Like **BED New York**, it's another mattress-equipped dining room (yawn), but Duvet gets high marks for its very happening bar scene. Built with a faux ice bar, dynamic colored lighting and an aquarium full of jellyfish, it's a cool and contemporary place to ogle cleavage-wielding bottle-blonds and sip expensive cocktails. The gauze-curtained dining beds upstairs are reserved for diners and bottle service. Bring arm candy and beware: weekends are strictly Bridge and Tunnel.

## EAST SIDE COMPANY BAR

49 Essex St (at Grand), Lower East Side

☎ 212.614.7408 🖥 No Website     🗺 L1 #24

Über mixologist Sasha Petraske (**Milk and Honey**) has another hit on his hands with this egalitarian DJ lounge that stresses function over form. Powerfully made and perfectly poured, the drink's the thing in this compact rectangle storefront that's

*Duvet*

literally on the straight and narrow. Cross your fingers for one of the few wooden tables, or satisfy yourself with standing at the never-too-crowded bar.

## EMPLOYEES ONLY

510 Hudson St (at Christopher), Greenwich Village

☎ 212.242.3021 🌐 employeesonlynyc.com     🗺 H2 #25

EO harks back to speakeasy days with a small "Employees Only" sign on the door, a tarot card reader in the window, and a knack for creating some of the finest specialty cocktails anywhere. And the staff is great. Bartenders in chef's jackets lord over a spacious and enchanting art-deco style drinking room, built with mahogany walls, mood lighting and a dreamy fireplace. Food, which is served in a dining room and back garden, can be quite good, but somehow feels like an afterthought.

## FLATIRON LOUNGE

37 West 19th St (at Fifth), Flatiron District

☎ 212.727.7741 🌐 flatironlounge.com     🗺 H2 #26

Bartender/owner Julie Reiner's red leatherette and mirrored Flatiron Lounge is a class act; straight out of the heydays of cocktailing. The crowd can be hit-or-miss, but the swing-era atmosphere is perfect for dates, or friends who actually want

to talk. Gin is the poison of choice here, along with drinks crafted with perfectly muddled fruit. They even have "flights," in which you can sample a trio of similarly-themed creations. Don't even think of ordering a sugary cosmopolitan.

## G

225 West 19th St (at Seventh), Chelsea

☎ 212.929.1085 🌐 glounge.com     🗺 H2 #27

One of the few boy bars in the city completely devoid of any apparent element of sleaze, G is a thoroughly upscale and sophisticated hangout for the most stylish members of the rainbow flag coalition. There's nowhere really to sit except for a handful of chairs upfront, so people mingle around the circular bar. Expect a democratically mixed crowd after work and an avalanche of good-looking guys on weekends. It's a fashionable place, right down to the shirtless barhunks, frozen cosmopolitans and unisex bathrooms.

## HAPPY ENDING

302 Broome St (at Forsyth), Lower East Side

☎ 212.334.9676 🌐 happyendinglounge.com     🗺 L1 #28

The back-story is that this hard-working two-story party space was once an Asian "massage parlor" (omygod). Now it's a pink-lit bordello-themed club/lounge for DJ dancing and

*Flatiron Lounge*

heavy lounging. We like it for its Chinese signage, lively good vibe and copious alcove seating.

## HIRO

**Maritime Hotel, 363 West 16th St (at Ninth), Chelsea**

**☎ 212.242.4300 ⓦ themaritimehotel.com**　　　　**MAP G2 #29**

The white hot Maritime Hotel is the setting for this serious scenester lounge for rich reallyares (as opposed to wannabes). Once past the sometimes-serious door scene you'll find a spectacular, Japanese themed late-night lounge and dance club with eclectic music, wonderful drinks, überbunny waitresses and a cocktail made with amaretto and a trio of sakes that tastes like almond biscotti. While the best seats are reserved for bottle service, there are plenty of other sexy places for lounging.

## HOGS & HEIFERS

**859 Washington St (at 13th), Meatpacking District**

**☎ 212.929.0655 ⓦ hogsandheifers.com**　　　　**MAP G2 #30**

Equal parts Coyote Ugly and Easy Rider, Hogs & Heifers is a redneck chic Harley bar for keg bellied bikers that rates high on our Pig-O-Meter. Despite its distinctly Southern tone (Confederate flag, country-western music), H&H attracts a crazy mix, a fact that garnishes a lot of press when Julia Roberts, Harrison Ford or some other apparent incongruity walks through the door. Fridays and Saturdays bring hopping hoe-downs, complete with bar-top boogying.

## LATITUDE

**783 Eighth Ave (at 48th), Midtown**

**☎ 212.245.3034 ⓦ latitudebarnyc.com**　　　　**MAP D2 #31**

Hell's Kitchen, the neighborhood on Midtown's far west side is coming into its own with a new influx of bars and clubs playing to twenty- and thirty-somethings. With twenty giant flatscreens, six bars, a trio of lounges, a pair of rooftop terraces and a billiards room, Latitude is a multi-level nightlife theme park with something for everyone, from frat boys to home boys. And it has a reputation as a pickup scene for people looking to hit a speed hump. The bar opens early in the day, then becomes an after work hotspot and serves palatable pub food until midnight.

## LENOX LOUNGE

**288 Lenox Ave (at 124th), Harlem**

**☎ 212.427.0253 ⓦ lenoxlounge.com**　　　　**MAP A1 #32**

Lenox Lounge is a beautiful and legendary art deco dive bar (Billie Holiday and Miles Davis were regulars) offering a regular

MO Bar & Lobby Lounge

schedule of live local music in the rear Zebra Room. Despite its fame, the lounge has remained true to its neighborhood roots and remains a true Harlem experience.

## LEVEL V

**675 Hudson St (at 13th), Meatpacking District**

☎ 212.699.2410 🖥 brguestrestaurants.com          🗺 G2 #33

The lounge beneath Steve Hanson's **Vento** restaurant might not have a sign, but plenty of hipsters know how to find this cavernous space. Built with exclusive niches that were once horse stables, the lounge plays to platinum-packing creative types with a neon-lit bar, decent DJs and red lighting that makes all the beautiful people that much prettier. Like so many places these days, there are velvet ropes and a VIP section for bottle-service types, but entry is not draconian, plenty of other seating is available and the bar makes good mixed drinks. It's best from Tuesday to Thursday.

## LIVING ROOM

**154 Ludlow St (at Stanton), Lower East Side**

☎ 212.533.7235 🖥 livingroomny.com          🗺 L1 #34

Although it looks more like a finished basement than a living room, this snug space for live music gives a stage to singer-songwriters

almost every night of the week. This being New York, talent is often excellent, the sound is great and the audience is from all over the map. There's hardly ever a cover, but a jar comes around.

## LUNA PARK

**in Union Square Park (at 17th), Union Square**

☎ 212.475.8464 🖥 No website          🗺 I2 #35

From May through early-September this open-air bar and restaurant at the north end of Union Square Park bustles with junior bond traders quaffing draft beers and cocktails. Warm nights draw big crowds and pushing your way to the bar can be trying. But wiling away a beautiful day with a drink in the park is just this side of paradise.

## MARQUEE

**289 Tenth Ave (at 27th), Chelsea**

☎ 646.473.0202 🖥 marqueeny.com          🗺 G1 #36

Marquee is a beautifully dramatic club/lounge designed by architectural firm of Philip Johnson and Alan Ritchie. It's a huge hit with boldface names and beautiful people, many of whom head straight for the upstairs VIP rooms. There is usually plenty of dancing and atmosphere during the week too. If you're on the list, this is definitely one to check out.

Movida

## McSorley's Old Ale House

15 East 7th St (at Third), East Village

☎ 212.254.2570 Ⓦ No Website      MAP I2 #37

Opened in 1854, McSorley's is the second-oldest pub in New York (after Fraunces Tavern, 54 Pearl St). It's a hip-resistant institution with sawdust on the floor, a century of history on the walls and urinals that should be landmarked. Women weren't allowed in until the 1970s, and then only by court order. Only two kinds of beer are served—house-brand light and dark—in glasses so small you must order them in pairs. The crowd oscillates between frat-oriented biftads and alcohol-soaked Jerseyites who line-up around the block on weekends.

## Metropolitan Museum Roof Garden

1000 Fifth Ave (at 81st), Upper East Side

☎ 212.879.5500 Ⓦ metmuseum.org      MAP B2 #38

It's only open from May to October, and then only in dry weather, but when it is open, day or night, the Met's open-air balcony overlooking a slice of Central Park is one of the finest bars in the city. The sculpture-filled space is wonderful, the crowd is delicious and the vibe is pure New York. Go at sunset and the view will make you swoon.

## Milk and Honey

134 Eldridge St (at Broome), Lower East Side

Phone unlisted Ⓦ mlkhny.com      MAP L1 #39

Ring the bell of this unmarked door and you're buzzed into a hushed railroad car of a room with just a handful of wooden booths and one of the most serious cocktail bars in town. The drinks are the stars here; so much so that owner/mixologist Sasha Petraske (**East Side Company Bar**) claims not to carry cranberry juice so as not to have to make dreaded cosmopolitans. You're supposed to have a reservation but the wonderful gimmick here is that the phone number is unlisted, and they change it frequently.

## MO Bar & Lobby Lounge

Mandarin Oriental Hotel, 35th Fl., 80 Columbus Circle (at 60th), Upper West Side

☎ 212.805.8800 Ⓦ mandarinoriental.com      MAP D2 #40

The Central Park and Broadway view is the thing at this seriously chi-chi bar in Time Warner Center, on the lobby level of one of the finest hotels in Manhattan. There are two adjacent, equally wonderful rooms: the Lobby Lounge, an open space set with club chairs, and MO Bar, a more intimate and dimly lit space that's abuzz with wannabes, used-to-bes and really-ares. Both are comfortable, stunning and reassuringly expensive.

## Monkey Bar

Hotel Elysée, 60 East 54th St (at Madison), Midtown

☎ 212.838.2600 🌐 theglaziergroup.com    MAP E2 #41

Once a favorite watering hole of the rich and famous like Humphrey Bogart and Tennessee Williams, this revered hotel bar remains gloriously anchored in its Golden Age with trademark frolicking-monkey decor and olive-shaped barstools. Today's crowd is young, creative and ambitious and includes a lot of suspender-wearing hepcats from the publishing industry.

## Movida

28 Seventh Ave S (at Leroy), Greenwich Village

☎ 212.206.9600 🌐 movidanyc.com    MAP H2 #42

Imagine a futuristic and fashionable bi-level yacht, complete with deep purple banquettes, great music and psychedelic sunsets projected onto faux portholes. This DJ-owned dance club and lounge is a swanky place to dance and imbibe raspberry mojitos in a fun, pretension-free environment.

## Nuyorican Poets Cafe

236 East 3rd St (at Ave C), East Village

☎ 212.505.8183 🌐 nuyorican.org    MAP J2 #43

This home of the goatee is the contemporary poets' capital of the spoken word, known for edgy new talent, vocal audiences and high-energy poetry slams. Nobody reads here; everyone performs. It's best on Fridays, when the stage opens to all who wish to wax beat-poetish. Admission is free to $10.

## Odea

389 Broome St (at Mulberry), Little Italy

☎ 212.941.9222 🌐 odeany.com    MAP L1 #44

Odea is a sleek and chic bar-meets-lounge with avant architecture, sexy lighting, powerful watermelon martinis and upscale Italian finger foods like fried olives and crisp baby squid. A stylish oasis in otherwise untrendy Little Italy, the space is best for dates and singles up front, and small groups who can colonize the semi-private, candlelit party pods set with comfy couches.

## Old Town Bar

45 East 18th St (at Broadway), Flatiron District

☎ 212.529.6732 🌐 No website    MAP I2 #45

Old Town Bar is something of a pristine old-man's bar: a great neighborhood saloon with an authentically retro turn-of-the-century atmosphere. A long oak bar backed by an equally lengthy mirror sits opposite tight, private wooden booths where local PR and publishing workers drink beers and shots and tuck into burgers, sandwiches and fried calamari.

## Pianos

158 Ludlow St (at Stanton), Lower East Side

☎ 212.505.3733 🌐 pianosnyc.com    MAP L1 #46

An old piano shop is the setting for this highly polished live-music and DJ bar. The design is great, the sound is less so, and the black-jeaned clientele looks ready to rock. It's a stylish place for gourmet beers, cocktails in Y-shaped glasses and indie bands in the back room. Add this one to your crawl.

## PM

50 Gansevoort St (at Greenwich), Meatpacking District

☎ 212.255.6676 🌐 pmloungenyc.com    MAP G2 #47

Depending on your perspective, PM is either a snobby insult to humanity with brutal door goons, or an amazing tropical-theme DJ lounge with a wonderfully selective admittance policy that favors well-dressed hotties and friends of the Haitian owners. Despite "No Dancing" signs posted to comply with a silly Giuliani-era law, there is plenty of boogying going on, even on the tables and tufted leather settees where standard-issue sexpot waitresses deliver bottle service. Get on the list, plan on cashing in a long-bond to pay for it all and party until morning.

## Pravda

281 Lafayette St (at Prince), Nolita

☎ 212.226.4944 🌐 pravdany.com    MAP K1 #48

Once white hot (when it first opened, of course), Pravda has long since cooled and become better in the process. The lounge is a pseudo-satirical ode to the most enduring Soviet stereotypes, namely, Lenin, caviar and vodka, the latter of which is available in a variety of infusions and served from an icy bar. Opened by Keith McNally (**Balthazar, Lucky Strike, Pastis, Schiller's Liquor Bar),** it's a super comfortable, speakeasy-ish place with arched ceilings, leather club chairs and a second intimate bar upstairs.

## Rare View

Shelburne Murray Hill, 303 Lexington Ave (at 37th), Midtown

☎ 212.481.1999 🌐 rarebarandgrill.com    MAP I1 #49

Rooftop bars are all the rage in New York, though good weather helps if you want to enjoy them. Rare View, the 16th-floor bar above the Shelburne's Rare Bar & Grill, is an outstanding perch from which to imbibe mango margaritas while enjoying wonderful Midtown views of the Chrysler and

Royalton Lounge & Round Bar

Empire State buildings. It's popular with young trendies who live in the neighborhood and closes by midnight.

## RIFIFI

332 East 11th St (at Second), East Village

☎ 212.677.1027 ☒ rififinyc.com ⬛ I2 #50

When you're looking for some fun, offbeat entertainment with your budget cocktail, Rififi delivers with a full schedule of live performances that ranges from comedy and burlesque to indie-rock. Situated in the back room of a video store, set with foundling sofas and populated with mop-headed hipsters with novelty facial hair, this is a true New York experience.

## ROTHKO

116 Suffolk St (at Rivington), Lower East Side

☎ 212.475.7088 ☒ rothkonyc.com ⬛ L1 #51

A&R execs and others looking for the latest in the city's indie rock scene head to this fittingly downscale space with a good stage, a fine sound system and much needed chillout space

downstairs. The crowd is young (at 30, you're a senior citizen), drinks are cheap and bands are often served by the half-dozen.

## ROYALTON LOUNGE & ROUND BAR

Royalton Hotel, 44 West 44th St (at Fifth), Midtown

☎ 212.944.8844 ☒ royaltonhotel.com ⬛ E2 #52

Walk into the Royalton's playroom lobby, survey the noisy young scene (as everyone else does), then retreat to the soporific Round Bar, concealed on your right just by the front door. Looking very much like the inside of a genie's bottle, this tiny quilted gem is lined with a padded circular banquette that only seats a dozen. It's one of the happiest rooms in the city.

## RUSSIAN VODKA ROOM

265 West 52nd St (at Broadway), Midtown

☎ 212.307.5835 ☒ No website ⬛ D2 #53

We love this Russian mafia bar because it has more than a whiff of authenticity. It's snug and old fashioned, has a vast stock of vodkas (including lots of lethal home-infused varieties), serves martinis by the carafe and offers a terrific (and well-priced) caviar and blini menu. And, lest we forget, the beautiful straight-out-of Moscow waitresses are terrific.

## SAKAGURA

**211 East 43rd St (at Third), Midtown**

☎ 212.953.7253 ⓦ sakagura.com                    ᴍᴀᴘ E2 #54

Early in the evening, this hard-to-find bar/restaurant in the basement of a nondescript high-rise is jammed like a Tokyo subway car with *biznismen* snacking on *izakaya* (Japanese small plates) and pounding sake, some 200 brands of which are lined up behind the bar. But, rather than being a kitschy theme bar, Sakagura is a true cultural adventure.

## SINGLE ROOM OCCUPANCY

**360 West 53rd St (at Ninth), Midtown**

☎ 212.765.6299 ⓦ No website                    ᴍᴀᴘ D2 #55

Speakeasy chic, as you know, is all the rage in Manhattan and the diminutive SRO plays to type with an inconspicuous entrance, green sconce light, a discreet door buzzer and a hidden charm that is sorely missing in the Midtown neck of the woods. It's a long and narrow candlelit room in which only high-end beer and wine are served, a policy that plays fine with everyone from after work suits to black-clad trendies who would otherwise be drinking on the Lower East Side.

## SON CUBANO

**405 West 14th St (at Ninth), Chelsea**

☎ 212.366.1640 ⓦ soncubanonyc.com                    ᴍᴀᴘ G2 #56

Although it's primarily a restaurant, Son Cubano is best as a boisterous salsa bar, delivering great mojitos, sangria by the pitcher and a seriously sexy atmosphere to a party-loving crowd. As loud as it is unpretentious, the bar features live Latin bands most every night of the week, after which a DJ spins. Skip the bottle service and eat elsewhere.

## STANTON SOCIAL, THE

**99 Stanton St (at Ludlow), Lower East Side**

☎ 212.995.0099 ⓦ thestantonsocial.com                    ᴍᴀᴘ L1 #57

Richard Wolf (**Tao**) and Peter Kane (**Happy Ending**) teamed up to create this beautiful, harbinger of gentrification designed by avroKO (**Odea, Public**). Although it is equal parts restaurant and lounge, you'd do well to skip the ground floor dining room and head straight up to the candlelit bar, where you can enjoy the same small plates while relaxing on comfortable leather banquettes. It's perfect for dates.

## STARLIGHT LOUNGE

**167 Ave A (at 11th), East Village**

☎ 212.475.2172 ⓦ starlightbarlounge.com                    ᴍᴀᴘ I2 #58

The Starlight is the East Village's most attractive gay bar. Elevated banquettes and bar tables line the front room, in which young creative directors and ambisexterous others canoodle by the bar. It's separated by a velvet curtain from the rear performance space which gives its tiny stage to an eclectic variety of everybody from monologists and drag artists to DJs. Sundays feature one of the best girl parties in the city.

## STONE ROSE LOUNGE

**Time Warner Ctr., 10 Columbus Circle, 4th fl (at 60th), Upper West Side**

☎ 212.823.9769 ⓦ mocbars.com                    ᴍᴀᴘ D2 #59

Even people who avoid Rande Gerber's other nightspots (many of which are ensconced in W Hotels) flock to this uncommonly large and amazing space in which the spectacular views of Central Park and Columbus Circle are almost as stunning as the modelicious staff. You've probably never seen so many alpha earning "alcooliques" (rich corporate types drinking $20 cocktails from the top shelf). And eat too, because light meals are delivered by Jean-George Vongerichten's "V" Steakhouse, next door. If you want a table, reservations are a must.

## SUBA

**109 Ludlow St (at Delancey), Lower East Side**

☎ 212.982.5714 ⓦ subanyc.com                    ᴍᴀᴘ L1 #60

It's definitely worth venturing underground to check out the supercool grottoesque dining rooms, but we prefer to keep our feet on the ground floor, where great drinks and flamenco dancing heat up the design-heavy bar. Underlit and overcrowded on weekends, it's a very sexy and sceney place in which to sip sangria and cocktails, and maybe even enjoy a few plates of well-made Spanish tapas. Suba has "date" written all over it.

## TEMPLE BAR

**332 Lafayette St (at Bleecker), East Village**

☎ 212.925.4242 ⓦ templebarnyc.com                    ᴍᴀᴘ K1 #61

We love this beautifully designed space with a discreet entrance, low lighting and seductive angles that exude swanky intimacy. Chef-like bartenders concoct generous $15 Tanqueray martinis for platinum-card carrying artists, models and Uptown interlopers. Bar snacks include smoked salmon, oysters and beluga caviar.

*The Stanton Social*

## TRAILER PARK

**271 West 23rd St (at Eighth), Chelsea**

☎ 212.463.8000 🌐 No website     MAP H1 #62

White-trash meets hipster heaven at this redneck-chic theme bar in which Pabst Blue Ribbon is on tap, velvet blacklight "art" is on the walls and DJs spin chill-out tunes. It's a thoroughly tacky theme bar that winks at itself and works with tongue firmly in cheek.

## UNCLE MING'S

**225 Ave B, 2nd Fl (at 13th), East Village**

☎ 212.979.8506 🌐 unclemings.com     MAP J2 #63

Uncle Ming's started life as an illegal after-hours bar. Now gone legit, this second floor hideaway up an unmarked flight of stairs remains a good, if stark, place for neighborhood twentysomethings drawn by cheap drinks, Chippendalesque bartenders and, of course, the mystique. There's usually a DJ on weekends, but forget dancing because there's hardly any room to turn around.

## WHISKEY WARD

**121 Essex St (at Rivington), Lower East Side**

☎ 212.477.2998 🌐 No website     MAP L1 #64

Everyone on a Lower East Side crawl, it seems, ends up at Whiskey Ward sometime during the night. It's a fun and friendly jukebox/DJ bar with a pool table, a half-dozen beers on tap and a limited selection of good whiskeys at neighborhood-appropriate prices. We like the very social vibe that makes this a good destination to meet old friends and new.

## WHITE HORSE TAVERN

**567 Hudson St (at 11th), Greenwich Village**

☎ 212.989.3956 🌐 No website     MAP H2 #65

Open since 1880, this woody West Village pub is a bona fide landmark with a striking old New York interior and a terrific collegy, neighborhood vibe. The tavern's dubious claim to fame is that writer Dylan Thomas drank himself to death here. In summer, picnic tables pack-out the sidewalk and you can raise your pint to passers-by.

## XL

**357 West 16th St (at Ninth), Chelsea**

☎ 646.336.5574 🌐 xlnewyork.com     MAP G2 #66

There are, of course, lots of gay lounges in Chelsea, but XL gets our nod for avant design and a terrific heteroflexible crowd that can be counted on almost every night of the week. Taking its inspiration from both Miami and Las Vegas, this almost-club features an enormous aquarium in the unisex bathroom and a spectacular Trompe L'Oeil ceiling that changes moods as the evening progresses. It's best early and on weeknights when it is marginally less crowded.

# MICHAEL STIPE

*Both an enigmatic cult hero and mainstream pop icon, REM frontman Michael Stipe is one of the greatest artists of our time. In addition to a raft of smash hit records, Stipe has published a photo collection, and heads the feature film production company that yielded the acclaimed Being John Malkovich and American Movie. A military brat childhood and relentless touring as a band means Stipe is also an inveterate traveler who spends an inordinate amount of time in New York City.*

**Avant-Guide:** Which cities in the world do you think are the most avant?

**Michael Stipe:** NYC, Tokyo, Marrakech, Copenhagen. Add anywhere where its summer right now and you've got an itinerary... Talinn, Capetown, Perth with the parakeets, Berlin with the renovations, Belgrade, Vancouver, Arles during the photo exhibit [mid-summer].

=∧= What aspect of your profession do you most enjoy?

**MS** The travel. And meeting other artists, swapping ideas, listening. Figuring out what other people are doing and what motivates them to do so.

=∧= What five non-essential items do you never travel without?

**MS** I honestly don't travel with anything that is not essential. Maybe 4 magazines — 2 smart and 2 crap — and some flip flops in winter. That's non-essential but good fun, and you never know.

=∧= Describe your perfect hotel room of the future. What kind of architecture, furniture, facilities and services would you like it to have?

**MS** The windows open. The steam room works and smells good. A good coffee and a boiled egg doesn't cost $24. The bed is hard, the shower hot. The sheets are really good cotton and the pillows don't smell like someone else's bad cologne. No more beige, I'm so sick of the idea that beige is a neutral color. (It's not neutral, its sallow. I blame Coco Chanel for that, it was her idea. Beige carpet is particularly distasteful). Wireless internet is free. Dogs are allowed. Breakfast is served around the clock. The furniture is functional, smart, and not trendy. The TV is not the center of the room and the book in the bedside table is Beckett. No more glass-top low tables to trip over. And finally, the couch is not a backbreaker. Give me Tokyo-meets-Andre Balazs somewhere in the Marrakech Medina with a redeye to Copenhagen and I am happy.

=∧= Where is your favorite place in New York City to shop?

**MS** Steven Alan for Rogan, Italian toothpaste and pajamas by Cabane de Zucca; Opening Ceremony [35 Howard St] for New York City designers; 8th Street on a Saturday is always a blast for Technicolor shoes, people watching, and blang [cheap bling]; Alife, definitely; Other Music for great hard to find dub and underground CD's and the staff are great and helpful and enthusiastic; Chelsea is fun for galleries — Matthew Marks, Andrea Rosen and Bespoke galleries always have great stuff; Kid Robot in Soho for Japanese *kawaii* [cuteness]; Helmut Lang, APC and Flying A in Soho; Comme des Garcons in Chelsea; Washington Street in the Meat Packing District and Atlantic Avenue in Brooklyn for awesome furniture design.

=∧= What can you get in New York City that you can't get anywhere else?

**MS** 1-800-MATTRESS. The only place in the world that I'm aware of where, 24-hours a day, you can order a new mattress, they will deliver it within hours, pick up your old mattress and cart it away. And they stock organic cotton mattresses and pillows. Brilliant.

| Map | # | Venue | Address | Phone | Apres Work | Lounge | Good Food | Dance Club | DJ Bar | Brewpub/Beer Bar | Quiet Conversation | Gay | Live Music |
|---|---|---|---|---|---|---|---|---|---|---|---|---|---|
| | | **Chelsea** | | | | | | | | | | | |
| G1 | 9 | Bungalow 8 | 515 West 27th St | 212.629.3333 | ★ | | ★ | | | | | | |
| G2 | 10 | Cabanas, The | 88 Ninth Ave | 212.835.5537 | ★ | | ★ | | | | | | |
| G1 | 11 | Cain | 544 West 27th St | 212.947.8000 | ★ | | | ★ | | | | | |
| G1 | 20 | Crobar | 530 West 28th St | 212.629.9000 | | | | ★ | | | | | |
| H2 | 27 | G | 225 West 19th St | 212.929.1085 | ★ | ★ | | | | | | ★ | |
| G2 | 29 | Hiro | 363 West 16th St | 212.242.4300 | ★ | | ★ | | | | | | |
| G1 | 36 | Marquee | 289 Tenth Ave | 646.473.0202 | ★ | | ★ | | | | | | |
| G2 | 56 | Son Cubano | 405 West 14th St | 212.366.1640 | | | ★ | | | | ★ | | ★ |
| H1 | 62 | Trailer Park | 271 West 23rd St | 212.463.8000 | ★ | | | | | ★ | ★ | | |
| G2 | 66 | XL | 357 West 16th St | 646.336.5574 | ★ | | | | | | | ★ | |
| | | **East Village** | | | | | | | | | | | |
| I2 | 3 | Angel's Share | 2nd Fl., 8 Stuyvesant St | 212.777.5415 | | | | | | | ★ | | |
| I2 | 37 | McSorley's Old Ale House | 15 East 7th St | 212.254.2570 | ★ | | | | | | ★ | | |
| J2 | 43 | Nuyorican Poets Cafe | 236 East 3rd St | 212.505.8183 | ★ | | | | | | | | ★ |
| I2 | 50 | Rififi | 332 East 11th St | 212.677.1027 | | | | | | | | | ★ |
| I2 | 58 | Starlight Lounge | 167 Ave A | 212.475.2172 | ★ | | | | | | | ★ | ★ |
| K1 | 61 | Temple Bar | 332 Lafayette St | 212.925.4242 | ★ | ★ | | | | | ★ | | |
| J2 | 63 | Uncle Ming's | 225 Ave B, 2nd Fl | 212.979.8506 | ★ | | | ★ | | | | | |
| | | **Flatiron, Gramercy & Union Square** | | | | | | | | | | | |
| H1 | 1 | 40/40 | 6 West 25th St | 212.832.4040 | ★ | | | ★ | | | | | |
| H2 | 23 | Duvet | 45 West 21st St | 212.989.2121 | ★ | ★ | | | | | ★ | | |
| H2 | 26 | Flatiron Lounge | 37 West 19th St | 212.727.7741 | ★ | ★ | | | | | ★ | | |
| I2 | 45 | Old Town Bar | 45 East 18th St | 212.529.6732 | ★ | | ★ | | | ★ | ★ | | |
| I2 | 18 | Cibar | 56 Irving Pl | 212.460.5656 | ★ | | | | | | ★ | | |
| I2 | 35 | Luna Park | in Union Square Park | 212.475.8464 | ★ | | | | | | | | |
| | | **Greenwich Village** | | | | | | | | | | | |
| H2 | 16 | Chumley's | 86 Bedford St | 212.675.4449 | ★ | | | | | | ★ | | |
| H2 | 25 | Employees Only | 510 Hudson St | 212.242.3021 | ★ | ★ | | | | | ★ | | |
| H2 | 42 | Movida | 28 Seventh Ave S | 212.206.9600 | ★ | | | | ★ | ★ | | | |
| H2 | 65 | White Horse Tavern | 567 Hudson St | 212.989.3956 | | | | | | | ★ | ★ | |
| | | **Harlem** | | | | | | | | | | | |
| A1 | 32 | Lenox Lounge | 288 Lenox Ave | 212.427.0253 | ★ | | | | | | | ★ | ★ |
| | | **Lower East Side** | | | | | | | | | | | |
| L1 | 5 | Arlene's Grocery | 95 Stanton St | 212.995.1652 | | | | | | | | | ★ |
| L1 | 8 | Barrio Chino | 253 Broome St | 212.228.6710 | ★ | ★ | | | | | | | |
| L1 | 14 | Chibitini | 63 Clinton St | 212.674.7300 | | | | | | | ★ | | |
| L1 | 21 | Dark Room | 165 Ludlow St | 212.353.0536 | ★ | | | | ★ | ★ | | | |
| L1 | 22 | Delancey, The | 168 Delancey St | 212.254.9920 | ★ | ★ | | | | ★ | | | ★ |

| Map | # | Venue | Address | Phone | Apres Work | Lounge | Good Food | Dance Club | DJ Bar | Brewpub/Beer Bar | Quiet Conversation | Gay | Live Music |
|---|---|---|---|---|---|---|---|---|---|---|---|---|---|
| | | **Lower East Side** | | | | | | | | | | | |
| L1 | 24 | East Side Company Bar | 49 Essex St | 212.614.7408 | ★ | | ★ | | | | | | |
| L1 | 28 | Happy Ending | 302 Broome St | 212.334.9676 | | ★ | ★ | | | | | | |
| L1 | 34 | Living Room | 154 Ludlow St | 212.533.7235 | | | | | | ★ | | | ★ |
| L1 | 39 | Milk and Honey | 134 Eldridge St | unlisted | | | | | | | | ★ | |
| L1 | 46 | Pianos | 158 Ludlow St | 212.505.3733 | | ★ | | | | ★ | ★ | | ★ |
| L1 | 51 | Rothko | 116 Suffolk St | 212.475.7088 | | | | | | | ★ | | ★ |
| L1 | 57 | Stanton Social, The | 99 Stanton St | 212.995.0099 | ★ | ★ | | | | | ★ | | |
| L1 | 60 | Suba | 109 Ludlow St | 212.982.5714 | | | ★ | ★ | | | | | |
| L1 | 64 | Whiskey Ward | 121 Essex St | 212.477.2998 | | | | | | | ★ | | |
| | | **Meatpacking District** | | | | | | | | | | | |
| G2 | 2 | Aer | 409 West 13th St | 212.989.0100 | | | | ★ | | | | | |
| G2 | 4 | APT | 419 West 13th St | 212.414.4245 | ★ | | | ★ | ★ | | | | |
| G2 | 19 | Cielo | 18 Little West 12th St | 212.645.5700 | | | | ★ | | | | | |
| G2 | 30 | Hogs & Heifers | 859 Washington St | 212.929.0655 | | | | | | ★ | | | |
| G2 | 33 | Level V | 675 Hudson St | 212.699.2410 | ★ | | ★ | | | | | | |
| G2 | 47 | PM | 50 Gansevoort St | 212.255.6676 | ★ | | ★ | ★ | | | | | |
| | | **Midtown** | | | | | | | | | | | |
| D2 | 6 | Ava Lounge | 210 West 55th St | 212.956.7020 | ★ | | ★ | | | | | | |
| E2 | 13 | Campbell Apartment, The | Grand Central Terminal | 212.953.0409 | ★ | ★ | | | | | ★ | | |
| D2 | 31 | Latitude | 783 Eighth Ave | 212.245.3034 | ★ | ★ | | | | ★ | | | |
| E2 | 41 | Monkey Bar | 60 East 54th St | 212.838.2600 | ★ | ★ | | | | | ★ | | |
| I1 | 49 | Rare View | 303 Lexington Ave | 212.481.1999 | ★ | | | | | | ★ | | |
| E2 | 52 | Royalton Round Bar | 44 West 44th St | 212.944.8844 | ★ | ★ | | | | | ★ | | |
| D2 | 53 | Russian Vodka Room | 265 West 52nd St | 212.307.5835 | ★ | ★ | | | | | ★ | | |
| E2 | 54 | Sakagura | 211 East 43rd St | 212.953.7253 | ★ | | ★ | | | | ★ | ★ | |
| D2 | 55 | Single Room Occupancy | 360 West 53rd St | 212.765.6299 | ★ | | | | | | ★ | ★ | |
| | | **Nolita, Little Italy, Soho & Tribeca** | | | | | | | | | | | |
| L1 | 15 | Chibi's Sake Bar | 238 Mott St | 212.274.0054 | | | | | | | ★ | | |
| K1 | 48 | Pravda | 281 Lafayette St | 212.226.4944 | ★ | ★ | | | | | ★ | | |
| L1 | 44 | Odea | 389 Broome St | 212.941.9222 | ★ | ★ | | | | | ★ | | |
| K1 | 7 | Bar 89 | 89 Mercer St | 212.274.0989 | ★ | ★ | | | | | | | |
| K1 | 17 | Church Lounge | 2 Sixth Ave | 212.519.6664 | | ★ | | | | | ★ | | |
| | | **Upper East Side** | | | | | | | | | | | |
| B2 | 38 | MoMA Roof Garden | 1000 Fifth Ave | 212.879.5500 | ★ | | | | | | ★ | | |
| | | **Upper West Side** | | | | | | | | | | | |
| A2 | 12 | Calle Ocho | 446 Columbus Ave | 212.873.5025 | ★ | ★ | | | | | | | ★ |
| D2 | 40 | MO Bar & Lobby Lounge | Time Warner Center | 212.805.8800 | ★ | ★ | | | | | ★ | | |
| D2 | 59 | Stone Rose Lounge | Time Warner Center | 212.823.9769 | ★ | ★ | ★ | | | | ★ | | |

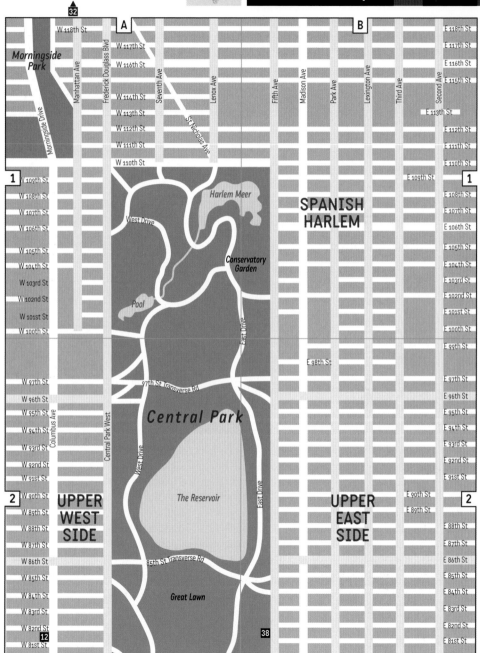

Morningside Park

W 118th St
W 117th St
W 116th St
W 114th St
W 113th St
W 112th St
W 111th St
W 110th St

Manhattan Ave
Frederick Douglass Blvd
Morningside Drive
Seventh Ave
St Nicholas Ave
Lenox Ave
Fifth Ave
Madison Ave
Park Ave
Lexington Ave
Third Ave
Second Ave

E 118th St
E 117th St
E 116th St
E 115th St
E 113th St
E 112th St
E 111th St
E 110th St

**1**

W 109th St
W 108th St
W 107th St
W 106th St
W 105th St
W 104th St
W 103rd St
W 102nd St
W 101st St
W 100th St
W 97th St
W 96th St
W 95th St
W 94th St
W 93rd St
W 92nd St
W 91st St

E 109th St
E 108th St
E 107th St
E 106th St
E 105th St
E 104th St
E 103rd St
E 102nd St
E 101st St
E 100th St
E 99th St
E 98th St
E 97th St
E 96th St
E 95th St
E 94th St
E 93rd St
E 92nd St
E 91st St

**1**

Harlem Meer

West Drive

**SPANISH HARLEM**

Conservatory Garden

Pool

East Drive

97th St Transverse Rd

Columbus Ave

Central Park West

West Drive

**Central Park**

**2**

W 90th St
W 89th St
W 88th St
W 87th St
W 86th St
W 85th St
W 84th St
W 83rd St
W 82nd St
W 81st St

**UPPER WEST SIDE**

The Reservoir

85th St Transverse Rd

Great Lawn

**UPPER EAST SIDE**

E 90th St
E 89th St
E 88th St
E 87th St
E 86th St
E 85th St
E 84th St
E 83rd St
E 82nd St
E 81st St
E 80th St

**2**

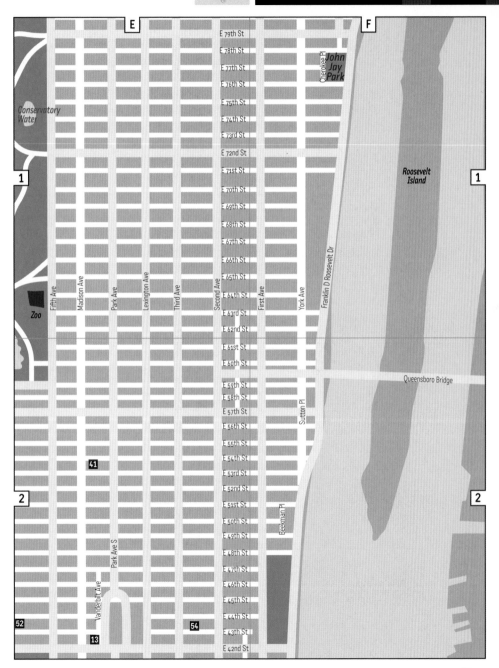

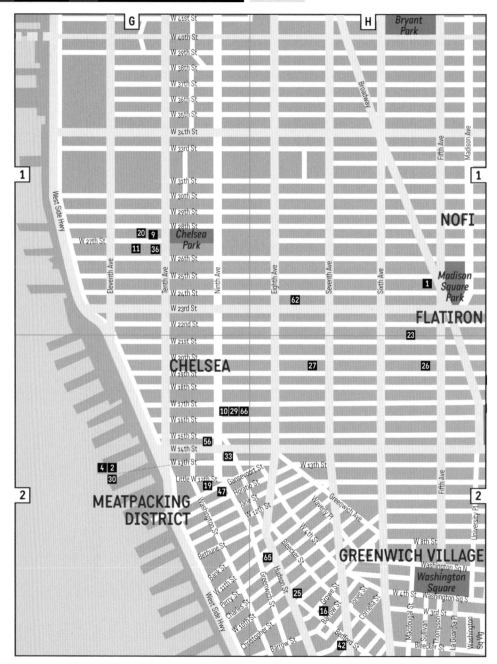

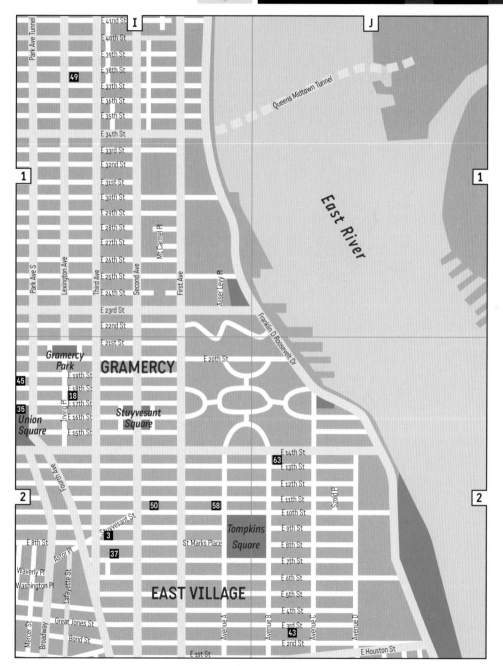

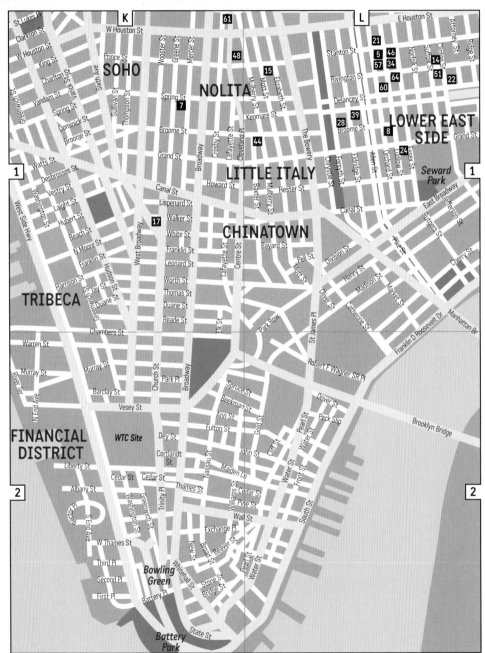

# EXPLORE

# 5

Ever since World War II, when artists and their enlightened benefactors turned New York into the Master of the Art Universe, the city has been one of the museum capitals of the world. And as they grow, the city's galleries keep getting better. There are lots of off-beat things to do around the city as well and don't overlook the museums' gift shops, as they are some of the best and most original stores in town.

# THE BEST OF NEW YORK...

## TOP NEW YORK EXPERIENCES
Brooklyn Bridge, The
Ellis Island Immigration Museum
Staten Island Ferry
Times Square
Yankee Stadium

## TOP MUSEUMS & GALLERIES
Frick Collection, The
Metropolitan Museum of Art
The Museum of Modern Art
Solomon R. Guggenheim Museum
Whitney Museum of American Art

## TOP SPECIAL-INTEREST MUSEUMS
Asia Society and Museum
Cooper-Hewitt National Design Museum
Jewish Museum, The
Museum at Fashion Institute of Technology
Museum of Arts & Design
Museum of the City of New York
Neue Galerie New York
Rubin Museum of Art
The Skyscraper Museum

## TOP OFFBEAT SIGHTS
The Cloisters
Federal Hall National Memorial
Federal Reserve Bank of New York
Lower East Side Tenement Museum
Morgan Library
Museum of Sex
World Trade Center Site

## TOP ARCHITECTURE & VIEWS
Empire State Building
Grand Central Terminal
Rockefeller Center

## TOP CHURCHES & CEMETERIES
Cathedral of St. John the Divine
Grace Church
Saint Patrick's Cathedral
Trinity Church

## TOP GARDENS & PARKS
Battery Park & The Esplanade
Central Park

## TOP PLACES TO TAKE KIDS
American Museum of Natural History
Central Park Zoo
Intrepid Sea-Air-Space Museum
Sony Wonder Technology Lab
South Street Seaport
Statue of Liberty National Monument
The United Nations

## THE BEST TOURS

**BIG ONION WALKING TOURS** | ☎ 212.439.1090 **W** bigonion.com | offers a comprehensive schedule that covers most of Manhattan. Their guides are mostly graduate students in American History from Columbia University. Itineraries run the gamut from an ethnic eating tour of the Lower East Side to a Gay and Lesbian History Tour.

**CIRCLE LINE** | ☎ 212.563.3200 **W** circleline42.com | is a classic New York sightseeing experience that sails all the way around Manhattan island in about three hours. Shorter excursions are also available. The company's eight uncomfortable boats are converted World War II Navy landing vessels. Tours depart Pier 83, at West 42nd Street on the Hudson River.

**HIP-HOP LOOK AT NEW YORK** | ☎ 212.714.3527 **W** hushtours.com | takes a musical and cultural look across three decades starting from the genre's local underground roots.

**LIBERTY HELICOPTER TOURS** | ☎ 212.967.6464 **W** libertyhelicopters.com | buzz around the city and the Statue of Liberty in late-model choppers. It departs from the heliport at Twelfth Ave and West 30th Street.

**THE MUNICIPAL ART SOCIETY** | ☎ 212.935.3960 **W** mas.org | runs walking tours which stress excellence in urban design and planning, and the preservation of the best of the city's past.

**NEW YORK GALLERY TOURS** | ☎ 212.946.1548 **W** nygallerytours.com | focus on some of the best art galleries in Manhattan. It meets only One Saturday per month at 526 West 26th Street.

**NOSHWALKS** | ☎ 212.222.2243 **W** noshwalks.com | offers international food tasting tours of restaurants, bakeries and food stores all around New York.

**WATSON ADVENTURES SCAVENGER HUNTS** | ☎ 212.726.1529 **W** watsonadventures.com | is a great way for families to have fun in the city. How quickly can you make it back with everything on the list?

*American Museum of Natural History*

## AMERICAN MUSEUM OF NATURAL HISTORY

Central Park West (at 79th), Upper West Side

☎ 212.769.5100 🖥 amnh.org　　　　　　　　MAP D1 #1

Of the 30 million or so artifacts that are stashed in this museum, we gravitate to the enormous collection of spiders, the rich gems and minerals department and the Biodiversity Wing, which explores the interconnectedness of nature. We also like to look at the stunning sphere-within-a-cube architecture of the Rose Center for Earth and Space that has become a global icon. Inside is a technologically advanced space show that's for astrophiles only. For kids, no matter how big this museum grows, dinosaurs will forever remain the star attractions. One of the world's largest collections of dinosaur bones is augmented by ginormous animatronic models, constructed in part with money donated by Jurassic Park director Steven Spielberg. It's best during the week, after 3pm, when school groups are not clogging the buildings' arteries. Guided tours depart from the African Mammals Hall throughout the day. Phone for times.

## ASIA SOCIETY AND MUSEUM

725 Park Ave (at 70th), Upper East Side

☎ 212.288.6400 🖥 asiasociety.org | CLOSED MON　　MAP E1 #2

Pakistani devotional music, Tibetan sand mandalas, the shooting death of a Japanese exchange student—no cultural subject is out of bounds for this wonderful small museum and cultural center that began as a pet project of John D. Rockefeller III. Frequently changing exhibitions are displayed on two floors. Guided talks are offered most afternoons (phone for times).

## BATTERY PARK & THE ESPLANADE

Hudson River, from Broadway to Chambers St, Financial District

☎ 212.267.9700 🖥 bpcparks.org　　　　　　　MAP K2 #3

Situated at the southernmost tip of Manhattan, Battery Park draws lots of tourists because it's the departure point for ferries to the Statue of Liberty and Ellis Island. It's worth strolling through the green for other reasons as well, not the least of which is to get close to the water and take in some

The Brooklyn Bridge

fabulous views. The circular, red sandstone fort in the center of the park is Castle Clinton, an 1811 structure that stood just offshore when it was built, but has since been surrounded by acres of landfill. Battery Park Esplanade stretches 1.2 miles (1.9 km) along the Hudson River, from Battery Park all the way up to Chambers Street. On warm, sunny days, this is one of the best places to stroll, bike or rollerblade and take-in a hidden part of the city that even most locals don't usually see.

## BROOKLYN BRIDGE, THE

Center St (at Park Row), Financial District    `MAP` L2 #4

Walking across the Brooklyn Bridge is one of the classic New York experiences. The main point is the beautiful structure itself and the incredible view of Manhattan; a dazzling portrait whose frame is as extraordinary as its subject. The best time to go is on a long summer evening around sunset. Designed in the 1860s by John Roebling, the man who invented wire cable, the stone-and-steel bridge includes an elevated pedestrian promenade for strollers and cyclists. Once on the other side the walkway forks. Take the left-hand path, walk down the stairs and turn left into Dumbo, Brooklyn's new Soho. Alternatively, turn right and you can explore Brooklyn Heights or take the #6 train back.

## CATHEDRAL OF ST. JOHN THE DIVINE

1047 Amsterdam Ave (at 111th), Harlem
☎ 212.316.7490 🌐 stjohndivine.org    `MAP` A1 #5

Begun in 1892, and not yet fully completed, the seat of the Bishop of the Episcopal Diocese of New York is one of the world's largest Neo-Gothic cathedrals; a grand Europeanesque stone affair, with stained glass galore and art ranging from Raphael tapestries to a Keith Haring painting. The adjacent Peace Garden is one of the most whimsical places in the city.

## CENTRAL PARK

59th to 110th St (btw Fifth Ave and Central Park West)
☎ 212.794.6564 🌐 centralparknyc.org    `MAP` A2 #6

Laid-out in 1858 by landscape architects Frederick Law Olmsted and Calvert Vaux, Central Park is widely regarded as one of the world's finest urban parks. The huge park blends rolling meadows, lakes, woods, formal avenues and rocky outcroppings, all the while ingeniously sinking roadways so that nature is uninterrupted. Places in the park especially worth discovering include Bethesda Terrace (mid-park at 73rd St), which offers an awesomely beautiful vantage over The Lake (where you can rowboat, in season); the Model Boathouse (east side at 74th St), where you can rent radio-controlled sailboats; and Wollman

*Central Park Wollman Rink*

Rink (east side at 63rd St), a dramatic place to ice skate under the trees and skyscrapers of Central Park South.

## CENTRAL PARK ZOO

Central Park, Fifth Ave at 64th St, Upper East Side
☎ 212.439.6500 🖳 centralparkzoo.com          MAP E1 #7

Especially great for kids, this pint-size zoo is divided by climate into three sections: rain forest, temperate zone and Arctic area. Frolicking sea lions take pride of place, along with the zoo's famously neurotic polar bear. There's an adjacent petting zoo as well.

## CLOISTERS, THE

Fort Tryon Park, Fort Washington Ave (at 190th), Washington Heights
☎ 212.923.3700 🖳 metmuseum.org | CLOSED MON          MAP A1 #8

The Cloisters is a group of buildings incorporating large sections of four European Gothic and Romanesque abbeys, set on a beautiful perch at the northern tip of Manhattan. Much of it was purchased in the 1930s by John D. Rockefeller, Jr. for the Metropolitan Museum of Art, transported to this site and filled with JP Morgan's priceless Medieval art collection. The result is a peaceful, even meditative, spot that seems a world away from the skyscrapers to the south. To protect its character,

Rockefeller even bought land in New Jersey, on the opposite side of the Hudson River, so that views from here would never be spoiled. The highlights of the Medieval art collection are the famed 16th-century Unicorn Tapestries.

## COOPER-HEWITT NATIONAL DESIGN MUSEUM

2 East 91st St (at Fifth), Upper East Side
☎ 212.849.8400 🖳 ndm.si.edu | CLOSED MON          MAP B2 #9

Situated in a 64-room Georgian mansion once owned by Andrew Carnegie and now run by the Smithsonian Institution, the Cooper-Hewitt has strong collections of textiles and wall coverings, along with what is said to be the world's largest assortment of architectural drawings. There is also jewelry, prints and, so we're told, a major hoard of antique pornography.

## ELLIS ISLAND IMMIGRATION MUSEUM

Ellis Island, New York Harbor
☎ 212.269.5755 🖳 ellisisland.com          MAP K2 #10

Between 1892 and 1954, some twelve million immigrants were processed at the Ellis Island Immigration Center, a castle-like Victorian building on an island situated a few hundred yards north of the Statue of Liberty. It's said that about 40-percent

*Empire and Chrysler_CVB*

of all living Americans can trace their roots to an ancestor who passed through here. The museum's centerpiece is the historic Great Hall, a beautiful, but eerie, tiled room where the anxious newcomers were sorted, diagnosed for disease, cross-examined, accepted or rejected and, on occasion, turned back. The room has been perfectly restored and contains no exhibits, only the ghosts of decades past. Flanking it are 30 galleries of artifacts offering a fascinating look at the immigrant experience that includes family photos, heirlooms, religious articles and exquisite clothing and jewelry. Don't miss the Academy Award-winning documentary Island of Hope, Island of Tears, which is screened at regular intervals throughout the day. The ticket booth for the ferry is located in Battery Park's Castle Clinton, but you can avoid the lines by purchasing tickets online.

## EMPIRE STATE BUILDING

350 Fifth Ave (at 34th), Midtown

☎ 212.736.3100 | esbnyc.com                    MAP H1 #11

Visiting the top of the Empire State Building may sound like a tourist trap, but it's actually one of New York's most thrilling attractions. At night, when the lights of New York are twinkling below, the view is as wonderful and awesome as any we've ever experienced. The 102-story office building itself is an icon

of American modernism and an Art Deco masterpiece that's the architectural cousin of the Chrysler Building and **Rockefeller Center**. Because it's quite small and completely enclosed, the view from the 102nd floor is inferior to the one on the 86th, and not worth the wait for the elevator. Lines are longest between 3pm and 9pm. But generous opening hours mean you can show up late and have Manhattan almost all to yourself.

## FEDERAL HALL NATIONAL MEMORIAL

26 Wall St (at Nassau), Financial District

☎ 212.825.6888 ⓦ nps.gov | CLOSED SAT–SUN          MAP K2 #12

A colonnaded building situated almost across the street from the Stock Exchange marks the site of George Washington's 1789 inauguration and America's first capital. Inside are several historical exhibits, including the bible on which every American president has placed his right hand and sworn the oath of office. New York's first City Hall was constructed on this site in 1702. Later, when the US Constitution was adopted by the thirteen original states, New York City became the capital of the new nation and City Hall became Federal Hall, the country's administrative headquarters. The departments of State, War and Treasury were all housed here, as was the Supreme Court. The present building was constructed in 1842 as the Customs House of the Port of New York. It's open Mon-Fri 9am-5pm and admission is free.

## FEDERAL RESERVE BANK OF NEW YORK

33 Liberty St (at William), Financial District

☎ 212.720.6130 ⓦ ny.frb.org | CLOSED SAT–SUN        MAP K2 #13

The New York Fed is a block-like fortress that's said to be the repository of one-third of the world's gold; about $100 billion dollars worth that exceeds the amount in Fort Knox. Most of the bullion is in the form of 27-lb (12 kilo) gold bars. They're stored in vaults resting some fifty feet underground that are accessible via a narrow passageway cut in a delicately balanced steel cylinder that revolves vertically in an enormous steel-and-concrete frame. The vault is opened and closed by rotating the cylinder 90 degrees. Free, hour-long tours visit the vaults and summarize the history of gold. Book a week in advance and bring photo ID.

## FRICK COLLECTION, THE

1 East 70th St (at Fifth), Upper East Side

☎ 212.288.0700 ⓦ frick.org | CLOSED MON            MAP E1 #14

The former home of steel tycoon Henry Clay Frick is the most wonderful place in the city to be alone with

Grand Central Terminal

art. The beautiful Fifth Avenue mansion is filled with the millionaire's extraordinary sculptures, paintings, rugs, furniture, porcelain and other possessions. Visitors are invited to stroll from room to room filled with paintings by European masters hung with casual elegance: a Titian here, two Goyas there, along with Van Dykes, Vermeers, Rembrandts and other Old Masters. Constructed in 1914, the block-long mansion itself is a masterpiece featuring intricate floors, crown moldings, carved ceilings and spectacular light fixtures.

## GRACE CHURCH

802 Broadway (at 10th), East Village

☎ 212.254.2000 🌐 gracechurchnyc.org | CLOSED MON          MAP I2 #15

The cutest Episcopal church in a city full of cute Episcopal churches. Grace is a Gothic Revival oasis of stained glass, with dark wooden pews, intricate mosaics, solid marble altar and a multi-spire storybook exterior that really wows. It was designed in the mid-19th century as the first commission of 23-year-old James Renwick, Jr., an architect who had never been to Europe but studied its great medieval Gothic cathedrals. He later went on to design St. Patrick's Cathedral. Phone for tour times.

## GRAND CENTRAL TERMINAL

15 Vanderbilt Ave (Park Ave and 42nd St), Midtown

☎ 212.340.2210 🌐 grandcentralterminal.com          MAP E2 #16

Completed in 1913, Grand Central is a majestic Beaux-Arts landmark that remains one of the city's most impressive pieces of public architecture. Primarily a terminus for trains to Westchester, the station's heart is its main concourse with the constellations of the winter zodiac painted on the vaulted blue ceiling, and iconic central clock. There are several good restaurants and bars here too, including **The Oyster Bar** and **The Campbell Apartment**. Free tours are offered regularly (phone for information) but beware: This place can get as crowded as, um, Grand Central Station.

## INTREPID SEA-AIR-SPACE MUSEUM

Pier 86, West 46th St (at West Side Hwy), Midtown

☎ 212.245.0072 🌐 intrepidmuseum.org          MAP C2 #17

New York City may seem like an unlikely location for a WWII-era aircraft carrier museum, and it is. More than 40 aircraft on the flattop include a Stealth bomber, an F-14 Super Tomcat, an F-16 Falcon and even one of the old Concord jets. There's an Iraqi tank too, captured in the first Gulf War. The *USS Intrepid* is flanked by the *USS Edson*, a destroyer from the Vietnam war;

*Metropolitan Museum of Art*

museum recreates a trio of cramped apartments to interpret the neighborhood's array of immigrant experiences. Tours depart every 30 minutes (phone for reservations) and, if you can, you should combine it with a walking tour of the neighborhood, offered on weekends for a small additional charge.

## METROPOLITAN MUSEUM OF ART

1000 Fifth Ave (at 82nd), Upper East Side

☎ 212.879.5500 🖥 metmuseum.org | CLOSED MON     MAP B2 #20

From teacups to temples, the museum's vast art and craft collections are some of the world's most complete and encyclopedic spanning the entire history of humanity. It's a one-stop shop for Egyptian tombs, ancient Roman coins, meditating bronze Buddhas, Renaissance master paintings, African ceremonial masks, muscular Greek torsos, Asian ceramics, Tiffany windows, European arms and armor... the list seems endless. Collections move from strength to strength, from Dutch masters like Vermeer and Rembrandt to Italian Renaissance works by Botticelli and Raphael to Impressionist paintings by Renoir, Gauguin, Cézanne, Manet and Monet. The riches are repeated with equally broad collections of Asian, Egyptian, African and Islamic art. Only the 20th century galleries lag, with a relatively small collection riddled with plenty of holes. Needless to say, the Met is way too big to see all in one go. The best strategy is to pick-up a floor plan and target specific collections. Better yet, latch on to one of the frequent, free docent tours, led by some of the most erudite and articulate volunteers anywhere (mid-September through mid-August only, from 10.15am to 3.15pm). During summer months, find your way to the wonderful **Metropolitan Museum of Art Roof Garden** where you can enjoy a drink as you watch the sunset over Central Park. And definitely check out the museum's amazing gift shop, a favorite of New Yorkers boasting one of the best catalogs in town.

and the *USS Growler*, a guided-missile submarine. Get there by taxi, foot or the M42 cross-town bus to the west end of West 42nd Street. It's closed Mondays in winter.

## JEWISH MUSEUM, THE

1109 Fifth Ave (at 92nd), Upper East Side

☎ 212.423.3200 🖥 thejewishmuseum.org | CLOSED SAT     MAP B2 #18

Situated in the elegant Gothic-style Warburg Mansion, and now over 100 years old, the Jewish Museum gets the Avant-Guide nod not so much for its enormous collection of Jewish art and Judaica, but for curating premier exhibits of cutting-edge art and regularly mounting provocative shows that range from modernism in literature and film to Sigmund Freud's influence on 20th century culture.

## LOWER EAST SIDE TENEMENT MUSEUM

108 Orchard St (at Delancey), Lower East Side

☎ 212.431.0233 🖥 tenement.org | CLOSED MON     MAP L1 #19

Providing an interesting counterpoint to New York's grand mansion-museums, this offbeat winner brings visitors into a typical Lower East Side tenement building; one which was home to 7000 people from 20 nations from 1863 to 1935. The

## MORGAN LIBRARY

29 East 36th St (at Madison), Midtown

☎ 212.685.0610 🖥 morganlibrary.org     MAP H1 #21

Constructed of pink marble, this money-was-no-object Italian-style palazzo was built in 1906 for financier JP Morgan to house his collection of rare and ancient books, manuscripts, autographs, drawings and art. It was designed by Charles McKim of McKim, Mead and White, the much lauded New York architectural firm responsible for the original Penn Station, wings of the Metropolitan Museum of Art and many other landmark buildings. Inside, you can still find many of Mr. Morgan's possessions, including books covered in gold and

*The Museum of Modern Art*

sapphires, manuscripts by Isaac Newton and Henry David Thoreau, and a 1455 Gutenberg Bible, one of the first books printed using movable type. It's worth latching on to a guided tour to gain admittance to the three-story library filled with Renaissance art and floor-to-ceiling bookcases. Stay for lunch at the spectacular, skylit Morgan Court Cafe.

## MUSEUM AT FASHION INSTITUTE OF TECHNOLOGY (FIT)

Seventh Ave (at 27th), Chelsea

📞 212.217.5800 🌐 fitnyc.edu | CLOSED SUN–MON          MAP H1 #22

Rotating exhibitions from America's finest fashion academy are culled from a tremendous collection of costumes and textiles that's said to be one of the worlds largest and most important. Shows usually emphasize 20th-century design from fine denim to fabric prints by Salvador Dali to a cashmere and mink evening ensemble by Halston.

## MUSEUM OF ARTS & DESIGN

40 West 53rd St (at Fifth), Midtown

📞 212.956.3535 🌐 madmuseum.org          MAP E2 #23

MAD showcases contemporary international work at the intersection of crafts, arts and design. And there's quite a lot

to like. Shows may focus furniture, lamps, art quilts, jewelry or any number of other applied arts. The uniting factors are the highest standards of mastery and innovation in the use of materials and processes. There's a great gift shop too.

## MUSEUM OF MODERN ART, THE

11 West 53rd St (at Fifth), Midtown

📞 212.708.9400 🌐 moma.org | CLOSED TUES          MAP E2 #24

The greatest collection of modern art in the world reads like a summary of the creative hits from the 1880s to the present day: Pollock, de Kooning, Rothko, Rauschenberg, Twombly and most every other well-known 20th century artist is represented, often by his or her very best work. While other museums thrill to have single canvases by masters like Monet, Matisse or Mondrian, MoMA's embarrassment of riches offers entire rooms filled with masterpieces and the chance to follow an artist's career in its entirety. Many icons of modern and contemporary art are always on display, including Vincent van Gogh's *The Starry Night*, Henri Matisse's *Dance*, Claude Monet's *Water Lilies*, Salvador Dali's *The Persistence of Memory*, Andy Warhol's *Gold Marilyn Monroe* and Andrew Wyeth's *Christina's World*. And frequent blockbuster exhibitions means that there

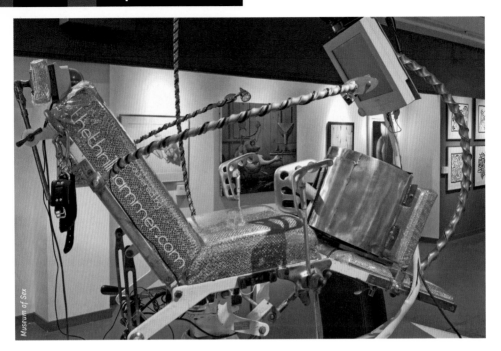

*Museum of Sex*

is always something new to look at. The museum has one of the most comprehensive collections of 20th century drawings anywhere, and boasts an industrial design collection that comprises objects ranging from appliances, furniture and tableware to tools, textiles, sports cars and even a helicopter. The new building by Japanese architect Yoshio Taniguchi is a resounding success too. Merciless crowds are our only gripe: Mondays, Fridays and Saturdays are cruelest.

## MUSEUM OF THE CITY OF NEW YORK

1220 Fifth Ave (at 103rd), Upper East Side

☎ 212.534.1672 ⓦ mcny.org | CLOSED MON          MAP B1 #25

New York City's history museum is an upbeat, even irreverent place, with both permanent and temporary exhibitions from historical times to the present day. Much of the floor space is given over to tremendous collections—silver, model ships, toys—which, for us, is a yawn. But other exhibits are phenomenal; like the luxuriously appointed Stettheimer Dollhouse, fitted with tiny furnishings, a teensy-weensy sculpture by Gaston Lachaise and a Lilliputian version of Marcel Duchamp's *Nude Descending a Staircase*. Other exhibits include a section of the plane that crashed into the Empire State Building

in 1945, and the News Zipper that wrapped around the old New York Times Building. On the top floor you can peek into John D. Rockefeller's antique-filled Japanese-style bedroom, which was moved here in its entirety when the Rockefeller townhouse was torn down to make way for MoMA.

## MUSEUM OF SEX

233 Fifth Ave (at 27th), Flatiron District

☎ 212.689.6337 ⓦ museumofsex.com          MAP H1 #26

This private museum wants to be a major cultural institution devoted to the history and continuing evolution of human sexuality. Lofty goals aside, it offers fairly titillating and eyebrow-raising exhibitions like the Origins of American Pornographic Film, Sex Machines and US Patent Office Sex Inventions that " prevent, improve or enhance sexual function."

## NEUE GALERIE NEW YORK

1048 Fifth Ave (at 85th), Upper East Side

☎ 212.628.6200 ⓦ neuegalerie.org | CLOSED TUE-WED          MAP B2 #27

Ronald Lauder's museum of early 20th century German and Austrian art is a beautiful place to get close to major works by Egon Schiele, Gustav Klimt and Paul Klee. The Fifth Avenue mansion itself is wonderful too, as is the museum's Cafe Sabarsky, an elegant Viennese-style kaffeehaus serving light lunches and excellent tortes.

## ROCKEFELLER CENTER
48th to 51st St (at Fifth), Midtown
☎ 212.698.2000 🖥 rockefellercenter.com     🗺 E2 #28

A masterpiece of modern design, Rockefeller Center is a limestone complex of 19 Art Deco buildings on 22 acres in the heart of Midtown. Mostly completed between 1932 to 1940, the Center is basically just a collection of office buildings. But its unique design and intricate styling create a compelling attraction. The best way to approach the complex is through the Channel Gardens that run from Fifth Avenue to the Sunken Plaza in the Center's middle. Lorded over by the fabulous and famous Prometheus statue, the Plaza is best from October to April when ice skaters glide around the **Rockefeller Center Ice Rink** (tel. 212.332.7654). The tallest building in the complex is the 65-story skyscraper known colloquially as "30 Rock." It's worth seeing the lobby, with its vast murals, gleaming black granite floors and lots of inlaid elements outlined in brass. Upstairs is the East Coast headquarters and studios of NBC television. You can take an elevator to the **Top of the Rock** observatory for fantabulous open-air views of Manhattan, and beyond. The complex also includes the Art Deco landmark **Radio City Music Hall**, 1260 Sixth Ave (tel. 212.307.7171), the largest and most dazzlingly theater in the US.

## RUBIN MUSEUM OF ART
150 West 17th St (at Seventh), Chelsea
☎ 212.620.5000 🖥 rmanyc.org | CLOSED MON     🗺 H2 #29

Himalayan art and culture are displayed and explored in this wonderful museum designed by Richard Blinder of Beyer Blinder Belle. Comprehensive collections of paintings, sculptures and textiles range in date over two millennia and include Bodhisattva statues, mandala paintings, dance masks and lots of ritual objects.

## SAINT PATRICK'S CATHEDRAL
14 East 51st St (at Fifth), Midtown
☎ 212.753.2261 🖥 ny-archdiocese.org     🗺 E1 #30

Opened in 1879, this imposing French Gothic style cathedral smack-dab in the center of Manhattan is the seat of the Archbishop of New York. It's a suitably grand structure with brilliant stained-glass windows and altars designed by Tiffany

*Rockefeller Center*

and Co. The Archbishops of New York are buried in a crypt under the high altar; their honorary hats, called galeros, hang from the ceiling over their tombs.

## SKYSCRAPER MUSEUM, THE
39 Battery Pl (at Little West St), Financial District
☎ 212.968.1961 🖥 skyscraper.org | CLOSED MON–TUE     🗺 K2 #31

It's fitting that this city of skyscrapers should have a museum devoted exclusively to the tallest form of architecture. The many dimensions of design are illustrated using architectural models, renderings, computer simulations, building material samples and plenty of graphics.

## SOLOMON R. GUGGENHEIM MUSEUM
1071 Fifth Ave (at 88th), Upper East Side
☎ 212.423.3500 🖥 guggenheim.org | CLOSED THU     🗺 B2 #32

The Frank Lloyd Wright-designed museum itself is what makes the Guggenheim so special. That's not to say that the art isn't world-class, it is. But, the landmark "chambered nautilus" advertecture seems to make almost anything inside seem like a masterpiece. The Guggenheim is great just because it's different, relatively small, quick and fun. Take the

## SONY WONDER TECHNOLOGY LAB

**550 Madison Ave (at 55th), Midtown**

☎ 212.833.8100 🖥 sonywondertechlab.com | CLOSED MON ▪MAP▪ E2 #33

Especially fun for kids, this hands-on technology museum is filled with exhibits that encourage visitors to "jam" with music artists, produce a mini movie trailer and "create" a video game. Admission is free.

## SOUTH STREET SEAPORT

**South St (at Fulton), Financial District**

☎ 212.732.8257 🖥 southstreetseaport.com ▪MAP▪ L2 #34

Don't let the cobblestone streets fool you, because the much-hyped corner of old New York is basically a redevelopment shopping mall with suburban-style chain stores, forgettable restaurants and bars that become after-work singles joints. But we like the wooden pier, the great views of the Brooklyn Bridge and the collection of life-size sailing and steam ships.

## STATEN ISLAND FERRY

**Whitehall Terminal, 1 Whitehall St (at South), Financial District**

☎ 212.639.9675 🖥 siferry.com ▪MAP▪ K2 #35

Whitehall Terminal, at the eastern edge of Battery Park, is where you board the boats to New York City's other big island. The orange ferries have been making the 5 mile, 25-minute trip to and from Staten Island since 1905. It's not a comfortable fleet, but it's the best-value romantic sightseeing ride in the city, offering stunning views of New York Harbor, Lower Manhattan, the Statue of Liberty and Ellis Island—free of charge. Despite what city boosters say, there's not much that's particularly worthwhile to do when you reach Staten Island's St. George Terminal, at least in comparison to what's happening back in Manhattan. Think about taking the cruise at sunset or after dark, when you can see Manhattan's office buildings emitting their fluorescent glow.

## STATUE OF LIBERTY NATIONAL MONUMENT

**Liberty Island, New York Harbor**

☎ 212.269.5755 🖥 statuereservations.com ▪MAP▪ K2 #36

The colossal bronze *Liberty Enlightening the World*, as she was originally called, was the life work of 19th-century French sculptor Frederic-Auguste Bartholdi. The artist toiled tirelessly not only to create it, but then to sell it to the French and American people who paid for it. Although the statue was dedicated in 1886, it wasn't until 1903, when Emma Lazarus' poem "The New Colossus" was inscribed on its base, that the statue became a symbol for immigrants. For the 12 million new

elevator to the top, then walk down the spiral ramp towards the exit. The majority of the main building is usually given over to one blockbuster temporary exhibition or another, often devoted to the work of a single significant modern artist. Side rooms are hung with the museum's own masterpieces of 20th-century art. The permanent collection began with Old Masters collected by mining magnate Solomon Guggenheim. Encouraged by his mistress, the eccentric artist Baroness Hilla Rebay von Ehrenwiesen, Guggenheim turned his sights towards the non-figurative art of Klee, Chagall, Kandinsky and others. In 1943, Rebay convinced Guggenheim to hire Frank Lloyd Wright—who was 74 at the time—to design a "Museum of Non-Objective Painting." By the time these doors finally opened sixteen years later, in 1969, both Lloyd Wright and Solomon Guggenheim were dead. Many of the paintings from the original collection now hang in the museum's tower annex, a 1992 addition that some purists say "wronged Wright." But the galleries inside are bright and spacious and allow visitors to step away from the art, which is impossible on the narrow ramp of the main building. The other paintings here are from a post-impressionist collection donated to the museum in the 1960s by art dealer Justin Thannhauser.

The Skyscraper Museum

Americans who sailed into New York Harbor in the late 19th and early 20th centuries, the "lady with the lamp" confirmed that they had arrived. These days "Your tired, your poor, your huddled masses yearning to breathe free" seems to refer to the throng of tourists jostling for position in lines and on boats. Woody Allen once joked that the last time he was inside a woman was when he took a tour of the Statue of Liberty. Unfortunately, visitors can no longer climb to the crown. But, that's OK, because the best views are from outside, along with vistas of Lower Manhattan. Ferries depart from Battery Park approximately every 30 minutes and stop at both Liberty Island and Ellis Island. Weekday mornings are the best times to go, as the tourist crush can be unbearable later in the day, as well as on Saturdays and Sundays (especially during July and August). The ticket booth is located in Battery Park's Castle Clinton, but you can avoid the lines by purchasing tickets online. While you're at it, make reservations for the free National Park Service tour.

## TIMES SQUARE

Broadway (between 42nd and 47th), Midtown      MAP D2 #37

So vast and demanding that it's impossible to take it all in with a single glance, the lights of Times Square are more spectacular than ever and remain a must-see after sundown. The deodorized intersection of Broadway and Seventh Avenue now has the cleanliness of a film set, but, mercifully, some things haven't changed. The district is still a nonstop circus plastered with wheatpasted posters. It's still Theaterland, home to the Broadway musical and the half-price TKTS booth. And the US Army still maintains a recruiting station right in the heart of the hustle, cleverly positioned to prey on runaways who slip past the chicken-hawkers at the nearby Port Authority Bus Terminal. The New Year's Eve ball drop, Times Square's most notable tradition, has survived too. While we hesitatingly approve of the kinder, gentler Times Square, we also openly hope that it will never be completely rid of pickpockets, prostitutes, porno parlors and psychodramatic panhandlers. And while we're happy that it's safer, cleaner and brighter, we're still wondering what to do with all our extra Peepland tokens.

## TRINITY CHURCH

74 Trinity Pl (at Broadway), Financial District

☎ 212.602.0800   🌐 trinitywallstreet.org      MAP K2 #38

The third Episcopal church to stand on land bequeathed to the city by England's King William III, tiny Gothic Revival Trinity

*Solomon R. Guggenheim Museum*

Church is one of the city's most historical buildings. Now surrounded by glass-and-steel skyscrapers, it's well worth a visit when exploring the Financial District. The building was completed in 1846 and remained the tallest building in Manhattan for the rest of the 19th century. Tombs in the surrounding burial yard date to 1681 and include American founding-father Alexander Hamilton, Engineer and Artist Robert Fulton, and Secretary of the Treasury Albert Gallatin.

## United Nations, The

First Ave (at 46th), Midtown

☎ 212.963.8687 🖵 un.org | CLOSED SAT–SUN FROM JAN–MAR 🗺 F2 #39

One of the most striking things about the United Nations is that the ethnic mixture inside looks very much like a microcosm of New York City. Of course, in here the hacks are not driving taxis, they are diplomats, which means they can drive even more recklessly and park anywhere they please with impunity. A UN tour may not be the most exciting event on the planet, but it's worth seeing where the countries of the world attempt to communicate with each other. Guided tours swing through the Security Council chambers and the iconic General Assembly Hall before being pointed in the direction of the gift shop, restaurant and UN post office's stamp counter. We also like the guides' uniforms, tailored navy blue suits for women and men designed by the Italian fashion house, Mondrian. Tours depart every 30 minutes, but be warned: Weekdays between 8am and 3pm the building is school group hell.

## Whitney Museum of American Art

945 Madison Ave (at 75th), Upper East Side

☎ 212.570.3676 🖵 whitney.org | CLOSED MON–TUE 🗺 E1 #40

Gertrude Vanderbilt Whitney founded her own museum in 1929 after the Metropolitan Museum of Art rejected her collection by American realist painters. The Whitney has been controversial from the get-go. Despite frequent popular successes, critics are routinely dismissive of the quality of the museum's exhibitions, a matter that's not helped by the building itself—a postmodern fortress by architect Marcel

World Trade Center Site

Breuer (complete with a concrete moat and bridge) that's loved as greatly as it is reviled. Temporary exhibits have included a retrospective of video art pioneer Bill Viola and a major Warhol show, and the museum's iconic Biennial always garners vehement criticism—both good and the other kind. The Permanent Collection Galleries include works by Jasper Johns, Claes Oldenburg and Ad Reinhardt, and entire rooms are dedicated to Edward Hopper, Georgia O'Keeffe and Alexander Calder. Few post-1945 holdings make it onto the walls (and floors, and ceilings...). Calder's restored "Circus" (1926-31) is spotlighted in a separate gallery, where whimsical circus performers and creatures made from tin, paperclips, springs, rags and clock movements are displayed along with a film of the artist as ringmaster, performing a show.

## WORLD TRADE CENTER SITE

Liberty St and Trinity Place, Financial District          MAP K2 #41

The building site continues to attract a huge crowd, especially on weekends. From Trinity Place, visitors can look into the Trade Center site through a screen-like grid of galvanized steel. On Liberty Street there is a series of large fiberglass panels with history and information on the building.

## YANKEE STADIUM

161st St and River Ave, Bronx

☎ 718.293.4300  🌐 yankees.com          MAP A1 #42

We can think of no true-bluer New York experience than to sit with the diehards in the bleachers of Yankee Stadium and learn the true meaning of a "Bronx cheer." Opened in 1923, the "house that Ruth built" is a classic piece of baseball architecture that still reverberates with the spirits of Yankee's past: Joe DiMaggio, Lou Gehrig, Mickey Mantle and the like. The Stadium is reached by subway on the 4 or D train to 161st Street. New York Waterway's popular Yankee Clipper service (tel. 201.902.8700) is a much more scenic way to the stadium from South Street Seaport, East 34th Street or East 90th Street. Phone for information about stadium tours too.

**Avant-Guide:** What five non-essential items do you never travel without, any why?

**Daniel Libeskind:** My complete Emily Dickinson poetry book (because that's all you need to read), a handmade toothbrush from Italy (I got it I think in Bologna), I have a brush-pen from Japan (a fountain pen with a brush at the end), watercolor paper, and an extra button. I always carry an extra button.

=Λ= Describe your perfect hotel room of the future.

**DL:** One in which I could instantly change its décor by pressing a button. That would be perfect.

=Λ= If you could take one restaurant with you to a deserted island from New York City, which one would it be?

**DL:** It's a small hole-in-the-wall, a dumpling restaurant right off Canal Street. I don't know the name, the readers will have to find it. It's literally a hole-in-the-wall and they do about a thousand different kinds of dumplings. And why? Because only New York City would have a restaurant with a thousand different kinds of dumplings! Vying for the position is Second Avenue Deli, you can't get pastrami like that from anywhere around the world—so many calories in just one sitting!

=Λ= What is your favorite place in New York City to shop?

**DL:** Definitely Grand Central [Terminal]. It's the most incredible civic edifice of architecture. You can get almost anything there, on the way in and out.

## DANIEL LIBESKIND

Architect Daniel Libeskind shot to stardom when he won the commission for his master plan design of the new World Trade Center project. His other distinguished projects include the Jewish Museum in Berlin, the Contemporary Jewish Museum in San Francisco and additions to the Denver Art Museum and the Royal Ontario Museum in Canada. A noted architectural theorist, Mr. Libeskind was named the first Cultural Ambassador for Architecture by the US Department of State and is credited with infusing a new philosophical discourse into the realm of architecture.

=Λ= What aspect of your profession do you most enjoy, and why?

**DL:** Well, that's a hard one. I like the creative aspect of architecture, which is almost everywhere to be found, whether it is fundraising, making a drawing, speaking to a client or inventing new spaces.

=Λ= What is your fallback job?

**DL:** Subway musician.

| Map | # | Area | Sight | Address | Phone | Closed |
|---|---|---|---|---|---|---|
| | | | **Top New York Experiences** | | | |
| L2 | 4 | Financial District | Brooklyn Bridge, The | Center Street | no phone | |
| H1 | 11 | Midtown | Empire State Building | 350 Fifth Ave | 212.736.3100 | |
| K2 | 35 | Financial District | Staten Island Ferry | 1 Whitehall St | 212.639.9675 | |
| D2 | 37 | Midtown | Times Square | Broadway | no phone | |
| A1 | 42 | The Bronx | Yankee Stadium | 161st St and River Ave | 718.293.4300 | SAT-SUN |
| | | | **Museums and Galleries** | | | |
| D1 | 1 | Upper West Side | American Museum of Natural History | Central Park West | 212.769.5100 | |
| E1 | 2 | Upper East Side | Asia Society and Museum | 725 Park Ave | 212.288.6400 | MON |
| B2 | 9 | Upper East Side | Cooper-Hewitt National Design Museum | 2 East 91st St | 212.849.8400 | MON |
| E1 | 14 | Upper East Side | Frick Collection, The | 1 East 70th St | 212.288.0700 | MON |
| B2 | 18 | Upper East Side | Jewish Museum, The | 1109 Fifth Ave | 212.423.3200 | SAT |
| L1 | 19 | Lower East Side | Lower East Side Tenement Museum | 108 Orchard St | 212.431.0233 | MON |
| B2 | 20 | Upper East Side | Metropolitan Museum of Art | 1000 Fifth Ave | 212.879.5500 | MON |
| H1 | 21 | Midtown | Morgan Library | 29 East 36th St | 212.685.0610 | |
| H1 | 22 | Chelsea | Museum at FIT | Seventh Ave and 27th St | 212.217.5800 | SUN-MON |
| E2 | 23 | Midtown | Museum of Arts & Design | 40 West 53rd St | 212.956.3535 | |
| E2 | 24 | Midtown | Museum of Modern Art, The | 11 West 53rd St | 212.708.9400 | TUES |
| B1 | 25 | Upper East Side | Museum of the City of New York | 1220 Fifth Ave | 212.534.1672 | MON |
| H1 | 26 | Flatiron District | Museum of Sex | 233 Fifth Ave | 212.689.6337 | |
| B2 | 27 | Upper East Side | Neue Galerie New York | 1048 Fifth Ave | 212.628.6200 | TUE-WED |
| H2 | 29 | Chelsea | Rubin Museum of Art | 150 West 17th St | 212.620.5000 | MON |
| K2 | 31 | Financial District | Skyscraper Museum, The | 39 Battery Pl | 212.968.1961 | MON-TUE |
| B2 | 32 | Upper East Side | Solomon R. Guggenheim Museum | 1071 Fifth Ave | 212.423.3500 | THU |
| E1 | 40 | Upper East Side | Whitney Museum | 945 Madison Ave | 212.570.3676 | MON-TUE |
| | | | **Parks & Gardens** | | | |
| K2 | 3 | Financial District | Battery Park & The Esplanade | Hudson River at Broadway | 212.267.9700 | |
| A2 | 6 | Uptown | Central Park | 59th to 110th St | 212.794.6564 | |
| | | | **Places to Take Kids** | | | |
| E1 | 7 | Upper East Side | Central Park Zoo | Fifth Avenue at 64th St | 212.439.6500 | |
| K2 | 10 | New York Harbor | Ellis Island Immigration Museum | Ellis Island | 212.269.5755 | |
| C2 | 17 | Midtown | Intrepid Sea-Air-Space Museum | Pier 86, West 46th St | 212.245.0072 | |
| E2 | 33 | Midtown | Sony Wonder Technology Lab | 550 Madison Ave | 212.833.8100 | MON |
| L2 | 34 | Financial District | South Street Seaport | South St | 212.732.8257 | |
| F2 | 39 | Midtown | United Nations, The | First Avenue | 212.963.8687 | SAT-SUN |
| K2 | 36 | New York Harbor | Statue of Liberty | Liberty Island | 212.269.5755 | |
| | | | **Offbeat Sights** | | | |
| A1 | 8 | Washington Heights | Cloisters, The | Fort Tryon Park | 212.923.3700 | MON |
| K2 | 12 | Financial District | Federal Hall National Memorial | 26 Wall St | 212.825.6888 | SAT-SUN |

| Map | # | Area | Sight | Address | Phone | Closed |
|-----|---|------|-------|---------|-------|--------|
| | | | **Offbeat Sights** | | | |
| K2 | 13 | Financial District | Federal Reserve Bank of New York | 33 Liberty St | 212.720.6130 | SAT-SUN |
| K2 | 41 | Financial District | World Trade Center Site | Liberty St | no phone | |
| | | | **Great Architecture** | | | |
| E2 | 16 | Midtown | Grand Central Terminal | 15 Vanderbilt Ave | 212.340.2210 | |
| E2 | 28 | Midtown | Rockefeller Center | 48th to 51st St | 212.698.2000 | |
| | | | **Churches, Synagogues & Cemeteries** | | | |
| A1 | 5 | Harlem | Cathedral of St. John the Divine | 1047 Amsterdam Ave | 212.316.7490 | |
| I2 | 15 | East Village | Grace Church | 802 Broadway | 212.254.2000 | MON |
| E1 | 30 | Midtown | Saint Patrick's Cathedral | 14 East 51st St | 212.753.2261 | |
| K2 | 38 | Financial District | Trinity Church | 74 Trinity Pl | 212.602.0800 | |

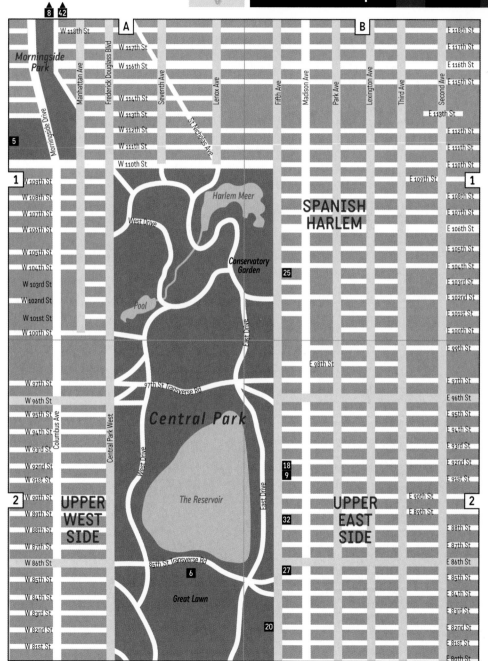

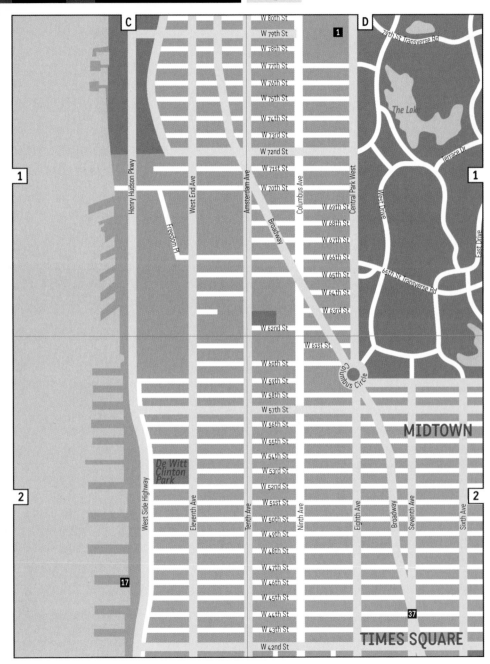

**C** **D**

1

W 80th St
W 79th St
W 78th St
W 77th St
W 76th St
W 75th St
W 74th St
W 73rd St
W 72nd St
W 71st St
W 70th St
W 69th St
W 68th St
W 67th St
W 66th St
W 65th St
W 64th St
W 63rd St
W 62nd St
W 61st St
W 60th St
W 59th St
W 58th St
W 57th St
W 56th St
W 55th St
W 54th St
W 53rd St
W 52nd St
W 51st St
W 50th St
W 49th St
W 48th St
W 47th St
W 46th St
W 45th St
W 44th St
W 43rd St
W 42nd St

79th St Transverse Rd
The Lake
Terrace Dr
East Drive
West Drive
65th St Transverse Rd
Central Park West

Henry Hudson Pkwy
Freedom Pl
West End Ave
Amsterdam Ave
Broadway
Columbus Ave
Columbus Circle

1

MIDTOWN

West Side Highway
Eleventh Ave
Tenth Ave
Ninth Ave
Eighth Ave
Broadway
Seventh Ave
Sixth Ave

De Witt Clinton Park

2

17

37

TIMES SQUARE

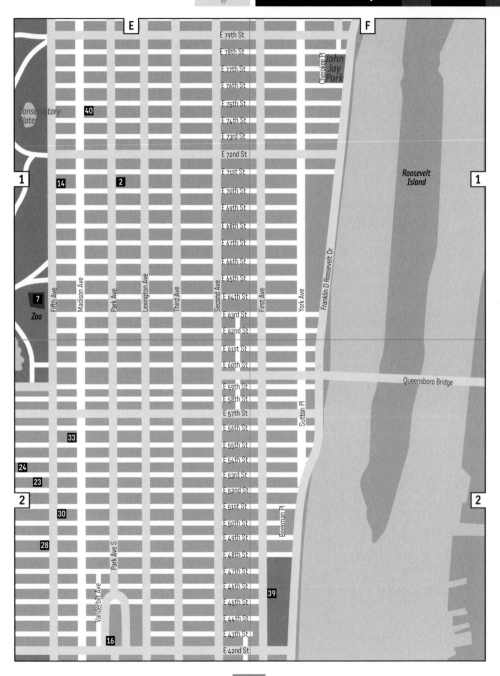

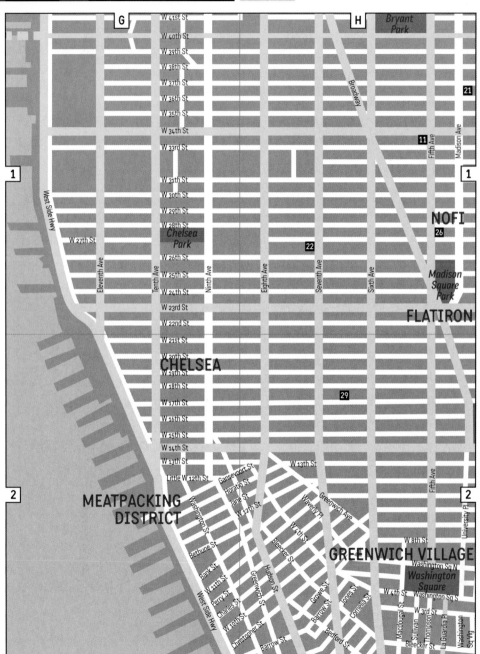

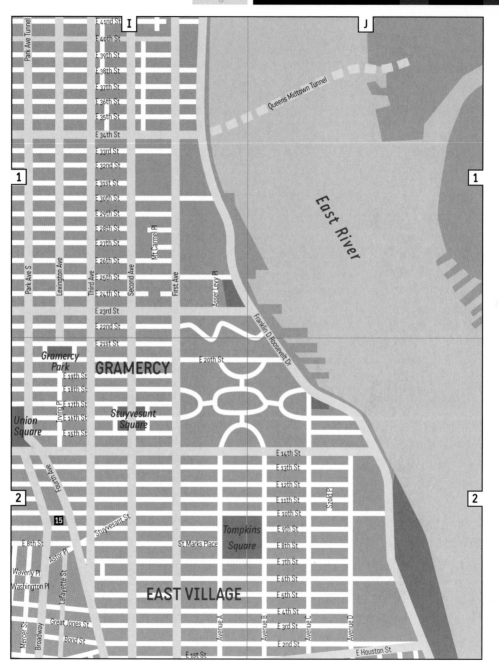

I

J

1

E 41nd St
E 40th St
E 39th St
E 38th St
E 37th St
E 36th St
E 35th St
E 34th St
E 33rd St
E 32nd St
E 31st St
E 30th St
E 29th St
E 28th St
E 27th St
E 26th St
E 25th St
E 24th St
E 23rd St
E 22nd St
E 21st St
E 20th St

Park Ave Tunnel
Park Ave S
Lexington Ave
Third Ave
Second Ave
Mt Carmel Pl
First Ave
Asser Levy Pl

Queens Midtown Tunnel

East River

Franklin D Roosevelt Dr

**Gramercy Park**
**GRAMERCY**
E 19th St
E 18th St
Irving Pl
E 17th St
E 16th St
**Stuyvesant Square**
E 15th St
**Union Square**

E 14th St
E 13th St
E 12th St
E 11th St
E 10th St
E 9th St
E 8th St
E 7th St
E 6th St
E 5th St
E 4th St
E 3rd St
E 2nd St
E 1st St

Fourth Ave

2

15

Stuyvesant St
E 8th St
Astor Pl
Waverly Pl
Washington Pl
Lafayette St
Mercer St
Broadway
Great Jones St
Bond St

St Marks Place
**Tompkins Square**

**EAST VILLAGE**

Avenue A
Avenue B
Avenue C
Avenue D
Szód Pl

E Houston St

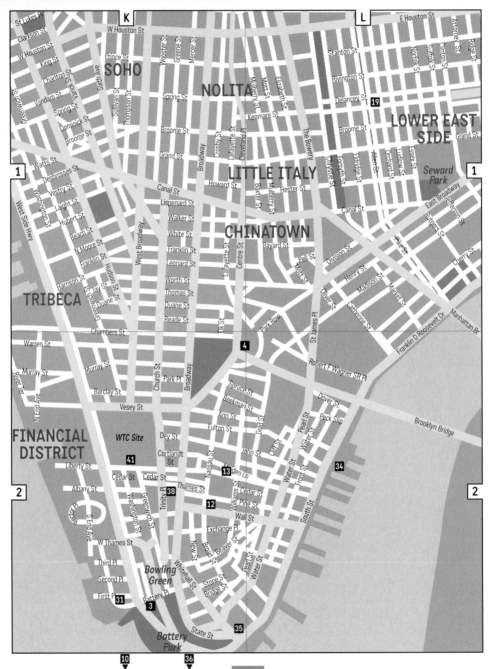

KNOW

6

Manhattan is a compact protrusion of rock that rises just a few hundred feet above sea-level. The southern tip and the center of the island are solid granite, which is why the city's tallest buildings are clustered in these two areas. Constrained by geography, the island was forced to build up. Viewed from across the river, it looks like a single architectural entity—a stone, glass, and steel ship or a cathedral of stalactites.

Financial District

## KNOW YOUR NEIGHBORHOODS
**See inside front cover for neighborhoods map**

CHELSEA | It's an old Manhattan story already: dilapidated industrial wasteland becomes hip cultural Mecca. But unlike Soho and Tribeca, the style fiends who've settled into this hot neighborhood are predominantly gay. Bounded by Sixth Avenue, the Hudson River, 14th and 28th streets, Chelsea's streets are lined with elegant brownstones and its avenues are packed with bustling restaurants, cafes, bars and shops. The city's best art galleries are clustered here too, on the far west side.

CHINATOWN | Centered on Canal and Mott streets, Chinatown is home to some 100,000 Chinese immigrants, as well as tens of thousands of settlers from Malaysia, Thailand, Cambodia, Vietnam and elsewhere who toil in the neighborhood's over-crowded sweatshops and hygienically-challenged restaurants. Once confined to a few blocks surrounding Mott Street, the neighborhood is more accurately described as Southeast Asiatown as it bursts its seams and expands in all directions. The area has enjoyed steady, continuous growth since 1883, when the Federal Chinese Exclusion Act was repealed. Today its tangle of narrow streets are humming, even by New York standards. The neighborhood is crammed with exotic-produce markets, street vendors hawking knock-off designer watches and

traditional pharmacies selling dried scorpions and flattened lizards like a page out of a Harry Potter spell book.

EAST VILLAGE | Former home to Beats and Punks, and more recently to adventurous young corporate types, the East Village still has plenty of edge and is one of the most interesting corners of the city. Situated east of Broadway, between 14th and Houston streets, the neighborhood continues to thrive with lower-income hipsters, unrepentant anarchists and earnest starving-artists living alongside older Ukrainian and Latino immigrants and the more than occasional Wall Streeter who's just here 'cause the rent is right. St. Mark's Place, one of the East Village's main drags, has long been the strip where the East Village meets the world. Leon Trotsky once lived in the windowless brick tenement at number 77. These days the strip is often crowded with suburban kids shopping for street-fashions and cheap sunglasses, both of which are in plentiful supply.

FINANCIAL DISTRICT | Also known as Lower Manhattan, the southern tip of the island is the site of the region's first European settlement and is now America's financial center. New Amsterdam was founded here by the Dutch West India Company in 1626 mainly for commercial reasons, and it hasn't looked back since. These narrow, historical and sometimes cobblestoned streets are home to the New York Stock Exchange, Battery Park and the World Trade Center site, as well as ferries to the Statue of Liberty, Ellis Island and Staten Island. Each morning, bond traders and stockbrokers roll in to this capital of capitalism in chauffeur-driven Lincoln Town Cars from all over the Tri-State area. Throughout the day, these suits with ulcers battle tourists for control of the sidewalks. After dark, the neighborhood becomes eerily empty and quiet—except for the odd strip club.

THE FLATIRON DISTRICT | Named for the Flatiron Building, the triangular-shaped terra cotta office tower that stands at Broadway and 23rd Street, the Flatiron District is very much the city's fashion center, home to model agencies, photographers' studios, film labs and many of the city's hottest restaurants and lounges.

GRAMERCY | This quiet residential district just southeast of Midtown is populated with some excellent bars and restaurants. Once home to the Astors and the Roosevelts, the area around Gramercy Park began life in the 1830s as one of New York's most fashionable addresses. Later on, the district attracted many successful writers and intellectuals, leading some to dub it an American Bloomsbury. The Communist Party moved their headquarters here and, in the 1960s, it was home to Andy Warhol's legendary Factory. Gramercy Park, at Lexington Avenue and 21st Street, is open only to neighborhood residents and shareholders who are given keys.

GREENWICH VILLAGE | The Village retains the character of its genteel name with beautiful 19th-century townhouses on tree-lined streets. Situated between Broadway and the Hudson River, and 14th and Houston streets, the neighborhood was built in the mid-19th century with beautiful upper-class homes and lots of little churches, shops, theaters, clubs and galleries. The founding of New York University on Washington Square Park added a youthful vibrancy, but only remnants of the area's famous bohemian lifestyle remain because you have to be rich to live here.

HARLEM | Situated between the rivers, from about 96th to 168th streets, Harlem is the spiritual and intellectual capital of black America. It's also a community that's relatively poor and politically impotent. Both these aspects attract curious visitors, who come up to see what makes this largely dilapidated corner of the world so famous. The east side, known as Spanish Harlem or East Harlem, is largely home to people from Puerto Rico, Mexico and Central America.

LITTLE ITALY | In the 19th-century, this neighborhood between Canal, Kenmare, Elizabeth and Lafayette streets was the locus of Italian immigration. Today, it's only a shadow of its former self and has been swallowed up by burgeoning Chinatown. What's left, primarily along Mulberry Street, has become something of a cannelloni Disneyland. Once home to some half-million, Italian-Americans, today the only Italian you'll witness here are the signs on the caffes and Ristoranti, "Kiss Me I'm Italian" T-shirts and, perhaps, the occasional Italian tourist. A mafioso can't even get gunned-down in one of the neighborhood's clam houses anymore. Still, each autumn, Little Italy puts on its best face, in the form of the San Gennaro Festival, an 11-day cacophony of bad music, garish carnival games and delicious sausage-and-pepper sandwiches. It's only a matter of time before Little Italy is a distant memory.

LOWER EAST SIDE | Bargain-shopping district by day, the Lower East Side transforms nightly into one of the most active bar scenes in the city. Ludlow and Orchard streets, just south of Houston Street, is the epicenter of the neighborhood, where you can easily floss in and out of almost a dozen bars in the course of a single night. Until recently, the cheap tenement housing and shifting demographics of the Lower East Side reflected the latest waves of immigration to New York. These days only a few vestiges of the neighborhood's illustrious past remain in discount clothing stores on Orchard Street and the random deli (Katz's, 205 East Houston St), bialy shop (Kossars Bialystoker, 367 Grand St), pickle stand (Gus', 35 Essex St), matzoh maker (Streit, 150 Rivington St) and knishery (Yonah Schimmel's, 137 East Houston St). Most of the locals now tend towards career-oriented "adultescents" wrestling with rebellion postponement. For them, "LES" is more because there's rarely a cover, and the off-center location ensures the crowd is never too haute—a plus in this gilded age of the velvet rope.

MEATPACKING DISTRICT | Roped-off lounges and stylish restaurants continue to open and prosper in this three-block-deep neighborhood below 14th Street at the Hudson River that has become the city's first self-contained night-life quarter. Only a few years ago this area was a shadowy sanctum of leather bars, transvestite prostitutes and full-service beef butchers. It's amazing how Disneyesque and B&T the area has become in so short of a time. Today you'll even find pedicabs that are more commonly associated with

New York Harbor

Times Square. By day, you'll find high end shopping on 14th Street in the visage of fashion stalwarts like Stella McCartney and Jeffrey. By night the locus shifts to the intersection of Greenwich and Gansevoort streets, where limos jostle for position outside restaurants and wannabes regularly get pagesix (drunk and crazy like a celebrity).

MIDTOWN | The area between 30th and 59th streets is the city's most densely commercialized. It's also an awesome place to explore. The eastern and western edges of Midtown are largely residential. In-between are the theaters of Broadway, the lights of Times Square, the Coca-colonized shops of Fifth Avenue, several concert halls, the skyscraping headquarters of dozens of Fortune 500 companies and the majestic architectural cousins, the Chrysler Building, the Empire State Building and Rockefeller Center.

NOLITA | Although these small handful of blocks are named for their location north of Little Italy, their character is much closer to its other geographic position, east of Soho. An enormous number of downtown designer shops are the main draw, attracting faux bohemians with Death Cab for Cutie on their iPods and platinum cards in their Rogan jeans and Lulu Guinness bags. By night the scene is somewhat more sedate, though the number and quality of the neighborhood's restaurants and lounges seems to be rising by the week.

SOHO | The area south of Houston and north of Canal Street, between Lafayette Street and the Hudson River, is an architectural landmark, foodie paradise and fashion statement all rolled into one. The fantastic cast-iron buildings that populate the neighborhood were converted from factories into living lofts and artists' studios long ago. Then the neighborhood abandoned its boho roots in favor of high-end restaurants and shops. What remains is one of the world's best places to shop and stroll; a chronically cool neighborhood whose style has come to define an entire genre of fashion designers from Marc Jacobs to Kirna Zabete.

TRIBECA | When real estate developers dubbed it the Triangle below Canal Street in the 1970s, there were fewer than 250 people living in this wasteland between Soho and the Financial District. Like Soho before it, Tribeca was transformed from a shadowy warehouse district to a genteel residential

*Upper West Side – Lincoln Center*

community in the space of a single decade. Once an important transfer point for goods moving through lower Manhattan, the neighborhood is still chock-full of loading docks protruding from beautiful cast-iron buildings, many of which have been renovated as living lofts. Although upscale restaurants have taken over entire blocks of Franklin and Hudson streets, stylish shops and eateries are not all lined-up in brightly-lit rows as they are in Soho, but are tucked away amongst still-operational commercial spaces.

UNION SQUARE | Full with lunchtime office workers and, later at night with destination restaurant-goers, the blocks surrounding the Union Square Park are so full with restaurants and shops that they warrant their own neighborhood designation.

UPPER EAST SIDE | Third-World nannies and ladies who lunch are the stereotypical images of 10021, the city's most prestigious zip code. The truth isn't too far behind, especially on Park Avenue, where white-gloved doormen hail cabs for their residents and Frédéric Fekkai ladies are groomed and pampered like best-in-show spaniels. Meanwhile on Madison, tourists loaded with eurogelt floss in and out of the world's most expensive designer boutiques. Many of Manhattan's most famous museums, including the Metropolitan Museum of Art, the Guggenheim and the Whitney are up here too. The northern and eastern reaches of the neighborhood are far less exclusive; Second and Third avenues in particular are full of late-model high-rises harboring ambitious executive-assistants, and there are plenty of raucous beer bars for those who can't be bothered to taxi downtown.

UPPER WEST SIDE | Home to Lincoln Center and the Museum of Natural History, the Upper West Side is primarily a residential neighborhood, popular with families and others who appreciate the abundance of services and the proximity to Central Park. It's also one of the city's wealthiest residential districts. There are some good clothing shops along Columbus Avenue and, at night, Amsterdam Avenue between 79th and 86th streets sports the neighborhood's best stretch of bars. But even these can be eerily quiet on weekdays.

*AirTrain*

## LEAVING THE AIRPORT

### JOHN F. KENNEDY INTERNATIONAL (JFK)

TAXI | The fastest and easiest way to Manhattan is by taxi. Yellow cabs line up in front of each terminal and charge a single flat fee to anywhere in Manhattan, plus toll and tip—a total of about $60.

AIRTRAIN | A light rail system connects the airport to the "A" subway train and to the Long Island Railroad (LIRR) every 4-8 minutes from 6am to 11pm, and every 12 minutes at other times. The trip is inexpensive and takes about 45 minutes. It's a good way to go during rush hours and if you are not carrying much luggage.

SHUTTLE VAN | At least two companies offer shared door-to-door service between the airport and the city. SuperShuttle Manhattan (tel. 800.258.3826) and Airlink (tel. 877.599.8200). Both operate nonstop and charge about $20.

LIMOUSINE | Several companies offer limo service so you can arrive in New York in style. Phone Dial 7 Car & Limo Service (tel. 212.777.7777) or Classic Limousine (tel. 631.567.5100).

### LA GUARDIA (LGA)

TAXI | The fastest and easiest way to Manhattan is by taxi. Yellow cabs line up in front of each terminal and cost $25-$35 to Manhattan, plus toll and tip, depending on how far you go.

SHUTTLE VAN | At least two companies offer shared door-to-door service between the airport and the city. SuperShuttle Manhattan (tel. 800.258.3826) and Airlink (tel. 877.599.8200). Both operate nonstop and charge about $15.

LIMOUSINE | Several companies offer limo service so you can arrive in New York in style. Phone Dial 7 Car & Limo Service (tel. 212.777.7777) or Classic Limousine (tel. 631.567.5100).

*New York Taxi*

Washington Square Greenwich Village are prefaced "East" or "West." Street numbering begins at Fifth Avenue. Thus, 345 East 59th Street is about three and a half blocks east of Fifth Avenue—and quite far from—345 West 59th Street, which is three and a half blocks west of Fifth Avenue. South of Washington Square streets are named rather than numbered and, with few exceptions, the east-west policy is substituted with sequential numbering. Avenues run north-south and buildings are numbered serially, starting from the south. Addresses on most avenues have no direct relation to the nearest cross street.

## LOCAL TRANSPORT

BY TAXI | The rivers of yellow Chevrolet Caprices and Ford Crown Victorias that flow along Manhattan's streets and avenues course like blood through the city's concrete veins. Hail a cab and tell the Punjabi driver where you want to go (when the center of the roof light is lit, the cab is available for hire). The average taxi fare in Manhattan is $8 and cabbies expect a 15% tip. There is a limit of four passengers per cab.

## NEWARK INTERNATIONAL (EWR)

TAXI | Taxis line up for passengers at each terminal and charge fixed-price fares to Manhattan ranging from $40-$60, depending on how far you go. The trip takes 30-60 minutes.

SHUTTLE VAN | At least two companies offer shared door-to-door service between the airport and the city. SuperShuttle Manhattan (tel. 800.258.3826) and Airlink (tel. 877.599.8200). Both operate nonstop and charge $15-$23.

BUS | Newark Liberty Airport Express busses (tel. 908.354.3330) connect the airport with the Port Authority Bus Terminal (42nd St and Eighth Ave), Grand Central Terminal (Park Ave and 41st St), Penn Station (34th St and Eighth Ave), Chinatown (Lafayette and Walker sts), and the Wall Street area (Church and Barclay sts). Most buses depart every 30 to 40 minutes from 5am to 1am. The trip takes 30-60 minutes and costs about $15.

## FINDING AN ADDRESS

Fifth Avenue runs from the "top" of Manhattan to Washington Square in Greenwich Village and divides Manhattan into East and West sides. Almost all street addresses north of

BY SUBWAY | More than 6000 cars stopping at 469 stations on 23 lines make the NYC subway system one of the largest in the world. It's also the most complicated, and can feel like the Disorient Express. Each line is marked by a letter or number and station entrances are signed to show which lines stop there. Platforms are also marked with the lines that service them, though re-routing and frequent track work often puts these signs a little out of whack. Local trains stop at every station along the particular line in Manhattan while express trains stop only at major stations—marked with a white circle on subway maps. "Bronx-bound" and "Queens-bound" trains are heading uptown and "Brooklyn bound" trains are heading downtown. The subway operates 24 hours a day, seven days a week. Metrocards are available from station booths, which also dispense free route maps.

BY BUS | The world's largest fleet of municipal buses criss-crosses the city 24 hours a day, seven days a week. Some locals prefer riding busses on the avenues to taking the subways below them. Buses are identified by a letter representing the borough it serves, followed by the number of its route. Most run every few minutes from 7am to 10pm, and on a reduced schedule throughout the night.

## HISTORY IN A HURRY

**1524** First European explorer, Giovanni da Verrazzano, reaches New York Harbor.

**1624** First shipload of Dutch settlers arrives.

**1625** Settlement founded and named New Amsterdam.

**1626** Dutch Governor Peter Minuit "buys" Manhattan Island from the Indians for $24.

**1664** The Dutch surrender New Amsterdam to British troops without bloodshed; city is renamed New York.

**1725** The city's first newspaper, the New York Gazette, is founded.

**1754** Founding of King's College, later renamed Columbia University.

**1775** Patriots take over city government, setting the stage for the Revolutionary War.

**1776-81** New York is the site of numerous battles and skirmishes during the War of Independence.

**1784-96** New York City serves as the state capital (later moved to Albany).

**1783** The British evacuate the city.

**1812** Construction of City Hall completed.

**1834** Brooklyn becomes a city.

**1837** The Northern Dispensary, a landmark clinic for the poor treats Edgar Allen Poe, for a head cold.

**1840-60** Major wave of immigrants, especially Irish and Germans, nearly triple city's size to 800,000.

**1844** First City police force organized.

**1846** Telegraph service opens between NYC and Philadelphia.

**1847** City College of New York opens.

**1856** Land purchased for Central Park.

**1861** New York joins the Union army under President Lincoln during the Civil War.

**1865** NYC Fire Department is founded.

**1869** Construction of Grand Central Station begins.

**1870** First subway opens on Broadway.

**1877** Alexander Graham Bell makes first interstate phone call from Fifth Avenue and 18th Street; President Rutherford B. Hayes opens the American Museum of Natural History.

**1879** First telephone installed at the New York Stock Exchange.

**1880** Metropolitan Museum of Art opens.

**1883** Brooklyn Bridge links Brooklyn and Manhattan.

**1886** Statue of Liberty dedicated in New York Harbor.

**1891** Carnegie Hall opens.

**1892** First immigrants arrive at Ellis Island.

**1896** NY's first automobile accident.

**1897** First cab company opens in New York City.

**1898** Manhattan, Brooklyn, the Bronx, Queens and Staten Island join to become boroughs of NYC.

**1902** Construction begins on the main branch of the New York Public Library.

**1908** First New Years' Eve celebration held in Times Square.

**1910** The Flatiron Building leases offices to the Socialist Labor Party.

**1911** Fire at the Triangle Waist Company factory kills 141 people.

**1913** Equipped with a pony for transportation, Weegee begins working as a street photographer and photographs Lower East Side children on weekends.

**1927** Holland Tunnel opens.

**1913** The 60-story Woolworth Building becomes the tallest in the country.

**1924** The first Macy's Thanksgiving Day Parade begins when the department store's employees dress in costumes and march with floats, live bands and animals borrowed from the Central Park Zoo.

**1927** Actress Mae West is sentenced to ten days in a New York jail for public obscenity. She gets two days off for good behavior.

| | |
|---|---|
| **1931** | Empire State Building completed; George Washington Bridge connects Manhattan with New Jersey. |
| **1933** | RCA Building (Rockefeller Center) opens; Fiorello LaGuardia elected mayor. |
| **1935** | Women are admitted to the NYPD as uniformed, gun-toting officers. |
| **1936** | Triborough Bridge opens. |
| **1937** | Lincoln Tunnel connects Manhattan to New Jersey. |
| **1938** | Radio broadcast *War of the Worlds* announces that Mars invades New York!: *"The mouth is V-shaped with saliva dripping from its rimless lips that seem to quiver and pulsate...."* |
| **1946** | United Nations begins meeting in New York. UN headquarters completed six years later. The New York Knickerbockers start playing basketball. |
| **1953** | New York adopts three-color traffic lights. |
| **1955** | The iconic "Don't Walk" signs are introduced to the streets of New York City. |
| **1959** | After a spate of stabbings, the song *"Mack the Knife"* is banned from WCBS Radio. |
| **1960** | Woody Allen becomes a writer for the TV show *Candid Camera*. |
| **1965** | The Great Blackout cuts power to the entire Northeast. |
| **1965** | Andy Warhol, then producer for Velvet Underground, hires the frontwoman Nico, but Lou Reed refuses to let her sing his songs. |
| **1969** | Police raid the gay bar Stonewall Inn, resulting in a drag-queen led riot that sparks the gay liberation movement. |
| **1971** | The New York Dolls take to the stage for the first time, at a homeless shelter on Christmas Eve . |
| **1973** | CBGB opens with the intention of giving a stage to Country BlueGrass and Blues. One of the first shows is a band called Television, ushering in the era of punk. World Trade Center completed. |
| **1974** | New York City is broke and so is the Metropolitan Transportation Authority, a boon for graffiti artists who "bomb" trains and public spaces with "throw up" bubble lettering. |
| **1975** | The TV show *Saturday Night Live* begins broadcasting. Its first host is George Carlin. |
| **1976** | Roosevelt Island Tramway begins operations. |
| **1977** | Edward Koch becomes mayor. Son of Sam serial killer David Berkowitz terrorizes city. |
| **1979** | Studio 54 closes with the arrest of owners Steve Rubell and Ian Schrager on tax fraud charges. |
| **1980** | John Lennon is shot dead in front of his apartment building, the Dakota. Frank Sinatra records his iconic version of *New York, New York*: *"I want to wake up in a city that never sleeps/And find I'm A-number-one, top of the list"* |
| **1985** | Radio jock Howard Stern is fired from NBC after airing a comedy sketch called "Bestiality Dial-A-Date." |
| **1990** | Transvestite performer RuPaul is voted "Queen of Manhattan" by local club owners, promoters and DJs. |
| **1992** | John Gotti, the Teflon Don, is convicted on counts of murder, loan sharking and more and sentenced to life imprisonment without possibility of parole. |
| **1993** | Rudolph Giuliani elected mayor. |
| **1998** | New York City celebrates 100th birthday. |
| **1999** | The Brooklyn Museum ends its controversial exhibit, "Sensation," after Mayor Giuliani threatens to cut off city funding. |
| **2000** | New York Yankees win the World Series in a subway series. Donald Trump sets records for having one of the world's biggest swooping comb-overs. |
| **2001** | World Trade Center attacked. Hillary Clinton becomes Junior Senator from New York; Former President, Bill, sets up offices in Harlem. Media mogul Puff Daddy changes his name to P Diddy. |
| **2003** | Mayor Michael Bloomberg forces smokers outside with some of the country's most restrictive anti-smoking legislation. |
| **2004** | Dick Clark makes his last toast hosting New Year's Eve in Times Square. |
| **2005** | P Diddy changes his name to Diddy. |
| **2011** | Rebuilding of the World Trade Center site is still being contested. |

# INDEXES

# BOOK INDEX

# MAP INDEX

# MAP INDEX

**=U=**

| | |
|---|---|
| Union Square Park | I2 |
| University Pl | H2 |
| Upper East Side | B2 |
| Upper West Side | A2 |

**=V=**

| | |
|---|---|
| Vandam St | K1 |
| Vanderbilt Ave | E2 |
| Varick St | K1 |
| Vesey St | K2 |
| Vestry St | K1 |

**=W=**

| | |
|---|---|
| Walker St | K1 |
| Wall St | K2-L2 |
| Warren St | K2 |
| Washington Pl | I2 |
| Washington Sq North | H2 |
| Washington Sq South | H2 |
| Washington Sq Vlg | H2 |
| Washington Square Park | H2 |
| Washington St | G2, K1, K2 |
| Water St | L2 |
| Watts St | K1 |
| Waverly Pl | H2, I2 |
| West 3rd | H2 |
| West 4th St | H2 |
| West 8th St | H2 |
| West 10th St | G2-H2 |
| West 11th St | G2 |
| West 12th St | G2-H2 |
| West 13th St | G2, H2 |
| West 14th St | G2 |
| West 15th St | G2 |
| West 16th St | G2 |
| West 17th St | G2 |
| West 18th St | G2 |
| West 19th St | G2 |
| West 20th St | G2 |
| West 21st St | G2 |
| West 22nd St | G1 |
| West 23rd St | G1 |
| West 24th St | G1 |
| West 25th St | G1 |
| West 26th St | G1 |

| | |
|---|---|
| West 27th St | G1 |
| West 28th St | G1 |
| West 29th St | G1 |
| West 30th St | G1 |
| West 31st St | G1 |
| West 33rd St | G1 |
| West 34th St | G1 |
| West 35th St | G1 |
| West 36th St | G1 |
| West 37th St | G1 |
| West 38th St | G1 |
| West 39th St | G1 |
| West 40th St | G1 |
| West 41st St | G1 |
| West 42nd St | D2 |
| West 43rd St | D2 |
| West 44th St | D2 |
| West 45th St | D2 |
| West 46th St | D2 |
| West 47th St | D2 |
| West 48th St | D2 |
| West 49th St | D2 |
| West 50th St | D2 |
| West 51st St | D2 |
| West 52nd St | D2 |
| West 53rd St | D2 |
| West 54th St | D2 |
| West 55th St | D2 |
| West 56th St | D2 |
| West 57th St | D2 |
| West 58th St | D2 |
| West 59th St | D2 |
| West 60th St | D2 |
| West 61st St | D2 |
| West 62nd St | D1 |
| West 63rd St | D1 |
| West 64th St | D1 |
| West 65th St | D1 |
| West 66th St | D1 |
| West 67th St | D1 |
| West 68th St | D1 |
| West 69th St | D1 |
| West 70th St | D1 |
| West 71st St | D1 |
| West 72nd St | D1 |
| West 73rd St | D1 |

| | |
|---|---|
| West 74th St | D1 |
| West 75th St | D1 |
| West 76th St | D1 |
| West 77th St | D1 |
| West 78th St | D1 |
| West 79th St | D1 |
| West 80th St | D1 |
| West 81st St | A2 |
| West 82nd St | A2 |
| West 83rd St | A2 |
| West 84th St | A2 |
| West 85th St | A2 |
| West 86th St | A2 |
| West 87th St | A2 |
| West 88th St | A2 |
| West 89th St | A2 |
| West 90th St | A2 |
| West 91st St | A2 |
| West 92nd St | A2 |
| West 93rd St | A2 |
| West 94th St | A2 |
| West 95th St | A2 |
| West 96th St | A2 |
| West 97th St | A2 |
| West 100th St | A1 |
| West 101st St | A1 |
| West 102nd St | A1 |
| West 103rd St | A1 |
| West 104th St | A1 |
| West 105th St | A1 |
| West 106th St | A1 |
| West 107th St | A1 |
| West 108th St | A1 |
| West 109th St | A1 |
| West 110th St | A1 |
| West 111th St | A1 |
| West 112th St | A1 |
| West 113th St | A1 |
| West 114th St | A1 |
| West 116th St | A1 |
| West 117th St | A1 |
| West 118th St | A1 |
| West Broadway | K1 |
| West Dr | A1, A2, D1 |
| West Houston St | K1 |
| West Side Hwy | G1, G2 |

| | |
|---|---|
| West Side Hwy | K1 |
| West Thames St | K2 |
| White St | K1 |
| Whitehall St | K2 |
| Williams St | K2 |
| Wooster St | K1 |
| Worth St | K1 |
| York Ave | F1 |

# AVANT**GUIDE**NEW YORK CITY

# **POCKET**INFORMER
discreet guide with maps for ultimate portability

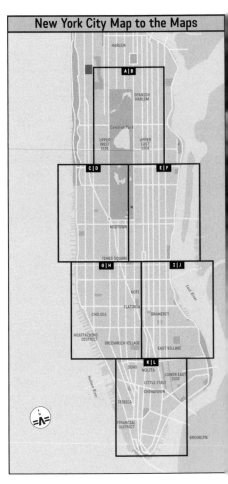

## New York City Map to the Maps

HARLEM

A | B

SPANISH HARLEM

Central Park

UPPER WEST SIDE

UPPER EAST SIDE

C | D

E | F

MIDTOWN

TIMES SQUARE

G | H

I | J

NOFI

FLATIRON

GRAMERCY

CHELSEA

MEATPACKING DISTRICT

GREENWICH VILLAGE

EAST VILLAGE

East River

K | L

SOHO

NOLITA

LOWER EAST SIDE

LITTLE ITALY

CHINATOWN

Hudson River

TRIBECA

FINANCIAL DISTRICT

BROOKLYN

| Map | # | Area | Hotel | Address | Phone | Website | Style Driven | Theme Driven | Club/Bar Scene | Spa | Pool | Business Sense | Kid Friendly |
|---|---|---|---|---|---|---|---|---|---|---|---|---|---|
| | | | **Inexpensive $** | | | | | | | | | | |
| H2 | 3 | Greenwich Village | Abingdon Guest House | 13 Eighth Ave | 212.243.5384 | abingdonguesthouse.com | | | | | | | ★ |
| H1 | 5 | Flatiron District | Arlington Hotel | 18 West 25th St | 212.645.3990 | hotelarlington.com | | | | | | | |
| I1 | 11 | Midtown | Carlton Arms | 160 East 25th St | 212.679.0680 | carltonarms.com | | | ★ | | | | |
| K1 | 16 | Tribeca | Cosmopolitan, The | 95 West Broadway | 212.566.1900 | cosmohotel.com | | | | | | | |
| J2 | 18 | East Village | East Village Bed and Coffee | 110 Ave C | 917.816.0071 | bedandcoffee.com | | | | | | | |
| H1 | 22 | Flatiron District | Gershwin, The | 7 East 27th St | 212.545.8000 | gershwinhotel.com | ★ | ★ | | | | | |
| I2 | 24 | Gramercy | Hotel 17 | 225 East 17th St | 212.475.2845 | hotel17ny.com | ★ | | | | | | |
| I1 | 25 | Midtown | Hotel 31 | 120 East 31st St | 212.685.3060 | hotel31.com | | | | | | | |
| H2 | 29 | Greenwich Village | Larchmont Hotel | 27 West 11th St | 212.989.9333 | larchmonthotel.com | | | | | | | |
| D2 | 38 | Midtown | Radio City Apartments | 142 West 49th St | 212.730.0728 | radiocityapartments.com | | | | | | | ★ |
| H1 | 44 | Midtown | Thirty-Thirty, Hotel | 30 East 30th St | 212.689.1900 | thirtythirty-nyc.com | ★ | | | | | | |
| | | | **Moderate $$** | | | | | | | | | | |
| C1 | 6 | Upper West Side | Beacon Hotel | 2130 Broadway | 212.787.1100 | beaconhotel.com | | | | | | | ★ |
| D2 | 7 | Midtown | Belvedere, The | 319 West 48th St | 212.245.7000 | belvederehotelnyc.com | | | | | | | |
| E2 | 8 | Midtown | Benjamin, The | 125 East 50th St | 212.715.2500 | thebenjamin.com | ★ | | | ★ | | ★ | ★ |
| D2 | 9 | Midtown | Blakely, The | 136 West 55th St | 212.245.1800 | blakelynewyork.com | | | | | | | ★ |
| H2 | 10 | Midtown | Bryant Park, The | 40 West 40th St | 212.869.0100 | bryantparkhotel.com | ★ | ★ | ★ | | | | |
| D2 | 12 | Midtown | Casablanca Hotel | 147 West 43rd St | 212.869.1212 | casablancahotel.com | ★ | | | | | | |
| H1 | 14 | Chelsea | Chelsea Hotel | 222 West 23rd St | 212.243.3700 | chelseahotel.com | | | | | | | ★ |
| D2 | 17 | Midtown | Dream Hotel | 210 West 55th St | 212.247.2000 | dreamny.com | ★ | ★ | | | | | |
| B2 | 20 | Upper East Side | Franklin, The | 164 East 87th St | 212.369.1000 | franklinhotel.com | ★ | | | | | ★ | ★ |
| D2 | 23 | Midtown | Hard Rock Hotel | 235 West 46th St | 212.764.5500 | hardrock.com | | | ★ | ★ | | | ★ |
| L1 | 26 | Lower East Side | Hotel on Rivington, The | 107 Rivington St | 212.475.2600 | hotelonrivington.com | ★ | | ★ | | | | |
| D2 | 27 | Midtown | Hudson | 356 West 58th St | 212.554.6000 | hudsonhotel.com | ★ | | ★ | | | | |
| I1 | 28 | Midtown | Kitano New York | 66 Park Ave | 212.885.7000 | kitano.com | | | ★ | | | ★ | ★ |
| G2 | 31 | Chelsea | Maritime Hotel, The | 363 West 16th St | 212.242.4300 | themaritimehotel.com | ★ | ★ | | | | | |
| I2 | 36 | Midtown | Park South Hotel | 122 East 28th St | 212.448.0888 | parksouthhotel.com | ★ | | | | | | |
| D2 | 37 | Midtown | QT Hotel | 125 West 45th St | 212.354.2323 | hotelqt.com | ★ | ★ | ★ | ★ | | | |
| E2 | 40 | Midtown | Roger Smith, The | 501 Lexington Ave | 212.755.1400 | rogersmith.com | | | | | | | ★ |
| D2 | 45 | Midtown | Time, The | 224 West 49th St | 212.320.2900 | thetimeny.com | ★ | ★ | | | | | |
| | | | **Expensive $$$** | | | | | | | | | | |
| K1 | 1 | Soho | 60 Thompson | 60 Thompson St | 212.431.0400 | 60thompson.com | ★ | ★ | ★ | | | | ★ |

| Map | # | Area | Hotel | Address | Phone | Website | Style Driven | Theme Driven | Club/Bar Scene | Spa | Pool | Business Sense | Kid Friendly |
|---|---|---|---|---|---|---|---|---|---|---|---|---|---|
| | | | **Expensive $$$** | | | | | | | | | | |
| I1 | 2 | Midtown | 70 Park Avenue | 70 Park Ave | 212.973.2400 | 70thparkave.com | ★ | | | | | ★ | ★ |
| E2 | 4 | Midtown | Alex Hotel, The | 205 East 45th St | 212.867.5100 | thealexhotel.com | ★ | ★ | | | | ★ | ★ |
| E2 | 13 | Midtown | Chambers, The | 15 West 56th St | 212.974.5656 | chambershotel.com | ★ | ★ | | | | ★ | |
| E2 | 15 | Midtown | City Club Hotel | 55 West 44th St | 212.921.5500 | cityclubhotel.com | ★ | | | | | | |
| G2 | 21 | Meatpacking Dist. | Gansevoort, Hotel | 18 Ninth Ave | 212.206.6700 | hotelgansevoort.com | ★ | ★ | ★ | ★ | ★ | | ★ |
| K1 | 32 | Soho | Mercer, The | 147 Mercer St | 212.966.6060 | mercerhotel.com | ★ | ★ | | | | ★ | ★ |
| H1 | 33 | Midtown | Morgans | 237 Madison Ave | 212.686.0300 | morganshotel.com | ★ | ★ | | | | ★ | |
| D2 | 34 | Midtown | Muse, The | 130 West 46th St | 212.485.2400 | themusehotel.com | ★ | | | | | ★ | |
| E2 | 35 | Midtown | New York Palace | 455 Madison Ave | 212.888.7000 | newyorkpalace.com | | | | | | ★ | ★ |
| D2 | 39 | Midtown | RIHGA Royal | 151 West 54th St | 212.307.5000 | rihgaroyalny.com | | | | | | ★ | ★ |
| E2 | 41 | Midtown | Royalton, The | 44 West 44th St | 212.869.4400 | royaltonhotel.com | ★ | ★ | | | | ★ | |
| K1 | 42 | Soho | Soho Grand | 310 West Broadway | 212.965.3000 | sohogrand.com | ★ | ★ | | | | ★ | |
| G2 | 43 | Meatpacking Dist. | Soho House New York | 29 Ninth Ave | 212.627.9800 | sohohouseny.com | ★ | ★ | ★ | ★ | ★ | | |
| K1 | 46 | Tribeca | Tribeca Grand Hotel | 2 Sixth Ave | 212.519.6600 | tribecagrand.com | ★ | ★ | ★ | | | ★ | |
| E2 | 48 | Midtown | W New York | 541 Lexington Ave | 212.755.1200 | whotels.com | ★ | ★ | ★ | ★ | | ★ | ★ |
| I1 | 49 | Midtown | W The Court | 130 East 39th St | 212.685.1100 | whotels.com | ★ | ★ | ★ | | | ★ | |
| D2 | 50 | Midtown | W Times Square | 1567 Broadway | 212.930.7400 | whotels.com | ★ | ★ | | | | ★ | ★ |
| | | | **Very Expensive $$$$** | | | | | | | | | | |
| E2 | 19 | Midtown | Four Seasons, The | 57 East 57th St | 212.758.5700 | fourseasons.com | ★ | | ★ | ★ | | ★ | ★ |
| D2 | 30 | Upper West Side | Mandarin Oriental | 80 Columbus Circle | 212.805.8800 | mandarinoriental.com | ★ | | ★ | ★ | ★ | ★ | ★ |
| D2 | 47 | Upper West Side | Trump International Hotel | 1 Central Park West | 212.299.1000 | trumpintl.com | ★ | | ★ | ★ | ★ | ★ | ★ |
| I2 | 51 | Union Square | W Union Square | 201 Park Ave South | 212.253.9119 | whotels.com | ★ | | ★ | ★ | | ★ | ★ |

| Pack it | | | | |
|---|---|---|---|---|
| aspirin | cd's | handcuffs | picnic blanket | sunglasses |
| backgammon set | clock | hat, scarf, gloves | playing cards | sunscreen |
| batteries | condoms | kite | power adapter | swim suit |
| beach towel | corkscrew | magazines | rolling paper | swiss army knife |
| binoculars | dvd's | massage oil | scented candles | umbrella |
| books | flip-flops | mp3 player | scrabble | video camera |
| camera | frisbee | phone charger | sexy underwear | warm sox |

▶▶▶ *Getting the best hotel deal is definitely avant. For the be*

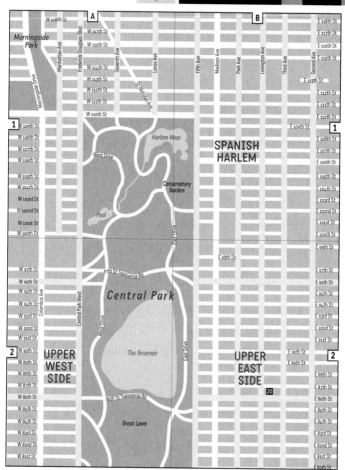

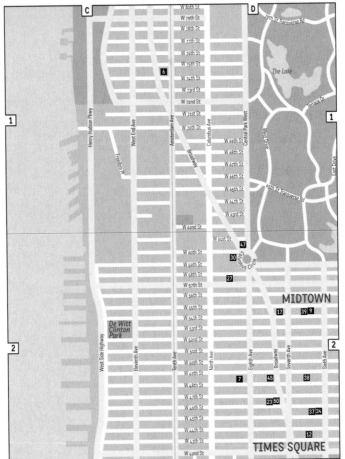

▶▶▶ *Getting the best hotel deal is definitely avant. For the b*

E 79th St
E 78th St
E 77th St
E 76th St
E 75th St
E 74th St
E 73rd St
E 72nd St
E 71st St
E 70th St
E 69th St
E 68th St
E 67th St
E 66th St
E 65th St
E 64th St
E 63rd St
E 62nd St
E 61st St
E 60th St
E 59th St
E 58th St
E 57th St
E 56th St
E 55th St
E 54th St
E 53rd St
E 52nd St
E 51st St
E 50th St
E 49th St
E 48th St
E 47th St
E 46th St
E 45th St
E 44th St
E 43rd St
E 42nd St

Conservatory
Water

Cherokee Pl
John Jay Park

Roosevelt Island

Zoo

Fifth Ave
Madison Ave
Park Ave
Lexington Ave
Third Ave
Second Ave
First Ave
York Ave
Franklin D Roosevelt Dr

Queensboro Bridge

Sutton Pl
Beekman Pl
Vanderbilt Ave
Park Ave S

**19**
**13**
**35**
**8**
**48**
**40**
**4**
**15**
**41**

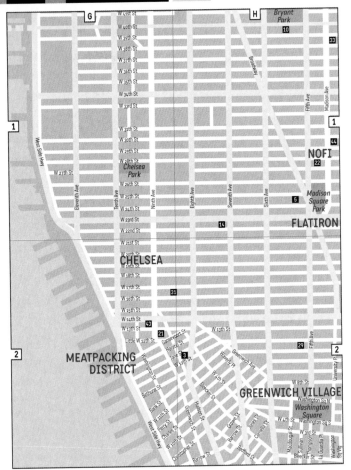

▶▶▶ *Getting the best hotel deal is definitely avant. For the be*

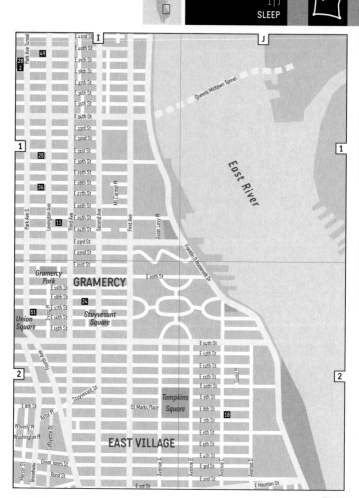

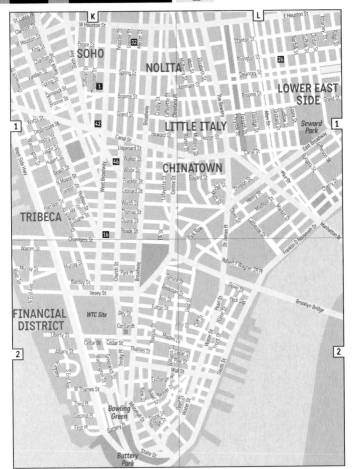

►►► Getting the best hotel deal is definitely avant. For the be...

| Map | # | Price | Cuisine | Restaurant | Address | Phone | Design Driven | Bar Scene | Celebrity Chef | Classic New York | Dining Alone | Date Place | Business Power | Kid Friendly | Outdoor Seating | Breakfast/Brunch | Dessert | After Midnight |
|---|---|---|---|---|---|---|---|---|---|---|---|---|---|---|---|---|---|---|
| | | | | **Chelsea** | | | | | | | | | | | | | | |
| G2 | 75 | $ | American | Pop Burger | 58 Ninth Ave | 212.414.8686 | ★ | ★ | | | | ★ | | | | | | ★ |
| H2 | 67 | $ | Pan Asian | Nooch | 143 Eighth Ave | 212.691.8600 | ★ | | | | | | ★ | ★ | ★ | | | |
| G1 | 8 | $$$ | American New | BED New York | 530 West 27th St | 212.594.4109 | ★ | ★ | | | | ★ | | | ★ | | | |
| G2 | 48 | $$$ | Italian | La Bottega | Maritime Hotel | 212.243.8400 | ★ | ★ | | | | ★ | | | | | | |
| G1 | 15 | $$$ | Italian Northern | Bottino | 246 Tenth Ave | 212.206.6766 | | | | | | | | | ★ | ★ | | |
| G2 | 59 | $$$ | Japanese | Matsuri | Maritime Hotel | 212.243.6400 | ★ | ★ | | | | | ★ | ★ | | | | |
| G1 | 79 | $$$ | Med-American | Red Cat | 227 Tenth Ave | 212.242.1122 | | | ★ | ★ | ★ | ★ | | | | | | |
| H1 | 9 | $$$$ | Asian New | Biltmore Room | 290 Eighth Ave | 212.807.0111 | ★ | | | | | | | | | | | |
| | | | | **Chinatown** | | | | | | | | | | | | | | |
| L1 | 74 | $ | Vietnamese | Pho Bang | 3 Pike St | 212.233.3947 | | | | | ★ | | | ★ | | | | |
| L1 | 32 | $$ | Dim Sum | Golden Unicorn | 18 East Broadway | 212.941.0911 | | | | | ★ | | | ★ | ★ | | | |
| | | | | **East Harlem** | | | | | | | | | | | | | | |
| B1 | 49 | $ | Mexican | La Casa De Los Tacos | 2277 First Ave | 212.860.6858 | | | | | ★ | ★ | | | | | | |
| | | | | **East Village** | | | | | | | | | | | | | | |
| I2 | 88 | $ | Japanese | SobaKoh | 309 East 5th St | 212.254.2244 | | | | | ★ | | | | | | | |
| I2 | 100 | $ | Ukrainian | Veselka | 144 Second Ave | 212.228.9682 | | | | ★ | ★ | | | ★ | | ★ | | ★ |
| I2 | 18 | $ | Venezuelan | Caracas Arepa Bar | 91 East 7th St | 212.228.5062 | | | | | ★ | | | | | | | |
| I2 | 87 | $$ | Delicatessen | Second Avenue Deli | 156 Second Ave | 212.677.0606 | | | | ★ | ★ | | | ★ | | ★ | | |
| I2 | 21 | $$ | Dessert | ChikaLicious | 203 East 10th St | 212.995.9511 | | | | | | ★ | | | | | ★ | |
| I2 | 78 | $$ | Greek | Pylos | 128 East 7th St | 212.473.0220 | | | | | | ★ | | | | | | |
| I2 | 26 | $$ | Korean | Dok Suni's | 119 First Ave | 212.477.9506 | | | | | | ★ | | | | | | |
| I2 | 38 | $$ | Thai | Holy Basil | 2nd Fl, 149 Second Ave | 212.460.5557 | | | | | | ★ | ★ | | | | | |
| I2 | 41 | $$$ | Vietnamese | Indochine | 430 Lafayette St | 212.505.5111 | | | | | | ★ | | | | | | |
| J2 | 6 | $$$ | Vietnamese New | Bao 111 | 111 Ave C | 212.254.7773 | ★ | | | | | ★ | | | | | | ★ |
| | | | | **Financial District** | | | | | | | | | | | | | | |
| K2 | 54 | $ | Pizza | Little Italy Pizza | 11 Park Pl | 212.227.7077 | | | | | | | ★ | ★ | | | | |
| | | | | **Gramercy** | | | | | | | | | | | | | | |
| H2 | 23 | $$ | American | Coffee Shop | 29 Union Sq. West | 212.243.7969 | ★ | | | | ★ | ★ | | | ★ | ★ | | ★ |
| I2 | 20 | $$ | Spanish Nuevo | Bar Jamón | 125 East 17th St | 212.253.2773 | | ★ | | | | ★ | | | | | | |
| I2 | 77 | $$$ | Raw Vegan | Pure Food and Wine | 54 Irving Pl | 212.477.1010 | | | | | | ★ | | | | | | |
| I2 | 91 | $$$ | S. American, Japanese | SushiSamba | 245 Park Ave South | 212.475.9377 | ★ | ★ | | | | ★ | | | | | | |
| I2 | 19 | $$$ | Spanish Nuevo | Casa Mono | 52 Irving Pl | 212.253.2773 | | ★ | | | | ★ | | | | | | |

| Map | # | Price | Cuisine | Restaurant | Address | Phone | Design Driven | Bar Scene | Celebrity Chef | Classic New York | Dining Alone | Date Place | Business Power | Kid Friendly | Outdoor Seating | Breakfast/Brunch | Dessert | After Midnight |
|---|---|---|---|---|---|---|---|---|---|---|---|---|---|---|---|---|---|---|
| | | | | | **Greenwich Village** | | | | | | | | | | | | | |
| H2 | 33 | $ | American | Gray's Papaya | 402 Sixth Ave | 212.260.3532 | | | | ★ | ★ | | | ★ | | | | ★ |
| H2 | 43 | $ | Pizza | John's Pizzeria | 278 Bleecker St | 212.243.1680 | | | | ★ | | ★ | | ★ | | | | |
| H2 | 22 | $$ | Asian | Chow Bar | 230 West 4th St | 212.633.2212 | ★ | | | | ★ | | | | | | | |
| H2 | 90 | $$ | English Modern | Spotted Pig, The | 314 West 11th St | 212.620.0393 | ★ | | | ★ | ★ | ★ | | ★ | | | | |
| H2 | 25 | $$ | Mexican | Diablo Royale | 189 West 10th St | 212.620.0223 | ★ | | | | ★ | | | ★ | | | | |
| H2 | 71 | $$ | Seafood | Pearl Oyster Bar | 18 Cornelia St | 212.691.8211 | | | | | ★ | ★ | | | | | | |
| G2 | 70 | $$$ | French Bistro | Pastis | 9 Ninth Ave | 212.929.4844 | ★ | ★ | | | ★ | | | | | | | |
| G2 | 72 | $$$ | French New | Perry Street | 176 Perry St | 212.352.1900 | ★ | | ★ | | | ★ | ★ | ★ | | | | |
| K1 | 57 | $$$ | Italian | Lupa | 170 Thompson St | 212.982.5089 | | | ★ | | ★ | | | | | | | |
| H2 | 92 | $$$ | S. American, Japanese | SushiSamba | 87 Seventh Ave South | 212.691.7885 | ★ | ★ | | | ★ | | ★ | | | | | |
| H2 | 4 | $$$$ | Italian | Babbo | 110 Waverly Pl | 212.777.0303 | | | ★ | | ★ | ★ | | | | | | |
| | | | | | **Little Italy** | | | | | | | | | | | | | |
| L1 | 29 | $ | Dessert Italian | Ferrara | 195 Grand St | 212.226.6150 | | | ★ | | | | | | | | ★ | |
| L1 | 73 | $ | Vietnamese | Pho Bang | 157 Mott St | 212.966.3797 | | | ★ | | ★ | | | | | | | |
| L1 | 50 | $$ | Mexican | La Esquina | 106 Kenmare St | 646.613.7100 | ★ | | ★ | ★ | | | | | | | | |
| | | | | | **Lower East Side** | | | | | | | | | | | | | |
| L1 | 55 | $ | American | LoSide Diner | 157 East Houston St | 212.254.2080 | | | ★ | | ★ | | ★ | ★ | | | | ★ |
| L1 | 40 | $ | Dessert | Il Laboratorio Del Gelato | 95 Orchard St | 212.343.9922 | ★ | ★ | | | | | | | | | ★ | |
| L1 | 86 | $$ | American | Schiller's Liquor Bar | 131 Rivington St | 212.260.4555 | ★ | | | ★ | | | | | | | | |
| L1 | 31 | $$ | American New | Freemans | Freeman Alley | 212.420.0012 | ★ | | | ★ | | | | | | | | |
| L1 | 42 | $$ | Italian | 'inoteca | 98 Rivington St | 212.614.0473 | ★ | | | | | | | | | | | |
| L1 | 85 | $$$ | Jewish | Sammy's Roumanian | 157 Chrystie St | 212.673.0330 | | | ★ | ★ | ★ | | | | | | | |
| L1 | 102 | $$$$ | Eclectic | WD-50 | 50 Clinton St | 212.477.2900 | ★ | | ★ | | | | | | | | | |
| | | | | | **Meatpacking District** | | | | | | | | | | | | | |
| G2 | 30 | $$ | French Bistro | Florent | 69 Gansevoort St | 212.989.5779 | | ★ | ★ | | | | | ★ | ★ | | | ★ |
| G2 | 58 | $$$ | Belgian | Markt | 401 West 14th St | 212.727.3314 | ★ | | | ★ | | ★ | | ★ | | | | |
| G2 | 99 | $$$ | Italian | Vento | 675 Hudson St | 212.699.2400 | ★ | | | ★ | ★ | ★ | ★ | ★ | | | | |
| G2 | 89 | $$$ | Southeast Asian | Spice Market | 403 West 13th St | 212.675.2322 | ★ | ★ | ★ | | | ★ | | | | | | |
| | | | | | **Midtown** | | | | | | | | | | | | | |
| H1 | 35 | $ | American | Gray's Papaya | 539 Eighth Ave | 212.904.1588 | | | | ★ | ★ | | | ★ | | | | ★ |
| C2 | 24 | $ | American Regional | Daisy May's BBQ USA | 623 Eleventh Ave | 212.977.1500 | | | | ★ | | | | | | | | |
| I1 | 82 | $ | Asian | Rice | 115 Lexington Ave | 212.686.5400 | | | | | ★ | | | | | | | |

▶▶▶ *Getting the best hotel deal is definitely avant. For the be*

| Map | # | Price | Cuisine | Restaurant | Address | Phone | Design Driven | Bar Scene | Celebrity Chef | Classic New York | Dining Alone | Date Place | Business Power | Kid Friendly | Outdoor Seating | Dessert | Breakfast/Brunch | After Midnight |
|---|---|---|---|---|---|---|---|---|---|---|---|---|---|---|---|---|---|---|
| D2 | 45 | $ | Pizza | John's Pizzeria | 260 West 44th St | 212.391.7560 | | | | | | ★ | | ★ | | | | |
| D2 | 51 | $ | Pizza | Little Italy Pizza | 55 West 45th St | 212.730.7575 | | | | | ★ | ★ | | ★ | | | | |
| E2 | 52 | $ | Pizza | Little Italy Pizza | 1 East 43rd St | 212.687.3660 | | | | | ★ | ★ | | ★ | | | | |
| I1 | 13 | $$ | American Regional | Blue Smoke | 116 East 27th St | 212.447.7733 | ★ | | | | | | | ★ | | | | |
| H1 | 47 | $$ | Korean | Kum Gang San | 49 West 32nd St | 212.967.0909 | | | | | ★ | ★ | | ★ | | | | |
| D2 | 7 | $$$ | American New | Bar Americain | 152 West 52nd St | 212.265.9700 | ★ | ★ | ★ | | | ★ | ★ | ★ | ★ | | | |
| E2 | 96 | $$$ | Asian | Tao | 42 East 58th St | 212.888.2288 | ★ | ★ | | | | ★ | ★ | | | | | |
| E2 | 16 | $$$ | French Brasserie | Brasserie | 100 East 53rd St | 212.751.4840 | ★ | | | | | ★ | ★ | ★ | ★ | | | ★ |
| H1 | 93 | $$$ | Indian New | Bread Bar at Tabla | 11 Madison Ave | 212.889.0667 | ★ | | | | | ★ | ★ | ★ | | | | |
| I1 | 28 | $$$ | Italian | English Is Italian | 622 Third Ave | 212.404.1700 | | ★ | | | | | | ★ | | | | |
| D2 | 37 | $$$ | Latin New | Hell's Kitchen | 679 Ninth Ave | 212.977.1588 | ★ | | | | | ★ | | ★ | | | | |
| F2 | 83 | $$$ | Mexican | Rosa Mexicano | 1063 First Ave | 212.753.7407 | | | | | | ★ | | ★ | | | | |
| D2 | 11 | $$$ | Seafood | Blue Fin | W Times Square | 212.918.1400 | ★ | | | | | ★ | ★ | | | | | |
| E2 | 69 | $$$ | Seafood | Oyster Bar, The | Grand Central Terminal | 212.490.6650 | | | ★ | ★ | | | ★ | | | | | |
| H1 | 46 | $$$ | Steakhouse | Keens Steakhouse | 72 West 36th St | 212.947.3636 | | | | ★ | | | ★ | ★ | | | | |
| E2 | 98 | $$$$ | American New | Town | Chambers Hotel | 212.582.4445 | ★ | | | | | | ★ | ★ | | | | |
| E2 | 63 | $$$$ | Chinese | Mr. Chow | 324 East 57th St | 212.751.9030 | | | | | | ★ | ★ | ★ | | | | |
| H1 | 93 | $$$$ | Indian New | Tabla | 11 Madison Ave | 212.889.0667 | ★ | | | | | | ★ | ★ | | | | |
| E2 | 66 | $$$$ | Japanese Peruvian | Nobu 57 | 40 West 57th St | 212.757.3000 | ★ | | ★ | | | ★ | ★ | ★ | | | | |
| E2 | 101 | $$$$ | Thai | Vong | 200 East 54th St | 212.486.9592 | ★ | | | | | | ★ | ★ | | | | |
| | | | | **Nolita** | | | | | | | | | | | | | | |
| L1 | 81 | $ | Asian | Rice | 227 Mott St | 212.226.5775 | | | | | | | | ★ | | | | |
| L1 | 76 | $$$ | Global | Public | 210 Elizabeth St | 212.343.7011 | ★ | ★ | | | | ★ | ★ | | | | | |
| | | | | **Soho** | | | | | | | | | | | | | | |
| K1 | 53 | $ | Pizza | Little Italy Pizza | 180 Varick St | 212.366.5566 | | | | | ★ | ★ | | ★ | | | | |
| K1 | 39 | $$ | Caribbean | Ideya | 349 West Broadway | 212.625.1441 | ★ | ★ | | | | ★ | ★ | | | | | |
| K1 | 56 | $$ | French Bistro | Lucky Strike | 59 Grand St | 212.941.0479 | | | | | | ★ | | | | | | ★ |
| K1 | 12 | $$$ | American New | Blue Ribbon | 97 Sullivan St | 212.274.0404 | | | | | | ★ | | | | | | ★ |
| K1 | 5 | $$$ | French Brasserie | Balthazar | 80 Spring St | 212.965.1414 | ★ | ★ | | | | ★ | | | | | | ★ |
| K1 | 61 | $$$ | French, American New | Mercer Kitchen | Mercer Hotel | 212.966.5454 | ★ | ★ | ★ | | | ★ | | | | | | |
| K1 | 2 | $$$ | Seafood | Aquagrill | 210 Spring St | 212.274.0505 | ★ | | | | | ★ | ★ | | ★ | | | |
| | | | | **Tribeca** | | | | | | | | | | | | | | |
| K1 | 103 | $ | Sandwiches | 'Wichcraft | 397 Greenwich St | 212.780.0577 | ★ | | ★ | | ★ | | | | ★ | | ★ | |

| Map | # | Price | Cuisine | Restaurant | Address | Phone | Design Driven | Bar Scene | Celebrity Chef | Classic New York | Dining Alone | Date Place | Business Power | Kid Friendly | Outdoor Seating | Breakfast/Brunch | Dessert | After Midnight |
|---|---|---|---|---|---|---|---|---|---|---|---|---|---|---|---|---|---|---|
| | | | | | **Tribeca** | | | | | | | | | | | | | |
| K1 | 1 | $$$ | Chinese | 66 | 241 Church St | 212.925.0202 | ★ | ★ | ★ | | | ★ | ★ | | | | | |
| K1 | 68 | $$$ | French Bistro | Odeon | 145 West Broadway | 212.233.0507 | ★ | | | ★ | | ★ | ★ | | ★ | ★ | | ★ |
| K1 | 36 | $$$ | Med-American | Harrison, The | 355 Greenwich St | 212.274.9310 | | | ★ | | | ★ | ★ | ★ | | | | |
| K1 | 27 | $$$ | Steakhouse | Dylan Prime | 62 Laight St | 212.334.4783 | ★ | | | | | | ★ | | | | | |
| K1 | 60 | $$$$ | Japanese | Megu | 62 Thomas St | 212.964.7777 | ★ | ★ | | | | ★ | ★ | | | | | |
| K1 | 64 | $$$$ | Japanese Peruvian | Nobu | 105 Hudson St | 212.219.0500 | ★ | | ★ | | | ★ | ★ | ★ | | | | |
| K1 | 65 | $$$$ | Japanese Peruvian | Nobu, Next Door | 105 Hudson St | 212.334.4445 | ★ | | ★ | | | ★ | ★ | ★ | | | | |
| | | | | | **Union Square** | | | | | | | | | | | | | |
| H2 | 80 | $ | Asian | Republic | 37 Union Square West | 212.627.7172 | ★ | | | | | | | ★ | | | | |
| H2 | 62 | $$$ | American Regional | Mesa Grill | 102 Fifth Ave | 212.807.7400 | ★ | ★ | | | | ★ | ★ | ★ | ★ | | | |
| H2 | 104 | $$$ | Mexican | Rosa Mexicano | 9 East 18th St | 212.533.3350 | ★ | ★ | | | | | ★ | ★ | | | | |
| H2 | 10 | $$$ | Seafood | BLT Fish | 21 West 17th St | 212.691.8888 | | | ★ | | | | ★ | | | | | |
| | | | | | **Upper East Side** | | | | | | | | | | | | | |
| B2 | 94 | $ | Bagels | Tal Bagels | 333 East 86th St | 212.427.6811 | | | | ★ | ★ | | | ★ | | ★ | | |
| B2 | 95 | $ | Bagels | Tal Bagels | 1228 Lexington Ave | 212.717.2080 | | | | ★ | ★ | | | ★ | | ★ | | |
| F1 | 44 | $ | Pizza | John's Pizzeria | 408 East 64th St | 212.935.2895 | | | | | | | | ★ | ★ | | | |
| D1 | 14 | $$$ | American New | Boat House | in Central Park | 212.517.2233 | | | | | | | | ★ | ★ | ★ | | |
| E1 | 3 | $$$ | Seafood | Atlantic Grill | 1341 Third Ave | 212.988.9200 | ★ | | | | | | | ★ | ★ | | | |
| | | | | | **Upper West Side** | | | | | | | | | | | | | |
| D1 | 34 | $ | American | Gray's Papaya | 2090 Broadway | 212.799.0243 | | | | ★ | ★ | | | ★ | | | | ★ |
| A2 | 17 | $$$ | Latin Nuevo | Calle Ocho | 446 Columbus Ave | 212.873.5025 | ★ | ★ | | | | ★ | | | | | | |
| D1 | 84 | $$$ | Mexican | Rosa Mexicano | 61 Columbus Ave | 212.977.7700 | | | | | | | | ★ | ★ | | | |
| D1 | 97 | $$$$ | American | Tavern on the Green | Central Park West | 212.873.3200 | ★ | | | ★ | | ★ | ★ | ★ | ★ | ★ | ★ | |

►►► *Getting the best hotel deal is definitely avant. For the b*

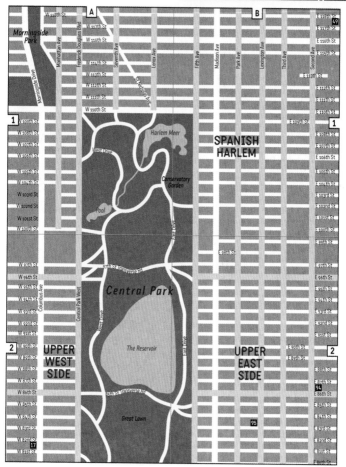

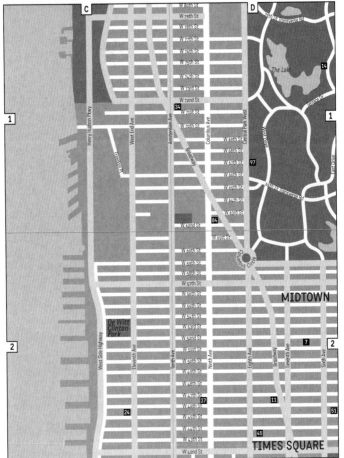

►►► *Getting the best hotel deal is definitely avant. For the b*

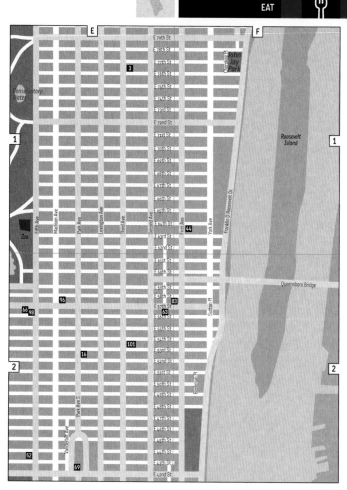

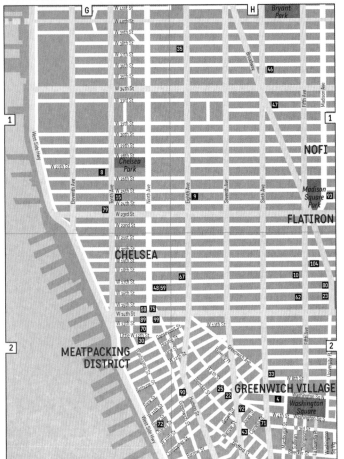

▶▶▶ *Getting the best hotel deal is definitely avant. For the bes*

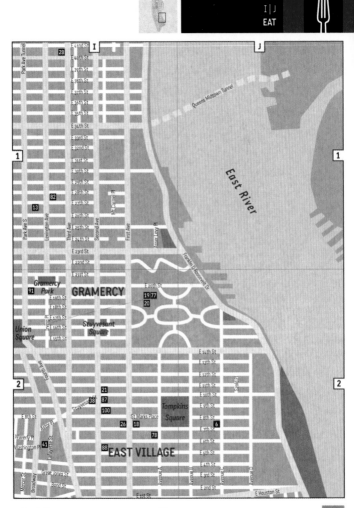

►►► *Getting the best hotel deal is definitely avant. For the be*

| Map | # | Area | Shop | Address | Phone | Design Driven | Celebrity Clientele | Legendary | Only in New York |
|---|---|---|---|---|---|---|---|---|---|
| | | | **FASHION & BEAUTY** | | | | | | |
| | | | **Accessories** | | | | | | |
| I2 | 82 | Lower East Side | Eugenia Kim | 203 East 4th St | 212.673.9787 | ★ | ★ | | ★ |
| D2 | 177 | Midtown | Swatch | 1528 Broadway | 212.764.5541 | ★ | | | |
| K1 | 10 | Soho | Add | 461 West Broadway | 212.539.1439 | | | | ★ |
| K1 | 12 | Soho | Agent Provocateur | 133 Mercer St | 212.965.0229 | | ★ | | |
| K1 | 107 | Soho | Jack Spade | 56 Greene St | 212.625.1820 | ★ | | | |
| K1 | 119 | Soho | Kazuyo Nakano | 117 Crosby St | 212.941.7093 | ★ | ★ | | ★ |
| E1 | 50 | Upper East Side | Brella Bar | 1043 Third Ave | 212.813.9530 | ★ | ★ | | ★ |
| | | | **Clothing—Basics** | | | | | | |
| G2 | 166 | Meatpacking District | Scoop | 430 West 14th St | 212.929.1244 | ★ | ★ | | |
| E2 | 34 | Midtown | Bebe | 805 Third Ave | 212.588.9060 | ★ | | | |
| D2 | 155 | Midtown | Quiksilver | 3 Times Square | 212.840.8534 | ★ | | | |
| K1 | 42 | Soho | Big Drop | 174 Spring St | 212.966.4299 | | ★ | | ★ |
| K1 | 165 | Soho | Scoop | 532 Broadway | 212.925.2886 | ★ | ★ | | |
| H2 | 33 | Union Square | Bebe | 100 Fifth Ave | 212.675.2323 | ★ | | | |
| E1 | 35 | Upper East Side | Bebe | 1127 Third Ave | 212.935.2444 | ★ | | | |
| E1 | 43 | Upper East Side | Big Drop | 1321 Third Ave | 212.988.3344 | | ★ | | ★ |
| E1 | 164 | Upper East Side | Scoop | 1275 Third Ave | 212.535.5577 | ★ | ★ | | |
| | | | **Clothing—Designer** | | | | | | |
| G1 | 61 | Chelsea | Comme des Garçons | 520 West 22nd St | 212.604.9200 | ★ | ★ | | |
| G2 | 173 | Chelsea | Stella McCartney | 429 West 14th St | 212.255.1556 | ★ | ★ | | |
| I2 | 65 | East Village | Daryl K | 21 Bond St | 212.529.8790 | ★ | ★ | | |
| I2 | 90 | East Village | Ghost | 28 Bond St | 646.602.2891 | ★ | | | |
| I2 | 168 | East Village | Selia Yang Bridal | 328 East 9th St | 212.254.9073 | ★ | ★ | | ★ |
| I2 | 169 | East Village | Selia Yang Ready to Wear | 324 East 9th St | 212.254.8980 | ★ | | | ★ |
| H2 | 63 | Greenwich Village | Cynthia Rowley | 376 Bleecker St | 212.242.3803 | ★ | ★ | | |
| H2 | 133 | Greenwich Village | Marc Jacobs | 403-405 Bleecker St | 212.924.0026 | ★ | | | |
| L1 | 51 | Little Italy | Built By Wendy | 7 Centre Market Pl | 212.925.6538 | ★ | ★ | | |
| G2 | 15 | Meatpacking District | An Earnest Cut & Sew | 821 Washington St | 212.242.3414 | | ★ | | ★ |
| G2 | 53 | Meatpacking District | Calypso | 654 Hudson St | 646.638.3000 | ★ | | | |
| G2 | 56 | Meatpacking District | Carlos Miele | 408 West 14th St | 646.336.6642 | ★ | ★ | | |
| G2 | 58 | Meatpacking District | Catherine Malandrino | 652 Hudson St | 212.929.8710 | ★ | | | ★ |
| H2 | 64 | Meatpacking District | Darling | 1 Horatio St | 646.336.6966 | ★ | | | ★ |
| G2 | 81 | Meatpacking District | Elizabeth Charles | 639 1/2 Hudson St | 212.243.3201 | | | | ★ |
| H2 | 128 | Meatpacking District | Lucy Barnes | 320 West 14th St | 212.255.9148 | ★ | | | ★ |
| E2 | 153 | Midtown | Prada | 45 East 57th St | 212.308.2332 | ★ | ★ | | |
| E2 | 154 | Midtown | Prada | 724 Fifth Ave | 212.664.0010 | ★ | ★ | | |
| E2 | 159 | Midtown | Robert Marc | 551 Madison Ave | 212.319.2000 | ★ | | | ★ |
| L1 | 11 | Nolita | A Detacher | 262 Mott St | 212.625.3380 | | | | ★ |
| L1 | 54 | Nolita | Calypso | 280 Mott St | 212.965.0990 | ★ | | | |
| L1 | 60 | Nolita | Christopher Totman | 262 Mott St | 212.925.7495 | | | | ★ |
| L1 | 129 | Nolita | Malia Mills | 199 Mulberry St | 212.625.2311 | ★ | ★ | | ★ |

| Map # | Area | Shop | Address | Phone | Design Driven | Celebrity Clientele | Legendary | Only in New York |
|---|---|---|---|---|---|---|---|---|
| | | **Clothing—Designer** | | | | | | |
| L1 150 | Nolita | Polo/Ralph Lauren | 31 Prince Street | 212.680.0181 | ★ | | | |
| K1 19 | Soho | Anna Sui | 113 Greene St | 212.941.8406 | ★ | | | |
| K1 20 | Soho | A.P.C. | 131 Mercer St | 212.966.9685 | ★ | | | |
| K1 25 | Soho | Barbara Bui | 115 Wooster St | 212.625.1938 | | ★ | | |
| K1 37 | Soho | Betsey Johnson | 138 Wooster St | 212.995.5048 | ★ | | | |
| K1 55 | Soho | Calypso | 424 Broome St | 212.274.0449 | ★ | | | |
| K1 57 | Soho | Catherine Malandrino | 468 Broome St | 212.925.6765 | ★ | ★ | | |
| K1 73 | Soho | Diesel | 135 Spring St | 212.625.1555 | ★ | | | |
| K1 75 | Soho | DKNY | 420 West Broadway | 646.613.1100 | ★ | | | |
| K1 77 | Soho | Dosa | 107 Thompson St | 212.431.1733 | ★ | ★ | | |
| K1 92 | Soho | Hotel Venus | 382 West Broadway | 212.966.4066 | ★ | ★ | | |
| K1 110 | Soho | J. Lindeberg | 126 Spring St | 212.625.9403 | ★ | | | |
| K1 134 | Soho | Marc Jacobs | 163 Mercer St | 212.343.1490 | ★ | | | |
| K1 136 | Soho | Miss Sixty | 386 West Broadway | 212.334.9772 | ★ | | | |
| K1 137 | Soho | Morgane Le Fay | 67 Wooster St | 212.219.7672 | ★ | ★ | | |
| K1 149 | Soho | Polo/Ralph Lauren | 379 West Broadway | 212.625.1660 | ★ | | | |
| K1 152 | Soho | Prada | 575 Broadway | 212.334.8888 | ★ | ★ | | |
| K1 157 | Soho | Reiss | 387 West Broadway | 212.925.5707 | ★ | | | |
| K1 158 | Soho | Robert Marc | 436 West Broadway | 212.343.8300 | ★ | | | ★ |
| H2 72 | Union Square | Diesel | 1 Union Square West | 646.336.8552 | ★ | | | |
| E2 39 | Upper East Side | Betsey Johnson | 251 East 60th St | 212.319.7699 | ★ | | | |
| B2 40 | Upper East Side | Betsey Johnson | 1060 Madison Ave | 212.734.1257 | ★ | | | |
| E1 52 | Upper East Side | Calypso | 935 Madison Ave | 212.535.4100 | ★ | | | ★ |
| E2 71 | Upper East Side | Diesel | 770 Lexington Ave | 212.308.0055 | ★ | | | |
| E2 74 | Upper East Side | DKNY | 655 Madison Ave | 212.223.3569 | ★ | | | |
| E1 130 | Upper East Side | Malia Mills | 1031 Lexington Ave | 212.517.7485 | ★ | ★ | | ★ |
| E1 138 | Upper East Side | Morgane Le Fay | 746 Madison Ave | 212.879.9700 | | ★ | | ★ |
| E1 147 | Upper East Side | Polo/Ralph Lauren | 867 Madison Ave | 212.606.2100 | ★ | ★ | | |
| E1 148 | Upper East Side | Polo/Ralph Lauren | 888 Madison Ave | 212.434.8000 | ★ | | | |
| D1 38 | Upper West Side | Betsey Johnson | 248 Columbus Ave | 212.362.3364 | ★ | | | |
| D1 131 | Upper West Side | Malia Mills | 220 Columbus Ave | 212.874.7200 | ★ | ★ | | ★ |
| D1 160 | Upper West Side | Robert Marc | 190 Columbus Ave | 212.799.4600 | ★ | | | ★ |
| | | **Clothing—Multilabel Stores** | | | | | | |
| H2 24 | Chelsea | Bang Bang | 147 Eighth Ave | 212.807.8457 | | | | ★ |
| G2 109 | Chelsea | Jeffrey | 449 West 14th St | 212.206.1272 | ★ | ★ | | ★ |
| I2 18 | East Village | Anna | 150 East 3rd St | 212.358.0195 | | | | ★ |
| I2 182 | East Village | Trash & Vaudeville | 4 St Mark's Pl | 212.982.3590 | | | | ★ ★ |
| I2 190 | East Village | Urban Outfitters | 162 Second Ave | 212.375.1277 | ★ | | | |
| H2 104 | Flatiron District | Intermix | 125 Fifth Ave | 212.533.9720 | ★ | ★ | | ★ |
| I2 23 | Greenwich Village | Bang Bang | 53 East 8th St | 212.475.8220 | | | | ★ |
| I2 79 | Greenwich Village | EdgeNY | 65 Bleecker St | 212.358.0255 | | | | ★ |
| H2 106 | Greenwich Village | Intermix | 365 Bleecker St | 212.929.7180 | ★ | ★ | | ★ |

▶▶▶ *Getting the best hotel deal is definitely avant. For the be*

| Map | # | Area | Shop | Address | Phone | Design Driven | Celebrity Clientele | Legendary | Only in New York |
|-----|---|------|------|---------|-------|:-:|:-:|:-:|:-:|
| K1 | 141 | Greenwich Village | Nom de Guerre | 640 Broadway | 212.253.2891 | ★ |  |  | ★ |
| H2 | 146 | Greenwich Village | Petit Peton | 27 West 8th St | 212.677.3730 | ★ |  |  | ★ |
| H2 | 189 | Greenwich Village | Urban Outfitters | 374 Sixth Ave | 212.677.9350 | ★ |  |  |  |
| L1 | 180 | Lower East Side | TG-170 | 170 Ludlow St | 212.995.8660 | ★ | ★ |  | ★ |
| E2 | 192 | Midtown | Urban Outfitters | 999 Third Ave | 212.308.1518 | ★ |  |  |  |
| K1 | 125 | Nolita | Label | 265 Lafayette St | 212.966.7736 |  |  |  | ★ |
| L1 | 170 | Nolita | SSUR Plus | 7 Spring St | 212.431.3152 |  |  |  | ★ |
| L1 | 175 | Nolita | Steven Alan | 229 Elizabeth St | 212.226.7482 | ★ | ★ |  |  |
| K1 | 97 | Soho | If | 94 Grand St | 212.334.4964 | ★ | ★ |  | ★ |
| K1 | 123 | Soho | Kirna Zabete | 96 Greene St | 212.941.9656 | ★ | ★ |  | ★ |
| K1 | 183 | Soho | Triple Five Soul | 290 Lafayette St | 212.431.2404 | ★ |  |  | ★ |
| K1 | 174 | Tribeca | Steven Alan | 103 Franklin St | 212.343.0692 | ★ | ★ |  |  |
| E1 | 16 | Upper East Side | Anik | 1355 Third Ave | 212.861.9840 | ★ |  |  |  |
| B2 | 17 | Upper East Side | Anik | 1122 Madison Ave | 212.249.2417 | ★ |  |  |  |
| E1 | 103 | Upper East Side | Intermix | 1003 Madison Ave | 212.249.7858 | ★ | ★ |  | ★ |
| D1 | 105 | Upper West Side | Intermix | 210 Columbus Ave | 212.769.9116 | ★ | ★ |  | ★ |
| A2 | 176 | Upper West Side | Steven Alan | 465 Amsterdam Ave | 212.595.8451 | ★ | ★ |  |  |
| C1 | 191 | Upper West Side | Urban Outfitters | 2081 Broadway | 212.579.3912 | ★ |  |  |  |
|  |  |  | **Clothing—Vintage & Thrift** |  |  |  |  |  |  |
| H2 | 93 | Chelsea | Housing Works Thrift Shop | 143 West 17th St | 212.366.0820 |  |  |  | ★ |
| I2 | 18 | East Village | Anna | 150 East 3rd St | 212.358.0195 |  |  |  | ★ |
| J2 | 161 | East Village | Rue St. Denis | 170 Ave B | 212.260.3388 |  |  |  | ★ |
| I2 | 167 | East Village | Screaming Mimi's | 382 Lafayette St | 212.677.6464 |  |  |  | ★ |
| I2 | 181 | East Village | Tokio7 | 64 East 7th St | 212.353.8443 | ★ |  |  | ★ |
| I1 | 94 | Midtown | Housing Works Thrift Shop | 157 East 23rd St | 212.529.5955 |  |  |  | ★ |
| E1 | 95 | Upper East Side | Housing Works Thrift Shop | 202 East 77th St | 212.772.8461 |  |  |  | ★ |
| C1 | 14 | Upper West Side | Allan & Suzi | 416 Amsterdam Ave | 212.724.7445 |  |  |  | ★ |
| D1 | 96 | Upper West Side | Housing Works Thrift Shop | 306 Columbus Ave | 212.579.7566 |  |  |  | ★ |
|  |  |  | **Clothing—Designer Outlet** |  |  |  |  |  |  |
| G2 | 85 | Chelsea | Find Outlet | 361 West 17th St | 212.243.3177 |  |  |  | ★ |
| I2 | 89 | East Village | Gabay's | 225 First Ave | 212.254.3180 |  |  |  | ★ |
| K2 | 59 | Financial District | Century 21 | 22 Cortlandt St | 212.227.9092 |  |  | ★ | ★ |
| L1 | 86 | Nolita | Find Outlet | 229 Mott St | 212.226.5167 |  |  |  | ★ |
| L1 | 99 | Nolita | Ina | 21 Prince St | 212.334.9048 |  |  |  | ★ |
| L1 | 101 | Nolita | Ina Men's Store | 262 Mott St | 212.334.2210 |  |  |  | ★ |
| K1 | 98 | Soho | Ina | 101 Thompson St | 212.941.4757 |  |  |  | ★ |
| E1 | 100 | Upper East Side | Ina | 208 East 73rd St | 212.249.0014 |  |  |  | ★ |
|  |  |  | **Cosmetics, Fragrance & Grooming** |  |  |  |  |  |  |
| I2 | 121 | East Village | Kiehl's | 109 Third Ave | 212.677.3171 | ★ | ★ |  |  |
| K1 | 12 | Soho | Agent Provocateur | 133 Mercer St | 212.965.0229 | ★ |  |  |  |
| D1 | 122 | Upper West Side | Kiehl's | 150 Columbus Ave | 212.799.3438 |  | ★ |  |  |
|  |  |  | **Eyewear** |  |  |  |  |  |  |
| I2 | 46 | East Village | Bond 07 | 7 Bond St | 212.677.8487 | ★ | ★ |  | ★ |

| Map | # | Area | Shop | Address | Phone | Design Driven | Celebrity Clientele | Legendary | Only in New York |
|---|---|---|---|---|---|---|---|---|---|
| | | | **Department Stores** | | | | | | |
| H2 | 30 | Chelsea | Barneys Co-Op | 236 West 18th St | 212.593.7800 | ★ | | | |
| E2 | 36 | Midtown | Bergdorf Goodman | 754 Fifth Ave | 212.753.7300 | | | ★ | ★ |
| E2 | 91 | Midtown | Henri Bendel | 712 Fifth Ave | 212.247.1100 | | | ★ | |
| K1 | 32 | Soho | Barneys Co-Op | 116 Wooster St | 212.965.9964 | ★ | | | |
| K1 | 45 | Soho | Bloomingdale's Soho | 504 Broadway | 212.729.5900 | | ★ | | |
| E2 | 29 | Upper East Side | Barneys | 660 Madison Ave | 212.826.8900 | ★ | | | |
| E2 | 44 | Upper East Side | Bloomingdale's | 1000 Third Ave | 212.705.2000 | | ★ | | |
| C1 | 31 | Upper West Side | Barneys Co-Op | 2151 Broadway | 646.335.0978 | ★ | | | |
| | | | **Handbags & Luggage** | | | | | | |
| E2 | 179 | Midtown | T. Anthony | 445 Park Ave | 212.750.9797 | ★ | ★ | | |
| L1 | 11 | Nolita | A Detacher | 262 Mott St | 212.625.3380 | | | | ★ |
| K1 | 10 | Soho | Add | 461 West Broadway | 212.539.1439 | | | | ★ |
| K1 | 107 | Soho | Jack Spade | 56 Greene St | 212.625.1820 | ★ | | | |
| K1 | 119 | Soho | Kazuyo Nakano | 117 Crosby St | 212.941.7093 | ★ | ★ | | ★ |
| | | | **Jewelry** | | | | | | |
| I2 | 46 | East Village | Bond 07 | 7 Bond St | 212.677.8487 | ★ | ★ | | ★ |
| I2 | 90 | East Village | Ghost | 28 Bond St | 646.602.2891 | ★ | | | |
| G2 | 81 | Meatpacking District | Elizabeth Charles | 639 1/2 Hudson St | 212.243.3201 | | | | ★ |
| L1 | 135 | Nolita | Me&Ro | 241 Elizabeth St | 917.237.9215 | ★ | ★ | | ★ |
| K1 | 10 | Soho | Add | 461 West Broadway | 212.539.1439 | | | | ★ |
| K1 | 12 | Soho | Agent Provocateur | 133 Mercer St | 212.965.0229 | ★ | | | |
| | | | **Lingerie** | | | | | | |
| G2 | 81 | Meatpacking District | Elizabeth Charles | 639 1/2 Hudson St | 212.243.3201 | | | | ★ |
| K1 | 12 | Soho | Agent Provocateur | 133 Mercer St | 212.965.0229 | ★ | | | |
| K1 | 126 | Soho | Le Corset | 80 Thompson St | 212.334.4936 | | ★ | | ★ |
| E1 | 48 | Upper East Side | Bra Smyth | 905 Madison Ave | 212.772.9400 | | ★ | | ★ |
| | | | **Shoes** | | | | | | |
| G2 | 109 | Chelsea | Jeffrey | 449 West 14th St | 212.206.1272 | ★ | ★ | | ★ |
| L1 | 114 | East Village | Jutta Neumann | 158 Allen St | 212.982.7048 | ★ | | | ★ |
| K1 | 141 | Greenwich Village | Nom de Guerre | 640 Broadway | 212.253.2891 | ★ | | | ★ |
| L1 | 13 | Lower East Side | Alife | 158 Rivington St | 212.375.8128 | ★ | | | ★ |
| L1 | 111 | Nolita | John Fluevog | 250 Mulberry St | 212.431.4484 | ★ | | | |
| K1 | 88 | Soho | Flying A | 169 Spring St | 212.965.9090 | ★ | | | |
| | | | **HOME** | | | | | | |
| | | | **Antiques & Auction Houses** | | | | | | |
| H1 | 142 | Chelsea | Olde Good Things | 124 West 24th St | 212.989.8401 | | ★ | | ★ |
| H2 | 9 | Flatiron District | ABC Carpet & Home | 888 Broadway | 212.473.3000 | | ★ | ★ | ★ |
| H2 | 143 | Greenwich Village | Olde Good Things | 19 Greenwich Ave | 212.229.0850 | | ★ | | ★ |
| K1 | 156 | Tribeca | R 20th Century Design | 82 Franklin St | 212.343.7979 | ★ | ★ | | ★ |
| | | | **Home Furnishings** | | | | | | |
| H1 | 142 | Chelsea | Olde Good Things | 124 West 24th St | 212.989.8401 | | ★ | | ★ |
| H2 | 9 | Flatiron District | ABC Carpet & Home | 888 Broadway | 212.473.3000 | | ★ | ★ | ★ |

| Map | # | Area | Shop | Address | Phone | Design Driven | Celebrity Clientele | Legendary | Only in New York |
|---|---|---|---|---|---|---|---|---|---|
| H2 | 143 | Greenwich Village | Olde Good Things | 19 Greenwich Ave | 212.229.0850 | | | ★ | ★ |
| G2 | 69 | Meatpacking District | Design Within Reach | 408 West 14th St | 212.242.9449 | ★ | | | ★ |
| K1 | 62 | Soho | Craft Caravan | 63 Greene St | 212.431.6669 | | | ★ | ★ |
| K1 | 70 | Soho | Design Within Reach | 142 Wooster St | 212.475.0001 | ★ | | | ★ |
| K1 | 87 | Soho | Flou | 42 Greene St | 212.941.9101 | ★ | | | |
| K1 | 112 | Soho | Jonathan Adler | 47 Greene St | 212.941.8950 | ★ | ★ | | |
| K1 | 139 | Soho | Moss | 146 Greene St | 212.204.7100 | ★ | ★ | | ★ |
| K1 | 140 | Soho | Muji at MoMA | 81 Spring St | 646.613.1367 | ★ | | | |
| K1 | 145 | Soho | Pearl River | 477 Broadway | 212.431.4770 | | | | ★ |
| K1 | 156 | Tribeca | R 20th Century Design | 82 Franklin St | 212.343.7979 | ★ | ★ | | ★ |
| B2 | 113 | Upper East Side | Jonathan Adler | 1097 Madison Ave | 212.772.2410 | ★ | ★ | | |
| E1 | 151 | Upper East Side | Porthault | 18 East 69th St | 212.688.1660 | ★ | ★ | | |
| | | | **Lighting** | | | | | | |
| H2 | 9 | Flatiron District | ABC Carpet & Home | 888 Broadway | 212.473.3000 | | ★ | ★ | ★ |
| G2 | 69 | Meatpacking District | Design Within Reach | 408 West 14th St | 212.242.9449 | ★ | | | ★ |
| K1 | 70 | Soho | Design Within Reach | 142 Wooster St | 212.475.0001 | ★ | | | ★ |
| K1 | 102 | Soho | Ingo Maurer | 89 Grand St | 212.965.8817 | ★ | ★ | | ★ |
| K1 | 139 | Soho | Moss | 146 Greene St | 212.204.7100 | ★ | ★ | | ★ |
| K1 | 163 | Tribeca | Schoolhouse Electric Co. | 27 Vestry St | 212.226.6113 | ★ | | | ★ |
| | | | **Kitchen & Tableware** | | | | | | |
| K2 | 124 | Flatiron District | Korin Japanese Trading Corp. | 57 Warren St | 212.587.7021 | | | | ★ |
| K1 | 145 | Soho | Pearl River | 477 Broadway | 212.431.4770 | | | | ★ |
| | | | **LIFESTYLE** | | | | | | |
| | | | **Books & Magazines** | | | | | | |
| I2 | 171 | East Village | Strand Bookstore | 828 Broadway | 212.473.1452 | | | | ★ |
| K2 | 172 | Financial District | Strand Bookstore | 95 Fulton St | 212.732.6070 | | | | ★ |
| I2 | 187 | Flatiron District | Universal News | 270 Park Ave South | 212.674.6595 | | | | ★ |
| E2 | 28 | Midtown | Barnes & Noble | 600 Fifth Ave | 212.765.0590 | | | | ★ |
| E2 | 184 | Midtown | Universal News | 676 Lexington Ave | 212.750.1855 | | | | ★ |
| D2 | 185 | Midtown | Universal News | 977 Eighth Ave | 212.459.0932 | | | | ★ |
| D2 | 186 | Midtown | Universal News | 1586 Broadway | 212.586.7205 | | | | ★ |
| K1 | 188 | Soho | Universal News | 484 Broadway | 212.965.9042 | | | | ★ |
| I2 | 26 | Union Square | Barnes & Noble | 33 East 17th St | 212.253.0810 | | | | ★ |
| H2 | 47 | Union Square | Books of Wonder | 18 West 18th St | 212.989.3270 | | | | ★ |
| B2 | 27 | Upper East Side | Barnes & Noble | 1280 Lexington Ave | 212.423.9900 | | | | ★ |
| | | | **Cameras & Electronics** | | | | | | |
| G1 | 41 | Midtown | B&H Photo | 420 Ninth Ave | 212.444.6615 | | | | ★ |
| | | | **Food & Drink** | | | | | | |
| G2 | 1 | Chelsea | Chelsea Market | 75 Ninth Ave | No phone | ★ | | | |
| L1 | 80 | Nolita | Eileen's Special Cheesecake | 17 Cleveland Pl | 212.966.5585 | | | ★ | ★ |
| K1 | 66 | Soho | Dean & DeLuca | 560 Broadway | 212.226.6800 | ★ | ★ | ★ | ★ |
| K1 | 108 | Soho | Jacques Torres Chocolate | 350 Hudson St | 212.414.2462 | ★ | | ★ | |
| I2 | 2 | Union Square | Greenmarket at Union Square | Broadway | 212.788.7476 | | | | ★ |

| Map | # | Area | Shop | Address | Phone | Design Driven | Celebrity Clientele | Legendary | Only in New York |
|---|---|---|---|---|---|---|---|---|---|
| | | | **Food & Drink** | | | | | | |
| B2 | 67 | Upper East Side | Dean & DeLuca | 1150 Madison Ave | 212.717.0800 | ★ | ★ | | ★ |
| E2 | 78 | Upper East Side | Dylan's Candy Bar | 1011 Third Ave | 646.735.0078 | ★ | ★ | | |
| A2 | 194 | Upper West Side | Zabar's | 2245 Broadway | 212.787.2000 | ★ | ★ | | ★ |
| | | | **Gifts, Novelties & Museum Stores** | | | | | | |
| I2 | 127 | East Village | Love Saves The Day | 119 Second Ave | 212.228.3802 | ★ | | | ★ |
| H1 | 178 | Midtown | Tannen's Magic Shop | 45 West 34th St | 212.929.4500 | | | ★ | ★ |
| K1 | 120 | Soho | Kidrobot | 126 Prince St | 212.966.6688 | ★ | | | |
| K1 | 140 | Soho | Muji at MoMA | 81 Spring St | 646.613.1367 | ★ | | | |
| | | | **Music & Video** | | | | | | |
| H2 | 84 | Greenwich Village | Fat Beats | 406 Sixth Ave | 212.673.3883 | | | | ★ |
| I2 | 144 | Greenwich Village | Other Music | 15 East 4th St | 212.477.8150 | ★ | | | |
| L1 | 49 | Lower East Side | Breakbeat Science | 181 Orchard St | 212.995.2592 | ★ | | | ★ |
| | | | **Musical Instruments** | | | | | | |
| D2 | 132 | Midtown | Manny's | 156 West 48th St | 212.819.0576 | ★ | | | ★ |
| D2 | 162 | Midtown | Sam Ash | 155 West 48th St | 212.719.2625 | ★ | ★ | | |
| | | | **Pet Supply** | | | | | | |
| K1 | 76 | Soho | DoggyStyle | 100 Thompson St | 212.431.9200 | ★ | | | ★ |
| | | | **Sex Shops** | | | | | | |
| H1 | 68 | Chelsea | DeMask | 135 West 22nd St | 212.352.2850 | ★ | | | |
| L1 | 22 | Lower East Side | Babeland | 94 Rivington St | 212.375.1701 | ★ | | | |
| K1 | 21 | Soho | Babeland | 43 Mercer St | 212.966.2120 | ★ | | | |
| | | | **Spas** | | | | | | |
| I2 | 7 | East Village | Russian and Turkish Baths | 268 East 10th St | 212.473.8806 | ★ | ★ | | ★ |
| E2 | 3 | Midtown | Bliss 57 | 19 East 57th St | 212.219.8970 | ★ | | | |
| E2 | 5 | Midtown | Cornelia Day Resort | 663 Fifth Ave | 212.871.3050 | ★ | | | ★ |
| H1 | 6 | Midtown | Juvenex | 25 West 32nd St | 646.733.1330 | | | | ★ |
| E2 | 4 | Soho | Bliss Soho | 568 Broadway | 212.219.8970 | ★ | | | |
| D2 | 8 | Upper West Side | Spa at the Mandarin Oriental | 80 Columbus Circle | 212.805.8800 | ★ | | | |
| | | | **Stationery** | | | | | | |
| H2 | 116 | Greenwich Village | Kate's Paperie | 8 West 13th St | 212.633.0570 | ★ | | | ★ |
| D2 | 118 | Midtown | Kate's Paperie | 140 West 57th St | 212.459.0700 | ★ | | | ★ |
| K1 | 115 | Soho | Kate's Paperie | 561 Broadway | 212.941.9816 | ★ | | | ★ |
| E1 | 117 | Upper East Side | Kate's Paperie | 1282 Third Ave | 212.396.3670 | ★ | | | ★ |
| | | | **Toys** | | | | | | |
| H2 | 193 | Greenwich Village | Village Chess Shop | 230 Thompson St | 212.475.9580 | | | | ★ |
| E2 | 83 | Midtown | FAO Schwarz | 767 Fifth Ave | 212.644.9400 | ★ | ★ | | |
| H1 | 178 | Midtown | Tannen's Magic Shop | 45 West 34th St | 212.929.4500 | | | ★ | ★ |
| K1 | 120 | Soho | Kidrobot | 126 Prince St | 212.966.6688 | ★ | | | |

▶▶▶ *Getting the best hotel deal is definitely avant. For the best*

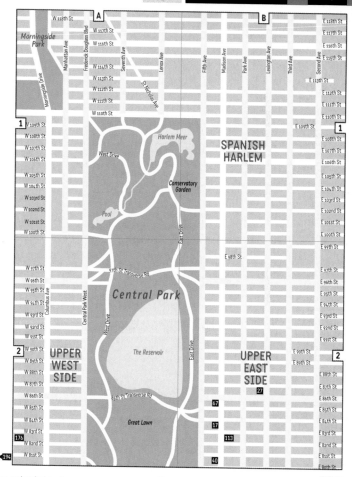

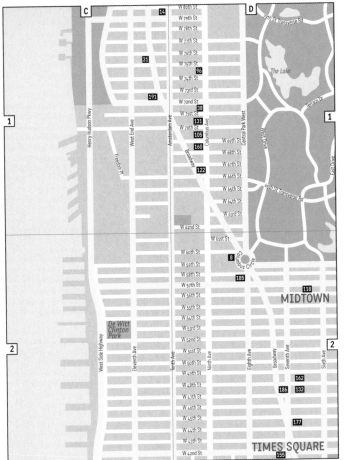

▶▶▶ *Getting the best hotel deal is definitely avant. For the bes*

EF
SHOP

▶▶▶ *Getting the best hotel deal is definitely avant. For the bes*

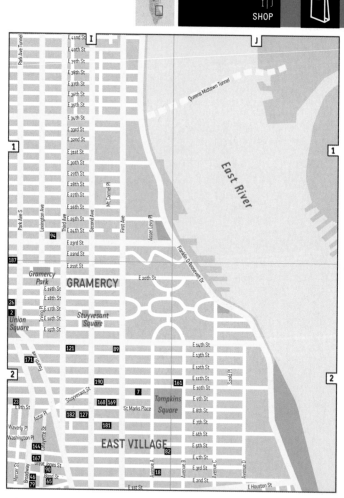

**Park Ave Tunnel**

E 41nd St
E 40th St
E 39th St
E 38th St
E 37th St
E 36th St
E 35th St
E 34th St
E 33rd St
E 32nd St
E 31st St
E 30th St
E 29th St
E 28th St
E 27th St
E 26th St
E 25th St
E 24th St
E 23rd St
E 22nd St
E 21st St

Queens Midtown Tunnel

East River

Park Ave S
Lexington Ave
Third Ave
Second Ave
Mt. Carmel Pl
First Ave
Asser Levy Pl
Franklin D. Roosevelt Dr

94

187

*Gramercy Park*

**GRAMERCY**

E 20th St
E 19th St
E 18th St
E 17th St
E 16th St
E 15th St

Irving Pl

26
2

*Union Square*

*Stuyvesant Square*

121    89

171

E 14th St
E 13th St
E 12th St
E 11th St
E 10th St
E 9th St
E 8th St
E 7th St
E 6th St
E 5th St
E 4th St
E 3rd St
E 2nd St

Szold Pl

190    161

Stuyvesant St

7

168 169

182 127

*St Marks Place*

*Tompkins Square*

181

**EAST VILLAGE**

23
E 8th St

Astor Pl

Waverly Pl
Washington Pl

Lafayette St

144

167

Mercer St
Broadway

Great Jones St
Bond St

82

18

Avenue A
Avenue B
Avenue C
Avenue D

46
79

90
65

E 1st St

E Houston St

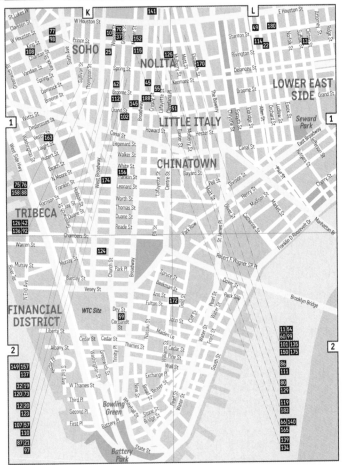

St Lukes Pl
Clarkson St

77
98

W Houston St

W Houston St

King St
Charlton St

108

Prince St

Sixth Ave

Sullivan St

Thompson St

Greene St

141

101
37

70

SOHO

152

25

115

NOLITA

125

Stanton St

Rivington St

Delancey St

E Houston St

49    180

114    22

Attorney St

Norfolk St

Suffolk St

Clinton St

Ridge St

13

Vandam St

Spring St

Dominick St

Broome St

Spring St

62

112

145

102

Broome St

45

188

Grand St

55

51

Mott St

Elizabeth St

170

Kenmare St

Mulberry St

Crosby St

Lafayette St

Mott St

LOWER EAST
SIDE

Grand St

Eldridge St

Allen St

Orchard St

Ludlow St

Essex St

Seward
Park

1

Watts St

Desbrosses St

Vestry St

163

Laight St

Hubert St

Beach St

N Moore St

West Side Hwy

Washington St

Greenwich St

West Broadway

LITTLE ITALY

Canal St

Howard St

Lispenard St

Walker St

White St

156

Hester St

Baxter St

Mulberry St

Centre St

CHINATOWN

Bayard St

Canal St

The Bowery

Chrystie St

Forsyth St

Eldridge St

Division St

East Broadway

Canal St

Ludlow St

Essex St

Jefferson St

Rutgers St

Pike St

East Broadway

Cherry St

1

75    76
158    88

TRIBECA

126    42
136    92

Franklin St

Leonard St

Worth St

Thomas St

Duane St

Reade St

Harrison St

Jay St

Staple St

Duane St

174

Hudson St

West Broadway

Chambers St

Lafayette St

Centre St

Elk St

Franklin St

Park Row

Pearl St

Henry St

Madison St

Market St

Catherine St

Franklin D Roosevelt Dr

Manhattan Br

Warren St

Murray St

124

Park Pl

Church St

Broadway

Spruce St

Beekman St

Ann St

172

Dover St

Pearl St

Peck Slip

Robert F. Wagner SR Pl

Brooklyn Bridge

Murray St

Barclay St

Vesey St

FINANCIAL
DISTRICT

WTC Site

N End Ave

River Ter

Dey St

Fulton St

John St

Cliff St

Gold St

59

Cortlandt
St

Fulton St

Water St

Front St

South St

11    54
60    99

101    135
150    175

2

Liberty St

Albany St

149    157
137

32    19
120    73

12    20
123

107    57
110

87    21
97

Cedar St

Battery Pl

Cedar St

Thames St

W Thames St

Third Pl

Second Pl

First Pl

Greenwich St

Washington St

Trinity Pl

Bowling
Green

Broadway

New St

Broad St

Stone St

Battery Pl

Maiden Ln

Pine St

Wall St

Exchange Pl

Beaver St

Pearl St

William St

Water St

State St

Water St

Bridge St

South St

Front St

Pearl St

86
111

80
129

119
183

66    140
165

139
134

2

Battery
Park

▶▶▶ *Getting the best hotel deal is definitely avant. For the be*

| Map | # | Venue | Address | Phone | Après Work | Lounge | Good Food | Dance Club | DJ Bar | Brewpub/Beer Bar | Quiet Conversation | Gay | Live Music |
|---|---|---|---|---|---|---|---|---|---|---|---|---|---|
| | | **Chelsea** | | | | | | | | | | | |
| G1 | 9 | Bungalow 8 | 515 West 27th St | 212.629.3333 | ★ | | ★ | | | | | | |
| G2 | 10 | Cabanas, The | 88 Ninth Ave | 212.835.5537 | ★ | | ★ | | | | | | |
| G1 | 11 | Cain | 544 West 27th St | 212.947.8000 | ★ | ★ | | | | | | | |
| G1 | 20 | Crobar | 530 West 28th St | 212.629.9000 | | ★ | | | | | | | |
| H2 | 27 | G | 225 West 19th St | 212.929.1085 | ★ | ★ | | | | | | ★ | |
| G2 | 29 | Hiro | 363 West 16th St | 212.242.4300 | ★ | ★ | | | | | | | |
| G1 | 36 | Marquee | 289 Tenth Ave | 646.473.0202 | ★ | ★ | | | | | | | |
| G2 | 56 | Son Cubano | 405 West 14th St | 212.366.1640 | | ★ | ★ | | | | | | ★ |
| H1 | 62 | Trailer Park | 271 West 23rd St | 212.463.8000 | ★ | | ★ | ★ | | | | | |
| G2 | 66 | XL | 357 West 16th St | 646.336.5574 | ★ | | | | | | | ★ | |
| | | **East Village** | | | | | | | | | | | |
| I2 | 3 | Angel's Share | 2nd Fl, 8 Stuyvesant St | 212.777.5415 | | | | | | | ★ | | |
| I2 | 37 | McSorley's Old Ale House | 15 East 7th St | 212.254.2570 | ★ | | | | | ★ | | | |
| J2 | 43 | Nuyorican Poets Cafe | 236 East 3rd St | 212.505.8183 | ★ | | | | | | | | ★ |
| I2 | 50 | Rififi | 332 East 11th St | 212.677.1027 | | | | | | | | | ★ |
| I2 | 58 | Starlight Lounge | 167 Ave A | 212.475.2172 | ★ | | | | | | | ★ | ★ |
| K1 | 61 | Temple Bar | 332 Lafayette St | 212.925.4242 | ★ | ★ | | | | | ★ | | |
| J2 | 63 | Uncle Ming's | 225 Ave B, 2nd Fl | 212.979.8506 | | ★ | | | | | | | |
| | | **Flatiron, Gramercy & Union Square** | | | | | | | | | | | |
| H1 | 1 | 40/40 | 6 West 25th St | 212.832.4040 | ★ | | ★ | | | | | | |
| H2 | 23 | Duvet | 45 West 21st St | 212.989.2121 | ★ | | ★ | | | | | | |
| H2 | 26 | Flatiron Lounge | 37 West 19th St | 212.727.7741 | ★ | ★ | | | | | ★ | | |
| I2 | 45 | Old Town Bar | 45 East 18th St | 212.529.6732 | ★ | | | | | ★ | ★ | | |
| I2 | 18 | Cibar | 56 Irving Pl | 212.460.5656 | ★ | | | | | | ★ | | |
| I2 | 35 | Luna Park | in Union Square Park | 212.475.8464 | ★ | | | | | | | | |
| | | **Greenwich Village** | | | | | | | | | | | |
| H2 | 16 | Chumley's | 86 Bedford St | 212.675.4449 | ★ | | | | | | ★ | | |
| H2 | 25 | Employees Only | 510 Hudson St | 212.242.3021 | ★ | ★ | | | | | ★ | | |
| H2 | 42 | Movida | 28 Seventh Ave S | 212.206.9600 | ★ | | ★ | ★ | | | | | |
| H2 | 65 | White Horse Tavern | 567 Hudson St | 212.989.3956 | | | | | | ★ | ★ | | |
| | | **Harlem** | | | | | | | | | | | |
| A1 | 32 | Lenox Lounge | 288 Lenox Ave | 212.427.0253 | ★ | | | | | | | ★ | ★ |
| | | **Lower East Side** | | | | | | | | | | | |
| L1 | 5 | Arlene's Grocery | 95 Stanton St | 212.995.1652 | | | | | | | | | ★ |
| L1 | 8 | Barrio Chino | 253 Broome St | 212.228.6710 | ★ | ★ | | | | | | | |
| L1 | 14 | Chibitini | 63 Clinton St | 212.674.7300 | | | | | | | ★ | | |
| L1 | 21 | Dark Room | 165 Ludlow St | 212.353.0536 | ★ | | | ★ | ★ | | | | |
| L1 | 22 | Delancey, The | 168 Delancey St | 212.254.9920 | ★ | ★ | | | ★ | | | | ★ |

| Map | # | Venue | Address | Phone | Apres Work | Lounge | Good Food | Dance Club | DJ Bar | Brewpub/Beer Bar | Quiet Conversation | Gay | Live Music |
|---|---|---|---|---|---|---|---|---|---|---|---|---|---|
| | | **Lower East Side** | | | | | | | | | | | |
| L1 | 24 | East Side Company Bar | 49 Essex St | 212.614.7408 | ★ | | | | | ★ | | | |
| L1 | 28 | Happy Ending | 302 Broome St | 212.334.9676 | | ★ | ★ | | | | | | |
| L1 | 34 | Living Room | 154 Ludlow St | 212.533.7235 | | | | | | | ★ | | ★ |
| L1 | 39 | Milk and Honey | 134 Eldridge St | unlisted | | | | | | | ★ | | |
| L1 | 46 | Pianos | 158 Ludlow St | 212.505.3733 | ★ | | | | | ★ | ★ | | ★ |
| L1 | 51 | Rothko | 116 Suffolk St | 212.475.7088 | | | | | | | ★ | | ★ |
| L1 | 57 | Stanton Social, The | 99 Stanton St | 212.995.0099 | ★ | ★ | | | | | ★ | | |
| L1 | 60 | Suba | 109 Ludlow St | 212.982.5714 | | ★ | ★ | | | | | | |
| L1 | 64 | Whiskey Ward | 121 Essex St | 212.477.2998 | | | | | | ★ | | | |
| | | **Meatpacking District** | | | | | | | | | | | |
| G2 | 2 | Aer | 409 West 13th St | 212.989.0100 | | ★ | | | | | | | |
| G2 | 4 | APT | 419 West 13th St | 212.414.4245 | ★ | | | ★ | | ★ | | | |
| G2 | 19 | Cielo | 18 Little West 12th St | 212.645.5700 | | | | ★ | | | | | |
| G2 | 30 | Hogs & Heifers | 859 Washington St | 212.929.0655 | | | | | | ★ | | | |
| G2 | 33 | Level V | 675 Hudson St | 212.699.2410 | ★ | | ★ | | | | | | |
| G2 | 47 | PM | 50 Gansevoort St | 212.255.6676 | ★ | | ★ | ★ | | | | | |
| | | **Midtown** | | | | | | | | | | | |
| D2 | 6 | Ava Lounge | 210 West 55th St | 212.956.7020 | ★ | | ★ | | | | | | |
| E2 | 13 | Campbell Apartment, The | Grand Central Terminal | 212.953.0409 | ★ | ★ | | | | | ★ | | |
| D2 | 31 | Latitude | 783 Eighth Ave | 212.245.3034 | ★ | ★ | | | | ★ | | | |
| E2 | 41 | Monkey Bar | 60 East 54th St | 212.838.2600 | ★ | | | | | | ★ | | |
| I1 | 49 | Rare View | 303 Lexington Ave | 212.481.1999 | ★ | | | | | | ★ | | |
| E2 | 52 | Royalton Round Bar | 44 West 44th St | 212.944.8844 | ★ | | | | | | ★ | | |
| D2 | 53 | Russian Vodka Room | 265 West 52nd St | 212.307.5835 | ★ | ★ | | | | | ★ | | |
| E2 | 54 | Sakagura | 211 East 43rd St | 212.953.7253 | ★ | | | | | | ★ | ★ | |
| D2 | 55 | Single Room Occupancy | 360 West 53rd St | 212.765.6299 | ★ | | | | | | ★ | ★ | |
| | | **Nolita, Little Italy, Soho & Tribeca** | | | | | | | | | | | |
| L1 | 15 | Chibi's Sake Bar | 238 Mott St | 212.274.0054 | | | | | | | ★ | | |
| K1 | 48 | Pravda | 281 Lafayette St | 212.226.4944 | ★ | ★ | | | | | ★ | | |
| L1 | 44 | Odea | 389 Broome St | 212.941.9222 | ★ | ★ | | | | | ★ | | |
| K1 | 7 | Bar 89 | 89 Mercer St | 212.274.0989 | ★ | ★ | | | | | | | |
| K1 | 17 | Church Lounge | 2 Sixth Ave | 212.519.6664 | ★ | | | | | | ★ | | |
| | | **Upper East Side** | | | | | | | | | | | |
| B2 | 38 | MoMA Roof Garden | 1000 Fifth Ave | 212.879.5500 | ★ | | | | | | ★ | | |
| | | **Upper West Side** | | | | | | | | | | | |
| A2 | 12 | Calle Ocho | 446 Columbus Ave | 212.873.5025 | ★ | ★ | | | | | | | ★ |
| D2 | 40 | MO Bar & Lobby Lounge | Time Warner Center | 212.805.8800 | ★ | ★ | | | | | ★ | | |
| D2 | 59 | Stone Rose Lounge | Time Warner Center | 212.823.9769 | ★ | ★ | ★ | | | | ★ | | |

▶▶▶ *Getting the best hotel deal is definitely avant. For the be...*

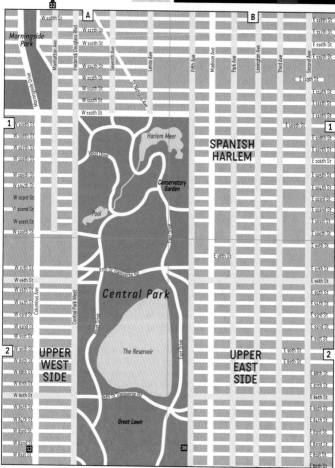

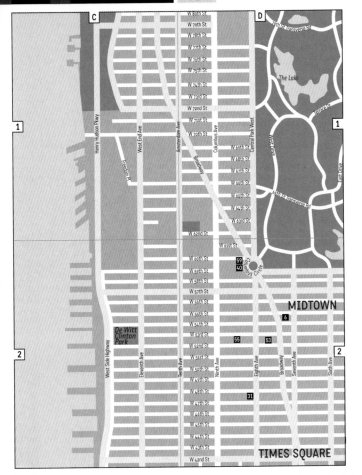

▶▶▶ *Getting the best hotel deal is definitely avant. For the be*

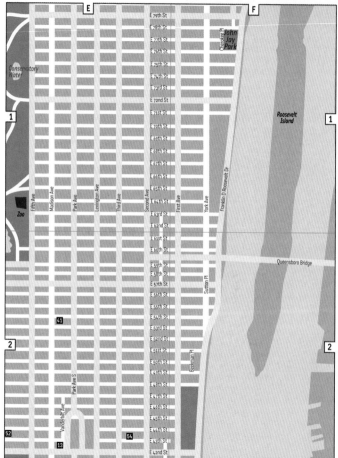

E 79th St
E 78th St
E 77th St
E 76th St
E 75th St
E 74th St
E 73rd St
E 72nd St
E 71st St
E 70th St
E 69th St
E 68th St
E 67th St
E 66th St
E 65th St
E 64th St
E 63rd St
E 62nd St
E 61st St
E 60th St
E 59th St
E 58th St
E 57th St
E 56th St
E 55th St
E 54th St
E 53rd St
E 52nd St
E 51st St
E 50th St
E 49th St
E 48th St
E 47th St
E 46th St
E 45th St
E 44th St
E 43rd St
E 42nd St

Conservatory Water

Zoo

Fifth Ave
Madison Ave
Park Ave
Lexington Ave
Third Ave
Second Ave
First Ave
York Ave
Franklin D Roosevelt Dr

Roosevelt Island

John Jay Park
Cherokee Pl

Queensboro Bridge

Sutton Pl
Beekman Pl

Park Ave S
Vanderbilt Ave

**41**
**13**
**54**
**52**

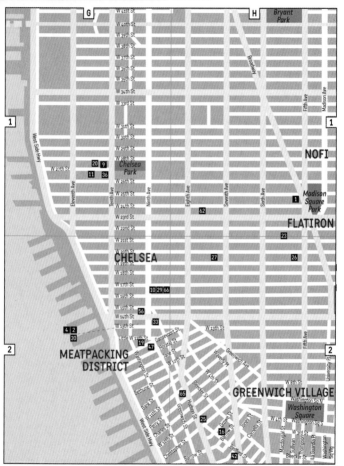

▶▶▶ *Getting the best hotel deal is definitely avant. For the best*

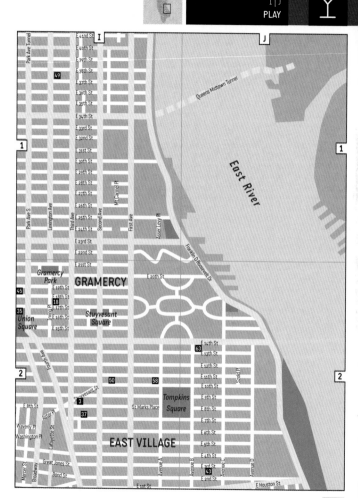

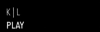

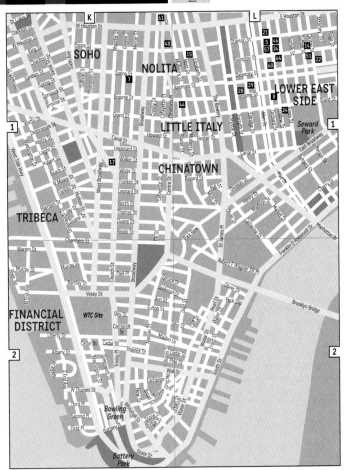

▶▶▶ *Getting the best hotel deal is definitely avant. For the bes*

| Map | # | Area | Sight | Address | Phone | Closed |
|---|---|---|---|---|---|---|
| | | | **Top New York Experiences** | | | |
| L2 | 4 | Financial District | Brooklyn Bridge, The | Center Street | no phone | |
| H1 | 11 | Midtown | Empire State Building | 350 Fifth Ave | 212.736.3100 | |
| K2 | 35 | Financial District | Staten Island Ferry | 1 Whitehall St | 212.639.9675 | |
| D2 | 37 | Midtown | Times Square | Broadway | no phone | |
| A1 | 42 | The Bronx | Yankee Stadium | 161st St and River Ave | 718.293.4300 | SAT-SUN |
| | | | **Museums and Galleries** | | | |
| D1 | 1 | Upper West Side | American Museum of Natural History | Central Park West | 212.769.5100 | |
| E1 | 2 | Upper East Side | Asia Society and Museum | 725 Park Ave | 212.288.6400 | MON |
| B2 | 9 | Upper East Side | Cooper-Hewitt National Design Museum | 2 East 91st St | 212.849.8400 | MON |
| E1 | 14 | Upper East Side | Frick Collection, The | 1 East 70th St | 212.288.0700 | MON |
| B2 | 18 | Upper East Side | Jewish Museum, The | 1109 Fifth Ave | 212.423.3200 | SAT |
| L1 | 19 | Lower East Side | Lower East Side Tenement Museum | 108 Orchard St | 212.431.0233 | MON |
| B2 | 20 | Upper East Side | Metropolitan Museum of Art | 1000 Fifth Ave | 212.879.5500 | MON |
| H1 | 21 | Midtown | Morgan Library | 29 East 36th St | 212.685.0610 | |
| H1 | 22 | Chelsea | Museum at FIT | Seventh Ave and 27th St | 212.217.5800 | SUN-MON |
| E2 | 23 | Midtown | Museum of Arts & Design | 40 West 53rd St | 212.956.3535 | |
| E2 | 24 | Midtown | Museum of Modern Art, The | 11 West 53rd St | 212.708.9400 | TUES |
| B1 | 25 | Upper East Side | Museum of the City of New York | 1220 Fifth Ave | 212.534.1672 | MON |
| H1 | 26 | Flatiron District | Museum of Sex | 233 Fifth Ave | 212.689.6337 | |
| B2 | 27 | Upper East Side | Neue Galerie New York | 1048 Fifth Ave | 212.628.6200 | TUE-WED |
| H2 | 29 | Chelsea | Rubin Museum of Art | 150 West 17th St | 212.620.5000 | MON |
| K2 | 31 | Financial District | Skyscraper Museum, The | 39 Battery Pl | 212.968.1961 | MON-TUE |
| B2 | 32 | Upper East Side | Solomon R. Guggenheim Museum | 1071 Fifth Ave | 212.423.3500 | THU |
| E1 | 40 | Upper East Side | Whitney Museum | 945 Madison Ave | 212.570.3676 | MON-TUE |
| | | | **Parks & Gardens** | | | |
| K2 | 3 | Financial District | Battery Park & The Esplanade | Hudson River at Broadway | 212.267.9700 | |
| A2 | 6 | Uptown | Central Park | 59th to 110th St | 212.794.6564 | |
| | | | **Places to Take Kids** | | | |
| E1 | 7 | Upper East Side | Central Park Zoo | Fifth Avenue at 64th St | 212.439.6500 | |
| K2 | 10 | New York Harbor | Ellis Island Immigration Museum | Ellis Island | 212.269.5755 | |
| C2 | 17 | Midtown | Intrepid Sea-Air-Space Museum | Pier 86, West 46th St | 212.245.0072 | |
| E2 | 33 | Midtown | Sony Wonder Technology Lab | 550 Madison Ave | 212.833.8100 | MON |
| L2 | 34 | Financial District | South Street Seaport | South St | 212.732.8257 | |
| F2 | 39 | Midtown | United Nations, The | First Avenue | 212.963.8687 | SAT-SUN |
| K2 | 36 | New York Harbor | Statue of Liberty | Liberty Island | 212.269.5755 | |
| | | | **Offbeat Sights** | | | |
| A1 | 8 | Washington Heights | Cloisters, The | Fort Tryon Park | 212.923.3700 | MON |
| K2 | 12 | Financial District | Federal Hall National Memorial | 26 Wall St | 212.825.6888 | SAT-SUN |

| Map | # | Area | Sight | Address | Phone | Closed |
|---|---|---|---|---|---|---|
| | | | **Offbeat Sights** | | | |
| K2 | 13 | Financial District | Federal Reserve Bank of New York | 33 Liberty St | 212.720.6130 | SAT-SUN |
| K2 | 41 | Financial District | World Trade Center Site | Liberty St | no phone | |
| | | | **Great Architecture** | | | |
| E2 | 16 | Midtown | Grand Central Terminal | 15 Vanderbilt Ave | 212.340.2210 | |
| E2 | 28 | Midtown | Rockefeller Center | 48th to 51st St | 212.698.2000 | |
| | | | **Churches, Synagogues & Cemeteries** | | | |
| A1 | 5 | Harlem | Cathedral of St. John the Divine | 1047 Amsterdam Ave | 212.316.7490 | |
| I2 | 15 | East Village | Grace Church | 802 Broadway | 212.254.2000 | MON |
| E1 | 30 | Midtown | Saint Patrick's Cathedral | 14 East 51st St | 212.753.2261 | |
| K2 | 38 | Financial District | Trinity Church | 74 Trinity Pl | 212.602.0800 | |

▶▶▶ *Getting the best hotel deal is definitely avant. For the bes*

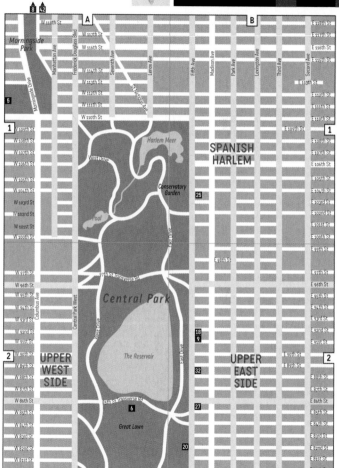

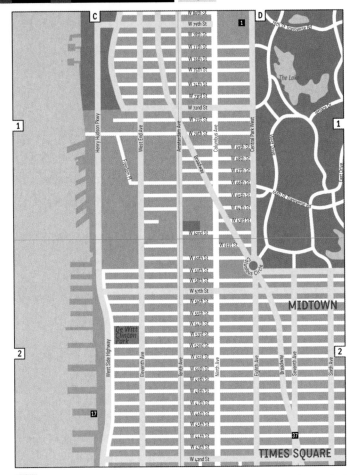

▶▶▶ *Getting the best hotel deal is definitely avant. For the b*

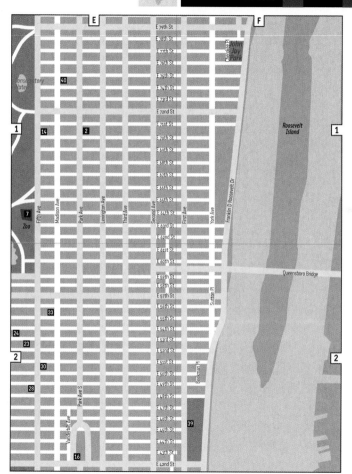

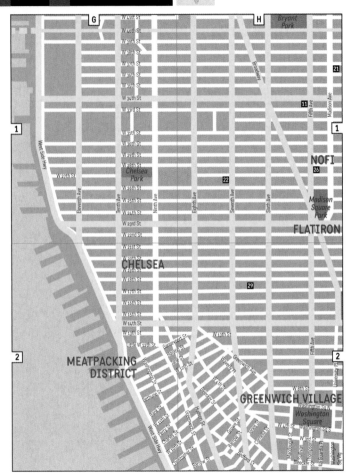

►►► *Getting the best hotel deal is definitely avant. For the be*

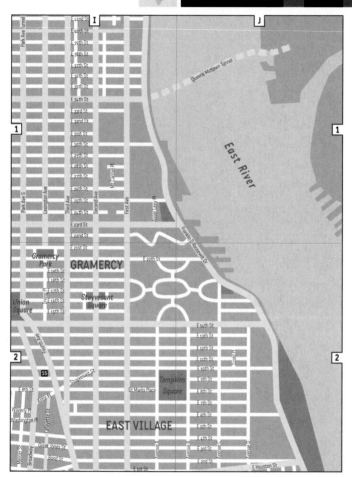

SOHO
NOLITA
LITTLE ITALY
CHINATOWN
LOWER EAST SIDE
TRIBECA
FINANCIAL DISTRICT
Seward Park
WTC Site
Bowling Green
Battery Park
Brooklyn Bridge

▶▶▶ *Getting the best hotel deal is definitely avant. For the b*

## MAP INDEX

▶▶▶ *Getting the best hotel deal is definitely avant. For the*

**MAP INDEX**